The Challenge of Democratic Representation in the European Union

The Challenge of Democratic Representation in the European Union

Edited by

Sandra Kröger
Marie Curie fellow,
Centre for European Governance,
University of Exeter, United Kingdom

and

Dawid Friedrich
Assistant Professor of International Relations,
Leuphana University of Lüneburg Germany

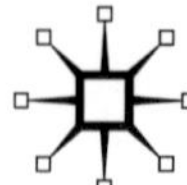

First published 2012 by
PALGRAVE MACMILLAN

Palgrave Macmillan in the UK is an imprint of Macmillan Publishers Limited, registered in England, company number 785998, of Houndmills, Basingstoke, Hampshire RG21 6XS.

Palgrave Macmillan in the US is a division of St Martin's Press LLC, 175 Fifth Avenue, New York, NY 10010.

Palgrave Macmillan is the global academic imprint of the above companies and has companies and representatives throughout the world.

Palgrave® and Macmillan® are registered trademarks in the United States, the United Kingdom, Europe and other countries.

ISBN: 978–0–230–29292–5

This book is printed on paper suitable for recycling and made from fully managed and sustained forest sources. Logging, pulping and manufacturing processes are expected to conform to the environmental regulations of the country of origin.

A catalogue record for this book is available from the British Library.

A catalog record for this book is available from the Library of Congress.

10 9 8 7 6 5 4 3 2 1
21 20 19 18 17 16 15 14 13 12

Printed and bound in Great Britain by
CPI Antony Rowe, Chippenham and Eastbourne

Contents

Tables

Figures

Abbreviations

A	Austria
AER	Assembly of European Regions
BverfG	Bundesverfassungsgericht (Federal Constitutional court)
CALRE	Conference of European Regional Legislative Assemblies
CAP	Common Agricultural Policy
CDU	Christlich Demokratische Union Deutschlands (Christian Democratic Union of Germany)
CEMR	Council of European Municipalities and Regions
CFSP	Common Foreign and Security Policy
CoE	Council of Europe
Com. Valenciana	Comunidad Valenciana (Region of Spain)
COPREPA	Conferencia de Presidentes de Parlamentos Autonómicos (Conference of the Chairmen of the Regional Parliaments)
CoR	Committee of the Regions (of the European Union)
COSAC	Conference of Parliamentary Committees for Union Affairs of Parliaments of the European Union
CSDP	Common Security and Defence Policy
CSO	Civil Society Organization
D	Germany
DK	Denmark
EAC	European Affairs Committee
EAPN	European Anti-Poverty Network
EC	European Community
ECJ	European Court of Justice
ECPRD	European Centre for Parliamentary Research and Documentation
EESC	European Economic and Social Committee
EGP	European Green Party
EN.CPS	European Network for Civil Peace Services

EP	European Parliament
EPF	European Party Federation
EPLO	European Peacebuilding Liaison Office
EPP	European People's Party
ESC	Economic and Social Committee
ESF	European Services Forum
ETUC	European Trade Union Confederation
EU	European Union
F	France
FoEE	Friends of the Earth Europe
GDP	Gross Domestic Product
ICT	Information and Communication Technology
IPEX	Interparliamentary EU Information Exchange
JCMs	Joint Committee Meetings
JPMs	Joint Parliamentary Meetings
LAUs	Local Administrative Units
MEP/MEPs	Member/s of the European Parliament
MF	Medlem av Folketinget (Member of the Danish Parliament)
MSCs	Meetings of Sectoral Committees
NA	National Assembly
NGO	Non-Governmental Organization
NP/NPs	National Parliament/s
NP	Nonviolent Peaceforce
NUTS	Nomenclature des Unités Territoriales Statistiques (Nomenclature of Statistical Territorial Units)
OMC	Open Method of Coordination
OP	Oikologoi Prasinoi (Ecological Greens)
ÖVP	Österreichische Volkspartei (Austrian People's Party)
PASOK	Panellinio Sosialistiko Kinima (Panhellenic Socialist Movement)
PES	Party of European Socialists
PDCI	Partners for Democratic Change International
QCEA	Quaker Council for European Affairs
RegLeg	Conference of European Regions with Legislative Powers
SD	Smer-Sociálna Demokracia (Direction Social Democracy)
SDKU	Slovenská Demokratická a Kresťanská Únia (Slovak Democratic and Christian Union)

SNAs	Sub-national authorities
SPD	Sozialdemokratische Partei Deutschlands
	(Social Democratic Party of Germany)
SPÖ	Sozialdemokratische Partei Österreichs
	(Social Democratic Party of Austria)
TD	Teachta Dála (Member of the Irish Parliament)
TEU	Treaty on the European Union
UK	United Kingdom
UMP	Union pour un Mouvement Populaire
	Union for a Popular Movement)
UNICE	Union des Industries de la Communauté européenne
	(European Association of Industries and Employers)
VAT	Value Added Tax
WIDE	Women in Development Europe
WPMLG	White Paper on Multi-Level Governance

Acknowledgements

This book would not have seen daylight without the help of a number of people and institutions that we would like to thank. First, we thank the contributors for their dedication to this project and the extremely timely delivery of the chapters which rendered the editorial work as easy as it gets. Second, we thank the Fritz-Thyssen-Foundation, without which we could not have organized a workshop that provided the opportunity to discuss first drafts of the present chapters; the book benefited substantially from the respective discussions. We also thank the Centre for the Study of Democracy of the Leuphana University of Lüneburg and the university's research service for additional funding for this workshop. Third, we are grateful for all the gentle and helpful support that Palgrave Macmillan has given us throughout the process. Finally, we thank a number of people who helped to realize this project at different stages: Dario Castiglione for invaluable inputs during the workshop; Niklas Tebbenhoff for administrative support before and during the workshop; Chris Engert, Rebecca Chan, and Christopher Gilley for proofreading; and Julia Holz for her editorial support.

Contributors

Pieter de Wilde is Senior Researcher at the Social Science Research Center Berlin. His interests include European integration theory, research methods, comparative politics, and democratic theory.

Cristina Fasone is a Ph.D. candidate in Comparative Public Law at the University of Siena, Italy. Her field of research interests include parliamentary law, in particular the role of parliaments in the EU democracy.

Dawid Friedrich is Assistant Professor for International Relations at the Center for the Study of Democracy, Leuphana University of Lüneburg. His main research interests cover the democratic legitimacy of European governance, European civil society and citizenship, and European citizen deliberation forums.

Elena Griglio is Research Fellow in Public Comparative Law at the Luiss Guido Carli of Rome. Her main research interests are comparative public law and regional assemblies in Europe.

Erik Jentges is Post-Doctoral Researcher at the Institute of Mass Communication and Media Studies at the University of Zurich. He is currently working on mediatization of political interest groups.

Håkan Johansson is Associate Professor at the School of Social Work, Lund University, Sweden, and holds a position as a senior researcher at NOVA – Norwegian Social Research. His main research interests relate to the representation and involvement of social NGOs in policymaking processes.

Sandra Kröger is Senior Researcher at the Jean Monnet Center for European Studies (CEuS) at the University of Bremen, Germany. Her main research interests are the re-configuration of democracy in the EU and the place of organized interests therein, and the critical political economy of European integration.

Asimina Michailidou is Post-Doctoral Researcher at ARENA Centre for European Studies, University of Oslo, Norway. Her main field of expertise is in online media and their impact on politics, particularly in relation to the European Union.

Simona Piattoni is Professor of European Integration Politics at the University of Innsbruck, Austria. Her main research focus is in regions and regional development in the European Union, multi-level governance, and clientelism.

Heiko Pleines is Head of the Section on Politics and Economy at the Center for Central and East European Studies, University of Bremen, Germany. His main research interests are political lobbying of non-state actors, trade unions, energy policy in Central and Eastern Europe, and corruption.

Johannes Pollak is Head of the Political Science Department at the Institute for Advanced Studies, Vienna. His research interests include European integration, theories of political representation, democracy beyond the nation-state, European energy politics, and parliamentarism.

Tapio Raunio is Professor of Political Science at the University of Tampere, Finland. His main research interests are national parliaments and parties and European integration, European Parliament and Europarties, the Finnish Parliament and party system, EU decision-making and the impact of integration on national political systems.

Meike Rodekamp is Researcher at the Collaborative Research Center 'Transformations of the State', University of Bremen, Germany and an affiliated Ph.D. candidate at the Bremen International Graduate School of Social Sciences. Her research interests include European civil society, EU democracy, and EU foreign policy.

Emmanuel Sigalas is Assistant Professor of European Union Politics at the Vienna Institute for Advanced Studies, Austria. His research interests include the European Parliament, European identity, EU education policy and EU space policy.

Stijn Smismans is Professor of Law and holder of the Jean Monnet Chair in European Law and Governance at Cardiff University, Wales, UK. He is particularly interested in EU law, EU studies, sociology of law, and socio-legal studies.

Hans-Jörg Trenz is Professor for Modern European Studies at the University of Copenhagen and adjunct professor at ARENA, Centre for European Studies, University of Oslo. His main research interests are in the areas of media, communication and public sphere, civil society, European civilization and identity, migration and ethnic minorities, cultural and political sociology, social and political theory, and democracy and constitutionalism in the European Union.

Introduction

1

Political Representation in the EU: A Second Transformation?

Sandra Kröger and Dawid Friedrich

Why representation?

Since the Maastricht Treaty (1992), the reality of a deepening European integration process has ended the (assumed) 'permissive consensus' among the European people that had sustained early phases of the integration process. Since then, an intensive debate about what is now called 'the EU's democratic deficit' has grown and continues to gain momentum. The legitimacy crisis of the EU appears to be too strong, as policy-making is seen as distant, non-transparent, and not in line with institutional checks and balances at the nation-state level. While increasingly affected by European integration, many European citizens believe that they have little say in European decision-making, a situation described as 'policies without politics' (Schmidt 2006: 5). Accordingly, several EU – related referenda have resulted in a majority of 'no' votes, clearly expressing that the people want to have a say and want to be represented in European policy-making.

For some observers, the lack of democratic representation at the EU level is not a significant problem, since in their perspective European governance tends to restrict itself to technical regulation (Majone 1999), or because it leaves the capacity of democratically elected Member State governments rather unscathed (Moravcsik 2008). Others, instead, point to the need for greater democratic legitimation of the EU (Kohler-Koch and Rittberger 2007) or question the capability of the EU to become truly democratic altogether (Offe 1998; Scharpf 1999).

We will argue that the EU is in need of more democratic representation if it wants to regain the support of its citizens. This normative conviction reflects the research focus of the present volume. In recent years, the governance discourse has dominated much of EU research.

Accordingly, in local, regional, national, trans- and supranational governance, a multitude of actors are heterarchically and polyarchically engaged in solving common problems, contributing to the betterment of both the legitimacy and effectiveness of European governance. Despite its obvious links to questions of EU democracy, this discourse has largely ignored issues of democratic representation.

We do not follow the understanding that 'governance' is the answer to the current empirical and theoretical challenges to representative democracy in the EU, nor that it supersedes representative government as such. Instead, we assume that democratic representation is a sine qua non for the legitimacy of any political system, including the EU, that is called democratic. No theory of democracy can reasonably disregard fundamental questions of democratic representation, such as who is represented in collective policy-making, by whom, and by what means (similar Saward 2010: 3). Democratic representation explicitly directs the attention to *ex ante* mechanisms in the policy process, which are processes involving authorization through constituencies, rather than insisting exclusively on *ex post* mechanisms, which have been the focus of recent work on accountability (Bovens 2007; Steffek and Ferretti 2009). Representation theory, instead, systematically links these two perspectives together.

Most recently, we have witnessed a renewed interest in issues of democratic representation, both in democratic theory (Mansbridge 2003; Rehfeld 2006; Saward 2006, 2010) and in regard to the EU (Crum and Fossum 2009; Kohler-Koch 2010; Lord and Pollak 2010). However, the theoretical literature on representation tends to focus on better understanding the nature of representation. It uses empirical evidence only with illustrative purpose, and is rather limited in regard to policy-making processes beyond the nation-state (Urbinati and Warren 2008). The EU-centred empirical literature, for its part, is still very much struggling with the question of the political order and the *finalité* of the EU and often neglects insights of political theory.

Representation is also a central concept regarding the way in which the EU understands its democratic legitimacy. The Lisbon Treaty specifies that the 'functioning of the Union is based on representative democracy' (Art. 10) which can, therefore, be understood as a meta-standard for evaluating politics in the EU. We have also seen, most recently, a variety of more or less institutionalized reactions to the perceived democratic deficit. Supranationally, the EU – more precisely the European Commission – has established a Commissioner for Communication, developed its Plan D (for dialogue), developed structured dialogues with Civil Society Organizations throughout its Directorates General (DGs), and increased its online consultations. Transnationally, there is an increase in interparliamentary committees and networks that signals the parliamentarians' desire to remain central actors of democracy. Nationally, the devolution of competences in many EU Member States pays tribute to a widespread desire to bring the power closer to where the people are.

Overall, the present volume contributes to the renewed theoretical and empirical interest in democratic representation. As a consequence of the unsettled political and social nature of the EU, it is a deliberate choice of the editors not to impose one common theoretical framework onto all the contributions, but to choose an inductive way of reasoning and to conceive of theoretical pluralism as an added value rather than a limitation. In the remaining sections of this introduction we will pursue three aims. First, we specify the concept of representation. We then elaborate on the contingent relationship of representation and democracy and how it is currently challenged. And, finally, we discuss recent developments in representation theory and show how the contributions to this book relate to the existing literature and the challenges previously sketched.

What is representation?

At a general level, representation is about making present that which is absent. Most authors would agree that representation involves a relationship between a represented and a representative, and concerns an *object* (interests, opinions, etc.) taking place in a particular *setting* (the political context) before a specific *audience*. The relationship involved, however, is context-specific and dependent on the cultural conditions and the assumptions of what is appropriate representation and what is not (Pitkin 1967; Saward 2006). Indeed, there is no representation 'out there', but only different ways of looking at representation. Also, representation is not per se democratic; democratic representation is only one form of representation among others (Rehfeld 2006: 2; Saward 2009).

In contemporary democracies, representation is generally perceived as the means of safeguarding the political equality of citizens. For centuries, we have differentiated between two main competing models for achieving representation: the delegate and the trustee models of representation. Delegate conceptions of representation, commonly associated with American anti-Federalists, require representatives to 'stand for', that is, to follow their constituents' preferences. Trustee conceptions of representation, on the other hand, commonly associated with Edmund Burke, require representatives to 'act for', that is, to follow their own judgement about the proper course of action. A delegate seeks to defend the interests of his or her constituency, and can therefore be expected to be responsive to the constituency's claims. The trustee aims at the public interest (instead of the interest of a particular constituency) as a result of deliberating with other representatives. (S)he is acting not in the light of foreseeable sanctions, but on the ground of civic virtue. The delegate model perceives politics as power conflict over diverging interests, whereas the trustee model perceives politics as deliberation about the common good. The former is primarily interested in the control of power, while the latter is primarily concerned with the exercise of self-rule (Rehfeld 2009).

Although this dispute is often concerned with the role of parliamentarians, political representation can also adopt different forms and has, consequently, been qualified by a variety of adjectives: from parliamentary to territorial: from formalistic to substantive; from anticipatory to promissory; as well as descriptive, symbolic, and advocacy representation (Dovi 2002; Mansbridge 1999; Pitkin 1967; Urbinati 2000). All these different forms of representation reveal a common understanding that modern democratic politics is linked to representation.

A historically grown link and its transformation

In everyday language, democracy is usually associated with representation. Conceptually and empirically, however, this link is not evident: 'Through much of their history both the concept and the practice of representation have had little to do with democracy or liberty' (Pitkin 1967: 2). Rather, the close linkage of representation with democracy was a product of contingent historical developments, more specifically of the gradual emergence of territorially confined nation-states (Decker 2002; Hobson 2008). The gradual emergence of nation-states increased both the number of people and the expanse of territory to such an extent that the direct participation in the agora-democracy lost its practical meaningfulness. The congruence of territorial borders, nations, and national economies facilitated the emergence of the institutions of modern liberal democracy, in which an institutional centre within a clearly-confined territory became the ultimate arena and target of political representation.

The French Revolution offered the intellectual and political context in which democratic government came to be envisioned and institutionalized as representative government (Hobson 2008; Urbinati 2004). Indeed, Abbé de Sieyès considered the establishment of representative government as the 'true object of the revolution' (Hobson 2008: 453). For him democratic rule could either be exercised directly or by delegation, and representation was a means of reactivating democracy in the context of territorial nation-states. From such a perspective, 'democracy *is* possible and *it is* desirable precisely because it *is* representative' (Hobson 2008: 466).

Representative government was to be realized through regular, free, and fair elections. Elections legitimate the authorization of political leaders and make them, theoretically, responsive and accountable to the electorate. For the limited time span of an election cycle, political authority is delegated to elected representatives through the voting act that follows the basic rule of political equality: namely, one person, one vote. Normatively, electoral cycles imply that power is conditional, and that its abuse can be sanctioned. Consequently, electoral competition, the independent and equal voting act, the responsiveness of the rulers to the demands and needs of the people, and the people's ability to hold the representatives to account have been perceived as the most convincing democratic mechanisms for large-scale political systems. Following this fusion of democracy and representation, democratic representation has been understood as a way of establishing the legitimacy of democratic institutions and of creating institutional incentives for governments to be responsive to citizens. Representative government, such conceived, has shown to be a practically feasible and normatively justifiable version of democracy: 'Seen in the *longue durée*, representation has been a decisive ally of democracy, insofar as it fundamentally helped to alter the latter's conditions of possibility' (Hobson 2008: 451).

Today we are arguably faced with another historical change, a second transformation of democracy (see Dahl 1989 for transformations of democracy). The transition from the national to the post-national constellation (Habermas 1998) has profound consequences on the conceptualization and institutionalization of democracy in general, and of representative democracy in particular. The modern territorial state, and with it the link between democracy and representation, is challenged through a variety of diversification processes, including that of supranational (European) integration which contributes to the dilution of traditional representative politics (Warren and Castiglione 2004):

(a) We are faced with geographical diversification as transnational and supranational decision-making arenas emerge beyond the reach of traditional territorial representation. This is particularly obvious in the case of the EU. The expansion and transcendence of social and territorial boundaries undermine the sovereign statehood of established European democracies (Habermas 1998), without replacing it at the EU level. It is this state between incomplete sovereignty and the lack of compensation at another level that is often perceived as the EU's democratic deficit by its citizens;

(b) We are witnessing a diversification of actors. Parliaments lose their exclusivity in representative politics and are increasingly accompanied by a broad range of more or less institutionalized and organized actors, such as interest groups, agencies, Civil Society Organizations, social movements, local short-term initiatives, citizen juries, and experts. In the light of increasingly blurred divisions between formal and informal representation, it is therefore argued by leading authors that representation cannot be restricted anymore to electoral representation and to representation in the nation-state alone, for such a conceptualization seems to no longer grasp political reality (Rehfeld 2006; Lord and Pollak 2010). This trend also holds for the EU. In particular, much attention has been given to Civil Society Organizations (CSOs), and to whether their inclusion in policy-making can be a means for democratizing EU politics (Kohler-Koch and Finke 2007). It is often believed that CSOs could serve as a remedy to the legitimacy crisis of the EU by bringing the political system closer to the citizens and vice versa. Along these lines, an increasing number of studies address the way CSOs participate in policy-making at the EU level (Della Sala and Ruzza 2007; Friedrich 2011; Hüller 2010), often referring to deliberative or participative democratic theories. In the present volume, we also find a number of contributions concerned with the involvement of CSOs in EU policy-making, however with a different theoretical perspective;

(c) We can observe a diversification of issues. An increasing number of issues are dealt with not only nationally, but also on a European or even global scale, such as poverty, gender equality, global warming, war crimes, human rights, and minority rights. In the EU, this is particularly marked in regard to anti-poverty policies, gender equality/mainstreaming, and global warming;

(d) There is a diversification of competences to bodies which are not always subjected to the same checks and balances as electoral representation. This is particularly the case for committees such the Economic and Social Committee, the Committee of the Regions, and the Economic Policy Committee, as well as agencies, such the

European Food Safety Agency (EFSA) (Klintmann and Kronsell 2010).

While the extent to which these diversification processes have challenged the historically contingent link between democracy and representation in the European states is an object of debate to which the Europeanization and compliance literatures testify, it is clear that they have had pronounced effects. Given the transfer of competences to the EU and its densely structured multi-level politics, both of which weaken the ability of national democracies to keep decision-making authority in their hands, the relationship between representation, democracy, and the nation-state in the EU is particularly strained.

The diversification processes provoke a situation in which new frontiers of representation develop (Urbinati and Warren 2008: 402), yet we know remarkably little about their implications for democratic practice and for democratic theory (Castiglione and Warren 2008; Hendriks 2009; Mansbridge 2003). In light of the diversification processes, the very fundamentals of democratic representation need to be re-thought. What shape does a constituency take if it is not a territorially bounded electorate? What new forms of representation, outside of voting, emerge beyond the state? Which actors claim to act as representatives of what constituency? Are representatives representative? How is the relationship between represented and representative organized? What role does the EU play in (re)shaping political representations? This book explores these key questions and attempts to provide answers to a few.

Contemporary representation theory

Representation theory has begun to react to the diversification processes of representation described above. We can distinguish three different research streams that point to specific aspects of representation: the semantics of representation; the relationship between the represented and the representative; and, normatively, mechanisms to improve the representativeness of weaker groups in society. Since these streams are not concerned with the EU in particular, we specify a fourth stream that focuses on the transformative power that the EU exerts, willingly or unwillingly, on forms and practices of representation.

Formalistic representation

First, there is research that targets the institutionalization of representation and democracy, and the way in which the two are combined in nation-states (Manin 1997; Pitkin 1967; Rehfeld 2009). In her seminal work, Hanna Pitkin (1967) differentiates four types of representation: formalistic, substantive, descriptive, and symbolic. *Formalistic* representation encompasses the institutional arrangements that precede and initiate representation. It has two dimensions: authorization and accountability. A focus on authorization insists that the actions of the agent(s) can be ascribed to the principal, and that the represented are bound by such acts. The focus on accountability is instead concerned with the reverse aspect of representation, namely how and to what extent the representatives can be held accountable by the represented. Authorization and accountability thus emphasize the initial and the final stages of the representative relationship. For representatives to be democratic, according to Pitkin, they must a) be authorized to act, b) promote the interests of the represented, and c) it must be possible for the represented to hold the representatives to account. Formalistic representation is thus concerned with questions such as: who is represented in policy-making; can the represented hold the representatives to account; and through which institutions and institutional arrangements is their relationship stabilized? A number of contributions in this volume deal with these sorts of questions in light of the EU. Who is actually represented in EU governance and with what sort of mandate? Can representatives be held to account and if so by whom and how? With which sort of formalistic representation are we dealing?

Emmanuel Sigalas and Johannes Pollak discuss whether one can categorize the European Party Federations as classical parties, which have traditionally been key actors in representative democracy, organizing the political representation of popular democracy (Mair 2006). They ask whether one can observe programmatic convergence for the European elections (2009) between the constituting elements of the European Party Federations (EPFs). Have the EPFs reached a stage where they direct, orchestrate, or coordinate the EP election campaigns in select Member States? Sigalas and Pollak conclude that the EPFs fail to meet the programmatic convergence condition: although there is some overlap between the European and national level manifestos, national parties emphasize different issues and promote different arguments in their electoral platforms. The EPFs would therefore 'offer no link between citizens and governmental choice, and they lack sufficient cohesion to behave as a party'. The consequence is that there will be no European politicization of EP elections and that the latter 'will continue to be contested along national lines'.

Parliaments have traditionally been *the* central venue for political representation in representative democracies. In her research on interparliamentary cooperation in the EU and its repercussions in the French and Italian parliaments, Cristina Fasone examines how European national parliaments react to the challenges of European integration in order to represent their constituencies under changing circumstances. She scrutinizes parliamentary rules of procedure, practices, and debates; the frequency, place, and media broadcasting of interparliamentary meetings; and the involvement of political parties and groups as manifestations of their 'expressive' and 'informing' functions. Interparliamentary cooperation, she finds, is rather 'ineffective in supporting democratic representation in the EU', as national parliaments failed to inform citizens who remained 'in the dark about interparliamentary activity'.

Simona Piattoni is interested in similar questions concerning representatives in the Committee of the Regions (CoR). Piattoni here identifies an inherent tension between an electoral and a functional form of representation: being composed of subnational political representatives, the committee is considered by the Treaties as a 'consultative committee' similar to many others. Grounded in empirical research, Piattoni discusses how the diverse bases of representation affect the representational function fulfilled by CoR members. She finds that 'CoR members feel indeed that they should represent not just their particular territory, but all subnational territories regardless of their economic and institutional situation', thereby upgrading 'subnational territorial representation to a higher level of generality'. The analysis shows that the interests of their own particular territory are filtered out, while the interests connected to the geographical position and socio-economic profile of their territory and partisanship are allowed to pass through.

In regard to democratic representation, new actors pose important questions, namely how the semantics of representation can be implemented in non-electoral representation. Where there are no regularized means of authorization such as elections, authorization can grow from the ability of groups to attract supporters (Saward 2009). Such a support can take different forms: memberships, petitions, voices, donations, public visibility, and so forth. It is difficult to picture neat forms of authorization when the constituency is inherently unclear. For this same reason, adapting the norm of accountability to CSOs is also a difficult exercise.

Two contributions in this volume are concerned with precisely these questions. Håkan Johansson discusses the representation of socially excluded people at the EU level. Using the European Anti-Poverty

Network (EAPN) as his empirical example, Johansson analyses the way European level networks of CSOs define their constituency and construct their representativeness. Representing the poor and socially excluded is obviously a difficult endeavour as they often lack the capacities to get involved in the representation of their interests. Johansson shows how EAPN has taken an 'active stance in forming members' (e.g. by restricting membership to one member per country), due in part to pressures from the European Commission to secure geographical representation, and, as a consequence, raising doubts about the network's representativeness. At the same time, it seems 'as if members have limited direct influence over EAPN's affairs and activities', thereby raising an additional question mark on the representativeness of EAPN. EAPN has sought to demonstrate its representativeness by participating in yearly roundtables in which socially excluded persons take part that had previously been identified by national member organizations of EAPN. Johansson's evaluation of these meetings, however, is critical. At best, he notes, 'the network seeks ways to introduce the perspectives of poor people into its internal operations and the general debate on poverty and social exclusion at EU level. ... At worst, the people involved end up in a "hostage situation", in which other actors use their experiences to push their agenda in a certain direction.'

Meike Rodekamp discusses the extent to which European umbrella organizations are meeting the increasing demand of representativeness, such as through the establishment of respective authorization and accountability structures. Taking the transmission belt rationale as the theoretical starting point in the field of the EU's external dimension as her case, Rodekamp addresses the link between CSOs and their members by asking questions such as: to what extent do the representatives of CSOs at EU level consult their members in the Member States? Do members have the possibility of holding their representatives to account? Do members feel that their interests are reflected in the advocacy work of their Brussels representatives? The results of the empirical analysis are mixed. Only half of the interviewees involve their members in operational decision-making and only in some cases are necessary formal structures in place in order for members to participate. However, the shortcomings in formalistic representation 'are accompanied by positive assessments of substantive representation' as the majority of members seems satisfied with the overall representation of their interests through the umbrella CSOs. Rodekamp therefore concludes that 'effectiveness of representation might be guaranteed but equality of representation is not'.

Substantive representation

The second research stream targets the way the relationship between represented and representative works (Saward 2006; Castiglione and Warren 2008). *Substantive* representation has traditionally been related to the trustee and delegate models sketched above. As Pitkin argues, there needs to be independence on both sides of the representative relationship in order for there to be representation in the form of a trustee or a delegate. However, both models focus one-sidedly on the representative while neglecting to address the represented.

More recently, Jane Mansbridge has argued that democratic representation should not be conceived as a monolithic but as a multiform concept (Mansbridge 2003). She differentiates between four types of representation. *Promissory* representation focuses on the responsibility of the agent to the principal on the one side, and on the control of the principal over the agent on the other. This standard model of representation is 'promissory' in that representatives are rewarded by voters if they fulfil their electoral promises, and punished if not. *Anticipatory* representation occurs when representatives focus on what they think voters will approve in the next elections. Anticipatory representation has certainly gained in importance with the development of information systems (e.g. public opinion polls) that allow the representative to be aware of future voter preferences. *Gyroscopic* representation occurs when representatives look within their personal background to derive interests and principles. Here the behaviour of representatives is to some degree predictable based on their observable characteristics (personal reputation, character, etc.). *Surrogative* representation occurs when representatives represent constituents outside their particular constituency (district, party, etc.), that is, constituents with whom they don't have any electoral relationship (e.g. monetary surrogacy). With these four forms of representation, Mansbridge shows that representation is more than a relationship between elected officials and constituents, and more than a simple, territorially based principal – agent relationship.

For Michael Saward, representation can be understood as *claims-making*, or as a constantly changing social dialogue in which different actors make claims to audiences which discuss, reject, or amend them (Saward 2006, 2010). His work is grounded on three assumptions. First, representation is not a relationship at precise moments, but must be thought of as a continuing process that evolves over time. Second, the core of representation is the practice of claims-making to be representative. Finally, constituents and representatives need not be members of electoral districts or elected parliamentarians respectively. Saward insists on the dynamic nature of the relationship and on the performative (rather than the institutional) side of representation in which both represented and representative play active roles. Such a conception of representation, according to Saward, is well suited to capture power and interests in political representation. The claims-making terminology certainly is useful in that it directs attention towards the public sphere and the representative as active agents of political representation. At the same time, the 'audience' gives citizens a much more passive role. The difficulty with this approach may be that it detracts from issues of accountability.[1]

In effect, representation does not exist per se, but needs to be constructed and continuously reconstructed. It is therefore important to examine how and with what success actors manage to offer themselves as representatives. In this volume, several contributions consider the intrinsically dynamic, socially constructed, and contextual nature of political representation. They address how and in which arenas representation comes about: how the constituency and the representative are constructed; what is the self-understanding of the different actors within the representative relationship; which incentives or disincentives for representative claims-making are produced by specific actors or institutions; and how claims-making functions, in particular across levels of governance.

Pieter de Wilde assesses the construction of constituencies within a claims-making perspective and presents a case study of strong and weak public spheres – parliaments and mass media – asking how far the 'operating logics of different public spheres' affect the practice of claims-making (i.e. who is claimed to be represented by whom). Drawing from analyses of the last three EU budget negotiations, de Wilde finds that the 'operating logics of both mass media and parliaments appear to stimulate a competitive representative space, where multiple constituencies are claimed to be represented by multiple claimants'. In mass media, the logic of news value seemingly brings about 'a plural representative space in newspaper coverage of EU budget negotiations,' while in parliament, interparty conflict works in favor of a plural representative space. The main finding is thus that both weak and public spheres, despite their different internal logics, produce plural representative spaces as a result of stimulating competition between representatives.

From a somewhat similar theoretical perspective, Asimina Michailidou and Hans-Jörg Trenz ask to what extent the Internet alters 'the act of representation among political agents, various constituents and audiences'.

Is there a new representative order online or is the online public sphere a mirror of the offline media debates, merely replicating the national public spheres? Does the Internet facilitate the representation and interaction of individuals within the complex transnational constituency of the EU electorate? Empirically, they examine several 'micro' web-spheres from 12 EU Member States and at the trans-European level in conjunction with the June 2009 European parliamentary elections. Michailidou and Trenz observe that the 'EP elections e-sphere is dominated by the voice of a category of actors that is largely absent in offline media, namely citizens' who, content-wise, 'refute the EU polity's right to claim representation *of* them'. At the same time, and also mirroring the findings by Sigalas and Pollak, online discussions about the EP elections 'remain a national affair', rooted in domestic topics and debates and representing national constituencies. The authors conclude that the results raise 'questions with regard to the ability of online media to re-present a constituency of democratic politics that is different from the community of co-national citizens and, therefore, to enable audiences to reach beyond the boundaries of nationally-framed political debates'.

Also adopting a claims-making perspective, Erik Jentges is interested in how CSOs construct their representativeness and how they become accepted by political decision-makers in Berlin and Brussels. Using a theoretical perspective that rests on Bourdieu's concept of political field as well as on Elias's concept of figuration, he analyses claims established by consumer associations and religious organizations in Germany. The contribution describes the processes and claims through which the organizations succeed in constituting themselves as representative of particular constituencies or diffuse interests. His analysis shows that that recognition by political institutions 'is a prerequisite and must come from those in power' before CSOs can actually negotiate in the name of their constituencies. To be accepted as representatives, organizations, according to CSO representatives, must have 'expert knowledge, personal contacts, and mutual trust'.

Descriptive representation

Issues of representation generate normative questions, which comprise a third area of research. Traditionally, these touched on the paradoxical presence and absence of representation, further developed in Urbinati's 'incompability theory' (2006: 6). Moreover, Bernard Manin categorizes representative democracy as a mixed government, rather than a strict democracy, as it is a 'machinery that combines democratic and undemocratic parts' (Manin 1997: 237). In a way, the fusion of representation and democracy into representative democracy created an uneasy trade-off: representation had to make room for equality, and democracy had to make room for delegation (responsiveness and accountability). We have long had lively debates over the weight that should be given to political equality and autonomy respectively (see Thaa 2008).

Most recently, normative representation theory has focused on the desirability and feasibility of the representation of weak interests, which often find their expression in identity politics, such as multiculturalism, religious pluralism, feminism, and the better representation of disadvantaged social interests in government (Kymlicka 1995; Young 2000). Pitkin discussed this type of representation as *descriptive*, referring to the degree to which the representative mirrors the characteristics of the represented (e.g. their gender, status, ethnicity, professional condition, etc.). In descriptive representation, 'the representative does not act for others, he "stands for" them, by virtue of a correspondence or connection between them, a resemblance or reflection' (Pitkin 1967: 61).

Along these lines, descriptive representation has attracted considerable attention in recent political theory. From the perspective of those who defend it, descriptive representation helps to address issues of equity or exclusion, thus providing arguments for disadvantaged groups to claim a seat at the decision-making table (Young 2000), who are often not proportionally represented through electoral representation. Considering representation as a differentiated relationship, Iris Marion Young has shown that representative institutions include groups as well as exclude. In other words, providing representation for some citizens and/or groups comes at the expense of others (ibid.). Representation, from this perspective, is as much about presence as it is about absence (see also Kymlicka 1995; Plotke 1997). Some of the authors concerned with descriptive representation argue that only socialization within a given group can make it possible to understand and represent the group's demands (Mansbridge 1999; Dovi 2002). In the same vein, Nadia Urbinati suggests an *agonistic* conception of representation that emphasizes the importance of disagreements and rhetoric. In her view, representation should not be about the aggregation of interests but the preservation of differences (Urbinati 2000).

Several of the contributions share an interest in normative questions of representative government. For instance, Håkan Johansson discusses the representation of socially excluded people at the EU level and its general feasibility. Sandra Kröger and Heiko Pleines (see below) show that, against official declarations, the activities of the Commission may contribute to sharpening the democratic deficit through its dialogue with CSOs rather than alleviating it.

The influence of the EU on practices of political representation

To these three research streams, we add a fourth that looks at the way the EU eventually transforms established forms and practices of political representation. This is an important issue insofar that institutions may function to deter political equality, a norm that democratic representation is meant to assure. Institutions need to select and therefore to restrict access to them (European Commission), or they can represent disproportionately (Council, European Parliament).

In his recent work, Stefano Bartolini (2005) identifies a 'system of representation' in the EU, which is markedly different from the one we find in Member States. The ensemble of structures organizes competition over inputs within a political system by upholding a representational relationship between those representatives that participate in the policy process and those whom they formally represent. Bartolini emphasizes three main channels of representation: *electoral, territorial,* and *interest-based* representation. Electoral representation is the standard model found in most contemporary democracies. Elections are expected to uphold the principle of political equality among citizens and ensure that political leaders stay responsive to the interests of the general public. Territorial representation seeks to secure equity between territories according to the principle of 'one state, one vote'. Interest representation, finally, is characterized by private actors who seek to influence policy development and to act as advocates through diverse lobbying activities (Beyers, Eising, and Maloney 2008). Should these three channels exist in different forms at the EU level than at Member-State level, there are reasons to believe that the interaction of both levels leaves neither one as it was before, possibly favouring some channels and ways of representation over others.

Tapio Raunio examines the influence of the European integration process on national parliaments. Utilizing an original data set of European Convention and COSAC documents, the chapter shows that when defining a role for national parliaments in the EU's political system, domestic members of parliament focus on policy-making and government oversight, while they see functions emphasizing the representation of citizens as 'clearly exceptional'. This may simply follow the process of European integration, as 'practically all of the rights and responsibilities assigned by the Treaties deal with government-related functions of parliaments – mainly with the functions of government oversight and law making'. Thus one observes that 'the electoral dimension of representation has clearly received less attention than government accountability – both at the European level…and in domestic debates on the role of national parliaments'. Raunio also shows that national parliaments are increasingly viewed as gatekeepers between national and EU politics, componded by the early warning system included in the Lisbon Treaty that reinforces the perception of domestic members of parliament acting as 'guardians of Treaties'.

Elena Griglio is interested in the extent to which regional assemblies have developed their capacities as well as displaying their willingness to interpret and carry out their role as representatives in EU affairs. She examines regional assemblies in Italy and Spain to understand whether they have managed to counterbalance the EU's intergovernmentalism and uncover spaces of intervention for parliaments to voice their popular will and promote regions in EU affairs. Her analysis shows that Spanish regional assemblies, often with a strong emphasis on autonomy, actively try to engage in the 'ascending subsidiarity' (i.e. try to engage in networks of interregional cooperation in order to directly influence EU affairs), while partially circumventing the national level. Italian regional assemblies, however, tend to follow the strategy of 'descending subsidiarity', that is, they try to strengthen their control function vis-à-vis the national level, rather than attempting to gain independent influence on EU policy processes.

Stijn Smismans analyses 'to what extent and how "representation" is an *explicit* concern of the EU institutions in their dealing with interest groups'. He argues that the EU's concern with the representative character of interest group participation takes two main forms, 'system representativeness' and 'organizational representativeness'. The former relates to the overall mosaic of interest representation, which should be as complete (representative) as possible, the latter to internal organizational features of CSOs. Smismans argues that there are severe problems with identifying criteria of representativeness and with knowing how to apply them to various organizations and consultative mechanisms, including traditional interest groups, social partners, and CSOs. Moreover, defining a clear standard for organizational representativeness had never been a major concern of the Commission. Instead, the Commission has a functional need 'for expertise, rather than a concern on how representative an organization is in relation to societal demands or in relation to the interests of its constituency'. An analysis of the recent Transparency Initiative illustrates that the Commission has deleted concepts such as representativeness or representativity, and has returned to more traditional concepts such as interest groups and lobbyists when speaking of CSOs. As a result of this shift, well-resourced organizations will undoubtedly gain strength and greater representation in EU policy-making.

Sandra Kröger focuses on the influence of the European Commission on CSOs' capacities to be democratically represenitive. She develops two ideal types of democratic representation – CSOs that represent people and CSOs that represent specific causes – and confronts them with the consultation and funding practices of the Commission. She argues that the Commission strives to support both effective governance and system integration, but does not necessarily have the goal of representing people or the specific causes identified. She shows that 'connecting EU policy processes to real-existing people in Member States, who could be democratically represented by CSOs, may move in far distance in the context of the multi-level structure and the pressure towards professionalization and adaptation'. Indeed, if patronage by the Commission allows CSOs to pursue their goals without members, why should they invest any effort in attracting membership? In such a scenario, she concludes, a constituency is increasingly rendered obsolete while weak interests largely remain dependent on the goodwill of powerful actors.

Heiko Pleines addresses the influence that EU membership has had on trade unions and their political representation among the newer post-socialist Member States. Using Poland, the Czech Republic, and Slovakia as his empirical cases, he shows that trade unions view the EU in an extremely positive light, and they acknowledge it to have had an important impact on their work. This is not surprising given that the EU supports them in their fight for more worker-friendly regulations. As Pleines shows, trade unions 'have partly been converted into representatives of EU prescriptions', as a sort of 'watchdog' for the EU Commission. While this eventually strengthens their position in domestic politics, it also 'limits their room for manoeuvre in the national political arena and it has the potential to alienate them from the national elites and from their original constituency'. Pleines argues that as an ally of the EU, trade union activities at the EU level have 'the potential to weaken the representative link between constituency and representatives', working against the Commission's rhetoric to activate civil society actors as a transmission belt between the citizens and Brussels.

This volume seeks to uncover dynamics of representation in the EU in several ways. It portrays representative claims made by different political actors engaged in European politics; it clarifies the representativeness of these actors; and it elucidates the transformative power of the

EU with regard to political representation. The analyses of these different contributions engender a number of conceptual questions that will be addressed in the concluding chapter, such as: how is the relationship between representatives and the 'to-be-represented' structured? What role(s) do European institutions play in representative politics? Do they sharpen or weaken the link between representatives and the represented? And what do the contributions tell us about the evolving link between democracy and representation in the EU?

Note

1. We would like to thank Dario Castiglione for pointing this out.

Part I

Who Represents Whom? Issues of Representativeness

2
Political Parties at the European Level: Do They Satisfy the Condition of Programmatic Convergence?

Emmanuel Sigalas and Johannes Pollak

Introduction

EU democracy cannot work without an element of representation, because 'no system can accommodate the participation of all relevant stakeholders' (Eriksen and Fossum 2007: 9). Parliamentary representation is a key mode of representation (Pollak et al. 2009) and is particularly relevant for the EU. As Article 8A of the Lisbon Treaty states, 'the functioning of the Union shall be founded on representative democracy' (European Union 2007: 14).

Within the context of representative democracy it is inconceivable that political parties will not have a role to play. Political parties serve two important functions indispensable for public representation, namely, aggregating individual preferences and transforming them into comprehensible policy programmes and enhancing public deliberation (Lord 2004 and 2010). The Treaty on the European Union itself states that '[p]olitical parties at the European level are important as a factor for integration within the Union. They contribute to forming a European awareness and to expressing the political will of the citizens of the Union' (Article 191, European Union 2006: 132). However, this statement can only apply to political associations that rightly bear the name 'parties', rather than to severely fragmented party federations.

The question of whether political parties at the European level are national party umbrella organizations instead of EU parties is open. On the one hand, the EU officially recognizes the European party federations (EPFs) as political parties and contributes to their funding from the EU budget. On the other, the link between European citizens and European-level parties is indirect and the latter cannot nominate candidates for the European elections. The ambiguity about the real as opposed to the nominal status of the European-level parties can be resolved if one looks at the necessary conditions that political parties need to meet in order to be properly labelled as such. We argue that a necessary, though not sufficient, condition is the programmatic convergence of the member parties. If the EPFs fail to adopt or, even worse, to agree on a common manifesto for the European elections, then it becomes evident that they lack the sufficient ideological cohesion that will allow them to operate as a party instead of a mere umbrella organization. As we explain in the ensuing sections, there are good reasons why EPFs should strive for the adoption of a common manifesto, but there are also good reasons why such an outcome is difficult, given the second-order character of the European elections (Schmitt 2009) and the different political priorities and sensitivities of the EU member states (Judge and Earnshaw 2008: 73).

This chapter is structured as follows: we commence by reminding the reader why political parties are integral to representative democracy; we then move to the debate in the literature as to whether the EPFs are integrated parties or party coalitions, and we propose two conditions that are necessary features of all parties. The remaining part of the chapter is dedicated to the presentation of our empirical research design and the analysis of the 2009 European election manifestos of the Party of the European Socialists (PES), the European People's Party (EPP), the European Green Party (EGP), and of the manifestos of their respective member parties. We find that although there is some overlap between the European- and national-level manifestos, the national parties emphasize different issues and promote mostly different arguments in their electoral platforms.

The importance of political parties in representative democracy

The importance of political parties is intimately linked with the importance of political representation in modern democracies. In mass democracies neither politics nor governance can function without some element of representation (e.g. Dalton 1985; Mair and Thomassen 2010), and representation requires political institutions that will channel communication and influence between represented and representatives.

This role is played primarily, though not exclusively (as is shown in the other chapters of this volume), by the political parties through the means of universal, regular, free, and fair parliamentary elections.

Historically, as Sartori (2005) has shown, party democracy and electoral democracy have gone together. The extension of suffrage to all the adult male and then later female population transformed parties-in-parliament into vote-seeking mechanisms and responsible government became responsive government (Sartori 2005: 16–21). Today political parties remain so deeply entrenched in systems of representative government and democracy that it is difficult to imagine the one without the other.

In a party democracy, where elections are universal, it is the whole citizenry and not just a fraction of it, as is the case with representation through interest and lobbying groups, that have the opportunity to influence policy-making. The regularity of elections ensures that parties are held accountable to the electorate at regular intervals, thus minimizing the threat of power abuse and maximizing congruence between the preferences of the represented and the choices of the representatives. Last but not least, conducting free and fair elections guarantees that the electoral choice and political message of the electorate will not be distorted or disregarded and that it will be reflected in the composition of the parliament.

Notwithstanding arguments about the decline of political parties (Whiteley 2011) or their alleged deterioration in 'their capacity and/or willingness to function as representative organizations' and their greater 'emphasis on their role as organizers of government' (Mair and Thomassen 2010: 25), political parties continue to link citizens to policy-making. The link is obviously indirect. Citizens do not instruct political parties what to do or how to decide on every single policy matter, but through their vote they can indicate whether they have been satisfied by the party's past performance and choices and whether they are in broad agreement with the proposed policy goals for the future.

Parties, furthermore, perform an aggregating function of choices that is crucial for the functioning of representative democracy. Effective representation requires a mechanism that allows the views, interests, and preferences of the many, of the represented, to be reflected in the choices of the elect few, the representatives. Political parties can help in this respect because, as Lord (2010: 5–6) explains, they enable (1) political competition around broad approaches to government; (2) the coordination of any two voters by simply voting for the same party; (3) the simplification of choices; and (4) judging representatives' performance over time. To perform these tasks, parties need to be able to agree on common programmatic objectives. It is a common political platform made public that allows voters to choose between parties that are closer to their own views and preferences. But the importance of agreement to a unique set of common principles, from which public policy preferences and choices may derive, goes beyond the objectives of electoral contestation. It is what distinguishes one party from another and, more importantly, what unites 'a body of men, for promoting by their joint endeavours the national interest', according to Burke's definition of political party (quoted in Sartori 2005: 8).

European party federations: political parties or umbrella organizations?

Our previous analysis made clear that political parties perform important tasks in systems of representative democracy. Since the EU's function is also based on the principles of representative democracy, as the Treaty of Lisbon stipulates, it should feature European-level political parties that can play a role analogous to the role of parties at the national level. The EU acknowledges the European party federations as political parties at the European level (EP and Council 2003; EP and Council 2007), but some scholars remain doubtful (e.g. Smith 1999; Lord 2004; Ladrech 2010).

According to the definition of Sartori (2005: 56), a 'party is any political group identified by an official label that presents at elections, and is capable of placing through elections (free or non-free), candidates for public office'. If we were to adhere strictly to the definition of Sartori, it is immediately obvious that the EPFs in their present form are not political parties. First of all, the EU lacks the office of a central government for which EPFs could have competed against each other. Secondly, the EPFs cannot nominate candidates for the European Parliament (EP) elections, or for the offices of the European Commission or the European Council President; these choices remain the prerogative of the national parties and governments, respectively.

Although being deprived of direct access to executive and legislative power removes the key incentive for political contestation, it may be premature to conclude that the EPFs are not political parties. They could be nascent parties with the potential of development (Hix 1996: 323). The 1996 Tsatsos EP report 'on the constitutional status of the European political parties' rightly observed that 'as we are in the midst of an evolutionary process, it would be a mistake to attempt any theoretical demarcation. There would be too great a risk of definitions unnecessarily excluding or inhibiting future forms of political organization' (Tsatsos 1999: 654). Thus, according to Tsatsos (ibid.), 'without providing a conclusive definition', a European-level party will have 'various features derived from the image of the political parties in the Union's member states and transferred – mutatis mutandis – to the level of the European Union' (ibid.).

Considering that the EPFs developed significantly over time (Hix 1996; Johansson and Zervakis 2002), Tsatsos's suggestion that the characteristics and functions of European-level parties may change further in the future is certainly useful for the appraisal of their status as political parties. But his recommendation to look for similarities between the parties at the national and European level is too vague for the purposes of empirical assessment. As Lord (2004) notes, using the degree of similarities as a criterion in order to determine if an EPF is a fully developed party or not is like trying to determine if the glass is half empty or half full. In favour of the party status of the EPFs count arguments such as those quoted in Lord (2006: 7): (1) the internal structures of the EPFs resemble those of the national parties; (2) the EU regulation 'governing parties at the European level' (EP and Council 2003) allows individual membership; (3) EPFs are officially recognized by the EU as European-level parties and are funded by the EU budget (EP and Council 2007); (4) EPFs produce manifestos for the European elections just as national parties produce manifestos for the national elections; (5) majority voting within the EFPs implies some loss of independence for the national member parties. However, all the previous arguments can be easily refuted to prove the opposite. Thus, individual membership may be allowed by the EU regulation, but the EPFs do not endorse it in practice (Smith 1999: 106). Furthermore, as Lord (2006: 7) argues, '[s]tructural resemblances between Europarties and conventional political parties may be mimetic only. Union resourcing may even be taken as a sign that Europarties lack roots in society that would allow them to do more to fund themselves. Accounts of how and where political preferences are formed are notoriously over-determined and therefore elusive. Majority voting is balanced by a lack of clear sanctions ... for those who do not follow the majority line.'

Instead of comparing the features of national- and European-level parties, it is conceptually and empirically more fruitful to assess if the EPFs fulfil the two necessary conditions that mark 'fully developed political parties in a liberal democratic system of governance' (Lord 2004: 47). The first necessary condition is that parties should provide an electoral connection between citizens and the political system (ibid.), and the second is that each party should be cohesive enough to present a common political platform.

Both Lord (2004: 54) and Hix, Noury and Roland (2007: 29) agree that the European elections offer no connection between citizens and political system. They are fought largely in national rather than European terms, and voter choice cannot be linked directly to the performance of the outgoing EP or the practically invisible programmatic commitments of the EPFs. Since the inability to satisfy the electoral linkage condition is attributed to the second-order character of the European elections (Lord 2004: 54; Hix, Noury and Roland 2007: 29), which is a persistent feature of European politics (Reif and Schmitt 1980; Marsh 1998 and 2005; Hix and Marsh 2007; Schmitt 2009) and largely beyond the influencing capacities of the EPFs, the electoral linkage connection condition is particularly difficult to meet under the present circumstances. This is why we focus on the performance of EPFs in relation to the second condition, which in theory should be easier to satisfy yet equally as important as the first: programmatic convergence for the European elections between the constituting elements of the EPFs.

Programmatic convergence as a necessary condition for parties at the European level

A degree of ideological cohesion which can lead to agreements on common political positions at the public level is absolutely necessary for a political association to act as a party. This means that internal disagreements and derogations should not prevent a party from declaring publicly its official positions, but it should be cohesive enough to formulate and pursue common policy-relevant proposals. Hence, if the EPFs are to be understood as something more than transactions cost-saving networks of national parties (Ladrech 2010: 138), they should be at least capable of agreeing on a common set of ideological and policy-relevant positions and their members should adhere to them.[1]

A high degree of ideological cohesion that is translated to common position should be reflected in the programmatic positions of the EFPs; in other words, in the European elections manifestos of the EFPs and of their member parties. The focus on the European election manifestos stems from the fact that the EPFs are normatively and practically closely linked to the European elections. It is mainly through and during the European election campaign process that the EPFs have the chance to play their prescribed roles as 'a key element in the process of forming and voicing European public opinion' (EP 2006: 3) and to reduce the 'gulf between many members of the public and the European institution' (ibid.).[2] Moreover, participation in the European elections, or the expressed intention to do so, is a precondition for the EPFs to be recognized as political parties by the EU and receive funding from its budget (EP and Council 2003; EP and Council 2007).

Agreeing on and adopting a common manifesto for the European elections entails a series of benefits for the EPFs and their member parties. For the EPF as a whole, and especially for its supranational core, it sends signals of party unity towards the voters and the rival EPFs. Furthermore, it gives the EPF some leeway in claiming that it is a political party in the traditional sense, and that it should be treated as such. At the EP level, having agreed on the stance the member parties should adopt on a number of policy areas increases the voting cohesion and the bargaining power of the EPFs' corresponding political group. For the national member parties agreeing on a common manifesto and drawing from it for their electoral campaign is a good occasion to show that they take their EPF membership seriously. It is also an opportunity to engage with new proposals and ideas that may prove useful to them and a channel of legitimization of their own policy proposals and choices (Ladrech 2010: 138).

Nevertheless, it cannot be taken for granted that the EPFs will manage to agree on a common manifesto for the European elections or that the member parties will use it in their own campaign. In the first three European elections the British and the Danish Labour parties exempted themselves from certain sections of the PES manifesto, and in 1994 a footnote clarified that the Danish party's agreement should be read in the light of the Danish opt-outs from the Treaty on the European Union (Smith 1999: 95). The EPFs lack a strong enforcement mechanism and they cannot force their members to consent to a manifesto they do not approve of, let alone oblige them to fully adopt the EPF manifesto as their own. The prospect of membership suspension is an extreme measure that offers no guarantee that member parties will comply with just any EPF decision, and it can be damaging to the EPF itself if the dissenting national party is large and influential. As a result, the drafting of the common manifesto takes place on the basis of broad consensus and by the time it reaches the stage of formal decision at the EPFs' congress, majority voting is a mere formality (Moschonas 2004: 116).

With the exception of the European Democrats, all the other EPFs managed to produce a common manifesto for the 2009 European elections. However, it is far from clear how many of their member parties really adopted it or to what extent. The second-order character of the European elections demands that the national parties focus their electoral campaign on domestic matters, priorities, and policies. Thus, a manifesto that has been designed to accommodate the views of all or most member parties may be unsuitable or even a liability for a campaign that evolves largely around country-specific topics. Since the EPFs cannot prescribe that their members stick to the political positions of the common manifesto, the disincentives to adopt it may outweigh the incentives. Therefore, the question whether the EPFs satisfy the condition of the programmatic convergence is subject to empirical verification.

Even though the analysis of the European election party manifestos is not something new, the extant literature has failed to tackle the question of similarities between the European- and national-level manifestos. Pennings (2006), Lefkofridi and Kritzinger (2008), Wüst and Schmitt (2007), and Wüst (2009) present some evidence of limited Europeanization of the national party manifestos, but increased references to the EU or Europe, or discussing issues in an EU frame, do not necessarily equate to convergence of political positions. Dorussen and Nanou (2006) address the issue of programmatic convergence of national parties, but their analysis focuses on the national elections and manifestos, leaving the convergence between EPF manifestos and national parties' European election manifestos aside. Our comparison of the political positions found in the EPF and national manifestos, therefore, hopefully covers a significant gap in the literature.

The research design

The question we seek to answer here is to what extent the EPFs and their member parties can present to the European electorate a common political platform for the 2009 European Parliament elections. Do we find the same or similar arguments in the manifestos of the EPFs and their national member parties, or do the national manifesto positions deviate from those commonly agreed at the European level? The parties we examine are the PES, the EPP, the EGP, and their respective national member parties in Austria, Denmark, France, Germany, Greece, Slovakia, and the UK. Our sample covers the two largest political federations and the Greens, and a selection of old and new, small and big EU member states.

We hand-coded the party positions through a detailed content analysis of the manifestos, and we classified the coded arguments to 50 broader political themes using the latter as reference points.[3] In total we analysed 23 documents that together were 564 pages long and yielded 6,691 coded arguments (Table 2.1).[4]

With the exception of the French Socialists (Parti Socialiste) and the Slovak Green party (Strana Zelených), who adopted a translated version of the respective EPF manifestos, all the other national parties in our study produced their own EP election manifesto. The comparative

Table 2.1 Descriptive statistics of the 2009 European elections manifestos

Federation	Party	Words	Rank	Quotations per 100 words	Rank
Party of European Socialists					
	PES (EU)	9426	5	3.925	13
	SPÖ (A)	3412	17	6.741	1
	SPD (D)	8764	7	4.096	10
	Socialdemokraterne (DK)	4265	14	2.11	18
	PASOK (GR)	3824	16	4.053	12
	SMER SD (SK)	2533	19	1.263	21
	Labour (UK)	8060	8	2.99	16
European Green Party					
	European Green Party (EU)	3847	15	5.017	5
	Die Grünen (A)	5613	12	4.543	7
	Die Grünen (D)	35968	1	4.412	8
	Sosialistisk Folkeparti (DK)	780	21	6.026	2
	Les Verts (F)	15102	3	4.079	11
	Oikologoi Prasinoi (GR)	3361	18	4.88	6
	Green Party UK	13440	4	3.876	14
European People's Party					
	EPP (EU)	19149	2	3.468	15
	ÖVP (A)	6616	10	4.187	9
	CDU (D)	5997	11	5.103	4
	Konservative (DK)	4594	13	2.068	19
	UMP (F)	1389	20	5.184	3
	SDKU (SK)	7160	9	2.011	20
	Conservatives (UK)	9355	6	2.918	17
Total		172655		3.875	

Notes: Authors' own data. The Conservatives are no longer an EPP member, but they are included in our analysis for comparison reasons.

analysis of 21 party manifestos is not a straightforward task. The parties did not only produce documents in different languages and formats, but also texts of different length and density in terms of arguments (Table 2.1). Thus the shortest manifesto is only 780 words long (Sosialistik Folkeparti, Denmark), whereas the longest extends to as many as 35,968 words (Die Grünen, Germany). In order to take into consideration the length differences between the different documents and get a more accurate view of the quantitative differences between them, we devised the index 'quotations per 100 words'. As the term suggests, the index takes into account both the number of coded arguments and the word-length of the manifesto. From this angle, shorter manifestos, such as that of the European Greens or the Social Democratic Party of Austria (SPÖ), appear particularly rich in terms of coded arguments (Table 2.1).

The sheer size of the coded arguments pool does not allow us to refer here to the actual political arguments mentioned in the manifestos. Instead, we opted for their synoptic presentation by employing an issue-salience scale and an argument-adoption rate. Thus we take a high programmatic convergence rate to have been achieved when the national manifestos focus largely on the same thematic families as the EPF manifestos, and when at least half of the EPF manifesto arguments have found their way in the national manifestos and figure prominently there.

Results

Tables 2.2 to 2.4 give us the first evidence that the member parties do not follow their EPF in the relative emphasis of the different topics in the manifestos. That is, certain thematic areas are addressed far more or far less frequently in the EPF manifesto than in the national manifestos. For reasons of simplicity we decided to concentrate on the ten most salient thematic areas in the EPF manifestos. The top ten code families cover more than 50 per cent of the EPF manifesto codes, which suggests that these are the issue areas where the European-level manifestos focus their attention.

As Table 2.2 shows, in the case of the Social Democrats the national party members touch upon more or less the same issues as the PES, but their emphasis differs and in some cases substantially so. The most salient issue for the PES is climate change, followed closely by foreign affairs and then by the financial crisis. When it comes to the top ten themes, the Labour manifesto offers the best match in terms of issue salience. The British manifesto covers all the PES priority areas and the

Table 2.2 Issue salience in the PES members' manifestos (per cent)

	PES	SPÖ	Social-demokraterne	SPD	PASOK	SMER SD	Labour
Top 10 code families							
Climate	9.89	3.26	1.11	3.03	0.68	0	6.11
Foreign affairs	9.32	3.72	4.44	8.79	10.14	0	5.68
Financial crisis	6.50	8.84	0	11.21	4.73	3.13	5.68
Energy	5.08	4.65	6.67	2.42	0	9.38	3.93
Job creation	5.08	4.19	4.44	1.21	2.70	9.38	4.80
Economy	4.80	3.72	3.33	3.64	1.35	12.50	4.80
Immigration	4.80	3.26	4.44	4.85	8.78	0	6.55
Social	3.95	4.65	3.33	5.45	4.05	25	2.18
Development	3.67	1.86	3.33	2.73	1.35	0	3.49
Job agreements	3.39	3.72	0	5.15	7.43	0	2.62
Total	56.50	41.86	31.11	48.48	41.22	59.38	45.85
Standard deviation of all code families issue salience		11.96	16.70	20.14	15.52	38.51	35.15

Notes: Authors' own data. The calculation of the standard deviation is not based on the population mean, but on the issue salience value of the EPF code family.

distribution of arguments among the top ten families does not differ so much from the PES code distribution. However, the large standard deviation suggests that in the remaining code families the Labour manifesto deviates from the PES manifesto pattern.

The standard deviation in the German and Austrian Social Democratic Party manifestos is among the lowest in the PES federation, indicating that both SPÖ and SPD emphasize more or less the same thematic areas as the PES manifesto. The main difference between the PES and the German and Austrian manifestos lies in the relative importance given to the financial crisis topic. Whereas this issue occupies 6.5 per cent of the PES manifesto, the SPD dedicates almost twice as much (11.21 per cent) of its space, and the SPÖ 8.84 per cent, thus putting financial crisis on the top of their agenda.

Deviation between the PES and the Slovak, Danish, and Greek member parties is greater. Table 2.2 illustrates that the Slovak party had prioritized completely different topics than the PES. To name but the most obvious examples, a quarter of its manifesto went to social affairs, compared to less than 4 per cent in the PES case, and the number one topic in the PES manifesto (climate change) hardly gets mentioned in the Slovak document. The deviation of the Danish and Greek documents is less dramatic but still discernible. Immigration gets the lion's share (8.78 per cent) in the PASOK manifesto and only 4.8 per cent in the PES manifesto. The Danish manifesto is one of the shortest in our study and as a result several topics are not mentioned at all. The Socialdemokraterne covered just seven of the top ten PES families and in total only 31 of the 50 categories.

Overall, from an issue-salience perspective the national member parties did not follow the pattern of the PES manifesto completely, but there are some striking similarities: foreign affairs, financial crisis, and energy issues figure prominently in almost all manifestos. There are, however, topic areas where the contrast between the PES and the national manifestos is unmistakable. For example, neither climate change nor foreign affairs, immigration, or development-related arguments featured in the Slovak manifesto, while public services and region-related topics appeared in the Austrian and German manifestos, but not in the PES document.

The situation in the EPP family is not fundamentally different from that of the PES. Some of the priority issues in the EPP manifesto figure highly on the national manifestos as well, but the national parties did not follow the European manifesto fully, and in several cases they opted to concentrate on their national priorities. However, the difference in issue salience between the EPP and its national members is greater than the differences in the PES family. As Table 2.3 shows, the top ten EPP themes cover more than 65 per cent of its manifesto, whereas they occupy less than 40 per cent, on average, of the national manifestos. Furthermore, the standard deviation is around 20 percentage units for all member parties in our EPP sample, which is also the case for the British Conservatives who are not an EPP member. Hence, not only is issue-emphasis variance greater among the EPP members compared to the PES, but membership in the Conservative and Christian Democrat federation does not seem to make any discernible difference in this respect.

With the exception of the ÖVP (Austria), all member parties placed foreign affairs high on their agenda, which is by far the most salient area in the EPP manifesto. When it comes to climate change, though, the second most prominent topic in the EPP document, it is found

Table 2.3 Issue salience in the EPP members' manifestos (per cent)

	EPP	ÖVP	Konservative	UMP	CDU	SDKU	Conservatives
Top 10 code families							
Foreign affairs	15.81	0.38	8.51	7.14	8.93	7.80	5.95
Climate	8.63	1.52	2.13	1.43	1.37	0	3.35
Energy	8.47	4.55	11.70	0	5.50	10.64	3.72
Financial crisis	5.91	10.23	2.13	14.29	7.22	1.42	2.60
Immigration	5.75	1.14	6.38	7.14	3.44	0	1.12
Job creation	5.27	0.76	1.06	2.86	0.69	2.84	0.37
Justice	4.79	2.27	8.51	4.29	4.47	0.71	4.83
Family	4.15	0.76	0	0	0	0.71	0
Agriculture	3.19	4.92	1.06	4.29	2.41	0	4.09
Social	3.19	7.58	0	1.43	3.78	5.67	1.49
Total	65.18	34.09	41.49	42.86	37.80	29.79	27.51
Standard deviation of all code families issue salience		26.88	26.75	29.53	19.90	23.49	20.10

Notes: Authors' own data. The calculation of the standard deviation is not based on the population mean, but on the issue salience value of the EPF code family.

low on the priority list of all the member parties. The only member party to have touched upon all the top ten EPP topics is the Austrian Conservative party, although there are clear differences between the ÖVP and the EPP in terms of issue emphasis. For instance, the financial crisis and social affairs cover nearly 18 per cent of all coded arguments in the ÖVP manifesto, while in the EPP manifesto they cover only half as many. The financial crisis and markets category stands out as one of the most important issues in the Austrian, French, and German manifestos, yet the EPP dedicates only 5.91 per cent of its space to it, putting it in the fourth position. In general, Table 2.3 reveals a picture of considerable diversity among the EPP federation manifestos. The member parties preferred to follow their own way in the election campaign by choosing to focus on the issues they may have deemed as more relevant for their national electorates.

The EGP decision to go for a short common manifesto in order to bridge (Sigalas et al. 2010), if not conceal, internal divisions seems to have paid off. As Table 2.4 shows, the distribution of coded arguments between parties is far more balanced in comparison to the other two EPFs, and the standard deviation from the EGP manifesto is lower for all parties. Only the Danish member party, which has observer status in the EGP (thus no voting rights), stands out by failing to put forward any arguments in as many as 29 code families. The remaining EGP member parties largely followed the pattern set out in the EPF manifesto, despite the fact that the EGP officially allowed its members to use the supranational manifesto in the national campaigns as they wanted (Sigalas et al. 2010: 16).

The issue-salience pattern of the manifestos is an informative measurement device of programmatic convergence, but it does not answer the question of how many arguments featured in the EPF manifestos were actually adopted by the national parties. In order to determine to what extent the national members integrated the EPF positions into their manifestos, we first identified the number of unique codes in each EPF manifesto, then checked how many of them were adopted in the

Table 2.4 Issue salience in the EGP members' manifestos (per cent)

	EGP	Die Grünen (A)	Les Verts	Die Grünen (D)	OP	Green Party	Sosialistik Folkeparti
Top 10 code families							
Financial crisis	6.99	6.64	3.28	3.58	4.38	4.76	2.13
Agriculture	5.91	2.07	6.56	1.89	1.88	2.98	2.13
Energy	5.91	7.47	4.75	5.28	4.38	5.95	8.51
EU democracy	5.91	1.66	2.30	1.95	6.25	0.40	2.13
Immigration	5.38	1.24	3.77	4.63	2.50	3.77	8.51
Discrimination	4.84	2.07	2.13	2.93	1.88	2.38	0
Social	4.84	7.05	3.11	1.82	5	4.17	6.38
Economy	4.30	2.49	4.10	1.24	3.75	4.17	0
Foreign affairs	3.76	10.37	2.13	8.14	3.13	2.98	10.64
Transport	3.76	3.32	4.10	2.02	1.25	4.96	2.13
Total	51.61	44.40	36.23	33.49	34.38	36.51	42.55
Standard deviation of all code families issue salience		13.40	20.29	13.80	13.26	12.13	19.93

Notes: Authors' own data. The calculation of the standard deviation is not based on the population mean, but on the issue salience value of the EPF code family.

national manifestos, and, finally, we identified the proportion of those common codes in the national manifestos.[5] The results of our analysis are summarized in Table 2.5.

The EPF manifesto adoption-rate evidence is in line with the findings of the issue-salience analysis. Similarities between the national and EPF manifestos are more frequent among the EGP federation than among the PES or EPP. As Table 2.5 illustrates, the Greens are much more likely to have arguments in their manifestos that are also found in the EGP manifesto. The German Green party, in particular, has the overwhelming majority (87 per cent) of its arguments in common with the EGP. The second and third best performers are the French and English Green parties, respectively. On average, the EGP member parties have adopted 39.4 per cent of the unique arguments found in the EGP manifesto. Even though they do not constitute the majority of arguments, they are still a substantial portion, especially if compared to the other two party families. For the PES member parties the average proportion of adopted arguments falls to 16.7 per cent and even lower for the EPP to 7.2 per cent.

The fact that the national parties adopted a certain number of arguments from the EPF manifesto does not automatically mean that they gave them a prominent position in their own manifestos. It is possible that the common arguments are only a small fraction of the total number of arguments found in the national texts. In such a case it would be misleading to talk about real adoption of the EPF arguments when the latter are effectively concealed behind the national positions. Table 2.5 shows that, on average, the share of the EPF manifesto

Table 2.5 Adoption rate of the European party federation manifesto (per cent)

	Austria	Denmark	France	Germany	Greece	Slovakia	UK	Average
EPF manifesto codes adopted								
PES	22.32	9.32	n/a	31.64	15.82	2.26	18.64	16.67
EPP	8.63	5.59	3.19	12.94	n/a	5.59	8.31*	7.19†
EGP	30.65	8.06	42.47	87.10	27.42	n/a	40.86	39.43
EPF manifesto codes in the national party manifesto								
PES	36.74	36.67	n/a	33.94	37.84	25	28.82	33.17
EPP	20.45	37.23	27.78	27.84	n/a	24.82	19.33*	27.62†
EGP	23.65	31.91	12.95	10.55	31.10	n/a	15.08	20.87

Notes: Authors' own data. n/a: not available.

*: Not an EPP member.

†: Excludes the UK Conservative party.

positions in the national manifestos ranges between 21 per cent (EGP) and 33 per cent (PES). Thus not only do the member parties draw selectively on the supranational manifesto, they introduce many more arguments in their own manifestos that have very little if anything to do with the positions agreed to at the European level.

Our manifesto analysis revealed also that when controlling for the relative share of the common arguments in the national manifestos, the differences between the EPFs are not only less pronounced, but also reversed. Whereas the EPP members used only 7 per cent of the supranational manifesto arguments available to them, the latter formed nearly 30 per cent of all the codes in the national manifesto. Similarly, 17 per cent of the PES manifesto positions are found also in the national documents, but they comprise almost 28 per cent of all codes. In contrast, the EGP parties adopted 39 per cent of the supranational manifesto positions but they form only 21 per cent of the total in the national manifestos.

Taking into account the values of all the indicators of manifesto convergence presented thus far, it is clear that there are very substantial differences between the commonly agreed manifesto at the European level and the manifestos the national parties produced for the 2009 European elections. The fact that the French Socialist party and the Slovak Green party adopted a translated version of the supranational manifesto is probably a sign of limited interest in, rather than evidence of, perfect programmatic overlap. Consequently, we conclude that neither the two largest European party federations nor the European Green Party meet the necessary condition of programmatic convergence which characterizes political parties.

Conclusion

The evidence we presented in this chapter illustrates that the national parties did not feel bound by the manifesto they consented to at the European level when they drafted their own electoral platform for the European elections. To a great extent the national manifestos emphasized topics other than those emphasized in the manifestos of the PES, EPP, and EGP. In addition, the national parties integrated only a small fraction of the supranational manifesto arguments, which were outnumbered by the national arguments. It is clear that the national parties adopted only those EPF manifesto arguments that suited their purposes. It may even be that the adopted positions were only those the member parties contributed in the drafting of the EPF manifesto. In any case, it is clear that agreeing on a common manifesto can only be taken as a sign of nominal programmatic convergence, not actual. The EPFs fail to satisfy not one but both conditions that are necessary to label a political association as a party. The supranational federations offer no link between citizens and governmental choice, and they lack sufficient cohesion to behave as a party. It comes as no surprise, therefore, that Külahci (2010) found the PES lacking sufficient cohesion in its stance towards the EU fiscal policy. We would argue that it is not only the PES but the EPP, and to a lesser extent the EGP, that face severe cohesion problems.

This has obvious repercussions in the contribution potential of the EPFs in the function of political representation and democracy at the EU level. If the main EPFs cannot manage to agree on a common set of positions around which their members will coalesce and campaign, then an EU-wide deliberation will not take place and the European elections will continue to be contested along national lines. The EPFs will remain loose and weak umbrella organizations subject to the interests and influence of their member parties. Consequently, they will have little influence in EU-level politics and probably limited chances in actively pursuing transnational forms of EU democracy.

Of course, it is possible that things will change in the future. Just because the national parties deviated from the supranational manifesto in the last elections does not mean that this will always be so. European integration is an evolutionary process and new opportunities and conditions in the future may facilitate the development of the EPFs. Thus far, however, and from a cohesion point of view, the progress of the EPFs has been rather slow. After more than 30 years of political life the programmatic convergence among the PES and EPP members continues to be very limited. The situation is slightly better in the Green federation, but it is still too early to talk of a truly European party. Promoting individual membership for EU citizens in the EPFs in combination with the introduction of transnational MEP candidate lists may boost the development dynamic of the EPFs. However, as long as the EPFs fail to produce evidence that convergence at the programmatic level has been achieved, the label 'political party at the European level' will remain a misnomer.

Notes

1. Lord (2004: 47) also names 'sufficient cohesion' as a necessary condition for a fully developed party, but he confines it to the 'groups of executive or legislative decision-makers'. In other words, Lord (2004) restricts this condition to

the parliamentary and office-holding branch of the party, whereas we argue that it is primarily at the broader party level that cohesion condition needs to be secured before it can be extended to the party-in-parliament and party-in-government.

2. As Smith (1999: 107) put it, 'European parties, essentially visible to the electorate only during the election campaigns... seem to disintegrate into their constituent national parties between elections'.
3. The full list of the thematic areas/code families can be found in Sigalas et al. (2010).
4. The French conservative party UMP and the Greek Greens produced two documents with their basic principles for the European elections which we merged and treated as a single manifesto in each case. The Greek conservative party Nea Dimokratia did not produce a manifesto for the 2009 EP elections. The French Parti Socialiste and the Slovak Strana Zelených parties did not produce their own manifesto, but used instead the translated version of the PES and European Greens manifesto, respectively. Finally, we included in our analysis the UK Conservative party, even though they are no longer members of the EPP. Their inclusion in the analysis is primarily for purposes of comparison.
5. By unique codes we mean codes that do not repeat themselves in the substance of their argument. Reworded codes that essentially promoted the same argument were treated as the same unique code.

3

Interparliamentary Cooperation and Democratic Representation in the European Union

Cristina Fasone

Introduction

This chapter asks the following question: how far is interparliamentary cooperation a useful tool in order to ensure democratic representation in the European Union (EU)? It aims at analysing how national parliamentarians perform their function of democratic representation when they act at supranational level, in the EU context, through the tool of interparliamentary cooperation. By interparliamentary cooperation, we mean the 'dialogue' both among national parliaments (NPs), and between them and the European Parliament (EP) without binding effects (both for the parliaments themselves and for national and European institutions). Consequently, we focus both on the activities of national legislatures at EU level, and also on the interparliamentary activities within the national parliaments. At both levels, the debate on EU matters should take place with a strong role for parliamentary representation, particularly after the Treaty of Lisbon.

Other powers that the new Treaty gives to national legislatures (the monitoring of the principle of subsidiarity: the participation in the procedures to revise the Treaties; the appeals to the Court of Justice; the involvement in the adhesion of new Member States; and the enforcement of the flexibility clause) are beyond the focus of this chapter, although they influence the carrying out of interparliamentary activities.

Dealing with the effectiveness of interparliamentary cooperation, problems arise when we look at the level of people's awareness of the existence and performance of this instrument. Excluding those members of parliament (MPs) who take part in interparliamentary meetings and parliamentary officials, very few people know that a significant European dimension of parliamentary activity exists (Palanza 2009: 252). It means that there is a mismatch between how MPs perform their role of representative at supranational level and what is reported back in the national arena in daily political debates and parliamentary work. We specifically deal with the case of the EU, which concerns the most considerable amount of interparliamentary meetings per year that has ever been experienced, on a huge range of matters.

The main argument of this chapter is that in the EU the role of national legislatures and that of the European Parliament (EP) are complementary in accomplishing the function of parliamentary representation on behalf of the people (both EU citizens and national residents) and that, as a result, interparliamentary cooperation is a necessity today. However, despite its potentiality and the amount of resources invested in it, the chapter will demonstrate that interparliamentary cooperation is, at present, quite ineffective in supporting democratic representation in the EU.

Section 2 provides the theoretical framework of analysis, the problem of democratic representation in a multi-level form of constitutionalism; Section 3 focuses on the newly affirmed supranational networking function which is performed through the more traditional 'expressive' and 'informing' functions; Section 4 describes how the interparliamentary cooperation in the EU is organized; Section 5 measures the diffusion of the interparliamentary cooperation in the EU at political and administrative levels; Section 6 considers the impact of interparliamentary activities on the French and the Italian parliaments; and Section 7 contains the conclusion.

Democratic representation in a multi-level constitutionalism: the need for interparliamentary cooperation

Interparliamentary cooperation can be considered as one of the most visible parliamentary reactions towards the transfer of decision-making powers to international and supranational organizations in which democratic representation is somewhat lacking (Peters 2009: 326).

Democratic representation is traditionally linked to parliaments. As pointed out (Castiglione and Warren 2008: 1), it is founded on three key factors: a principal-agent relationship: a form of political power that is responsible and accountable to citizens; and a right to elect the representatives. It is mainly the second feature of democratic representation which is particularly weak in the supranational[1] context of the EU. Indeed, the further the decision-maker is from the territorial communities to which the policies are addressed, the less these communities are able to control them and to participate in them.

Even though, as shown by many studies (Maurer and Wessels 2001; Auel and Benz 2005), parliaments, at domestic level, continue to have a say on supranational activity through the oversight of the government's conduct, national legislatures have become actively involved also in tasks that go beyond their mandatory area of influence, the national one, especially in interparliamentary cooperation. Such cooperation might affect democratic representation in the EU, which depends both on the European Parliament – the first interparliamentary assembly of the European Communities (Kreppel 2002) – and on the NPs.

Undoubtedly, since the time when David Marquand first talked about the 'democratic deficit' (1979) of the European Community, many things have changed (Mény 2002: 8). As some scholars have underlined, the problem of the democratic deficit in the EU has constantly decreased from a mere institutional point of view following every reform of the Treaties (Weiler et al. 1995; Majone 1998; Moravcsik 2002). We might even argue that, from a strictly legalistic perspective, democratic representation in the EU is perfectly guaranteed after the Treaty of Lisbon: the European Parliament is a legislator and enjoys a prominent role in the adoption of the EU budget; national legislatures and national governments take part in the EU decision-making process; despite not being elected directly to the Council, each national executive, when participating in the Council, assures democratic representation in the EU precisely because it is responsible to its NP, according to Article 10 TEU. However, we know de facto that there are still several problems of accountability in the EU architecture (for example, with the Commission): the lack of the involvement of the European citizens in EU policy-making and awareness of the outcomes of policy; the prevalence of technocratic, instead of political, procedures; and the adoption of policies which, although they have the support of the majority of the Member States, very often do not enjoy the support of most European citizens (Follesdal and Hix 2006; see also Kröger and Friedrich, Introduction to this volume).

Interparliamentary cooperation in the EU shows specific features which depend on the nature of this supranational organization. The EU legal order is characterized by the *complementarity* between national and supranational systems. As Ingolf Pernice argues, the European

Constitution is 'composed of two complementary constitutional layers, the European and the national, which are closely interwoven and interdependent' (Pernice 2002: 514). This intrinsic duality of the EU is also reflected in its institutions. National executives and parliaments (the latter, above all, after the entry into force of the Treaty of Lisbon) can be considered to be both national and European institutions (although, from a strictly legal point of view, European institutions are listed in Article 13 TEU), according to the place in which they act and the claims that they make.

From a parliamentary perspective, the existence of a 'multilevel parliamentary field' (Crum and Fossum 2009) is embedded in the fundamental principle of democratic representation established by the Treaties, and is implemented through both the EP and the NPs. The German Federal Constitutional Court has already recognized the existence of a dual and complementary channel of parliaments within the EU. In fact, if we admit that the EP is not really representative of European citizens, because its composition is based upon the principle of digressive proportionality (under-representing the people who live in the most populated states), the democratic representation in the EU cannot not be ensured without the direct involvement of NPs in the EU decision-making and public debate (*Maastricht Urteil* – BverfG, 2BvR 2134, 2159/92, 12 October 1993 – and much more so the *Lissabon Urteil* – BverfG, 2BvE 2/08, 30 June 2009).

Parliaments, including the EP, need to coordinate and organize their action in order to be influential, given the double channel of democratic representation in the EU: 'Deciding to give national parliaments a direct role (without executive intermediation)' has been interpreted as a response to the Dutch and the French referenda, as a claim to representation arising from citizens (Manzella 2009: 257). This was a reaction to the fact that policies had been transferred from national to EU level, continuing with the EP as co-legislator only for some of the policies, and with the role of the NPs being limited to the implementation of EU legislation.

New and traditional functions of parliaments

At the end of the nineteenth century, Walter Bagehot listed and described the functions carried out by the British House of Commons, which can concern any elective legislature in a democratic system even today (Bagehot 1873). The most important, according to this author, was the *elective function*, or, rather, the choice and the selection of the executive by parliamentary majority. Next, he considered the *legislative function*, the ability of parliaments to pass laws. Then he defined the *teaching function* as the capability of legislatures to influence and to modify society upon the basis of the most eminent ideas, the *expressive function* as the ability to communicate the opinions of the electorate on any topic to the other institutions, and, finally, the *informing function* through which parliaments make people aware of the decisions taken at political level and inform them of any new problems.

These parliamentary functions can be grouped in two main categories (Norton 1993): those related to the government – substantially, the *elective* and the *legislative functions* – and those dealing with the relationship between parliament and citizens, or, rather, between the representatives (democratically elected) and the represented (the voters). The *teaching*, the *expressive*, and the *informing* functions all fall within the latter category. We decided to circumscribe our analysis to the second category, usually less studied in the literature (Raunio 2009a: 4), by specifically focusing on the *expressive* and *informing* functions, because the *teaching* function is not directly related to the problem of democratic representation, but rather to the mission of educating people in a broad sense.

Recently scholars have pointed out the existence of a new function of parliaments, the '*international networking function*' (Raunio 2009a: 6 (my emphasis); see also Raunio in this volume), which has taken on an autonomous relevance from the historic ones investigated by Bagehot, in terms of purposes, and has, as a consequence, become a subject of study. It aims at promoting regional integration processes, exchanging best practices, supporting democratic transitions, representing the concerns of people in supranational decision-making processes and making them more understandable, and looking after national interests (Di Napoli 2009). However, in real terms this new function relies on traditional parliamentary means (mainly the informative and the expressive functions) in order to operate, since it implies the involvement of parliaments in bilateral or multi-lateral forms of cooperation with other parliaments, institutional actors, or organizations (see also Griglio in this volume). An increasing amount of financial and human resources from parliaments are dedicated to it, and the organization of parliamentary work is also affected because, in turn, MPs are engaged abroad and have to divide their time between national and international activities (Slaughter 2004: 104).

In relation to the democratic representation of parliaments, we understand the supranational networking function, in the EU, as being accomplished through the parliamentary 'expressive' and 'informing' functions (Bagehot 1873: 115). We may describe the *expressive function* in the case of the supranational activity of parliaments as the office of expressing the views of the very people who are subject to the supranational legal order on all matters which fall under the jurisdiction of the parliaments; thus, we can see a bottom-up movement of the people's claims, and, therefore, of the claims of the parliaments, from national to EU level.

However, it is through the *informing function* that parliaments ought to make people aware of the decisions and policies undertaken within the supranational legal order. This chapter particularly emphasises this function, since the representative role of parliaments cannot be seen as being fully accomplished – through a top-down movement of the feedback received about the people's claims – if the people at the national level are not properly informed about what is happening in the supranational context within interparliamentary arenas. Thus, the carrying out of the *informing function* directly affects the performance and the results of the claims.

The 'system' of interparliamentary cooperation in the EU and how it has been analysed

The emergence of a parliamentary dimension of international relations dates back to the end of the nineteenth century when the Interparliamentary Union was set up in 1889 (Šabič 2008). Since then the activity of parliaments beyond states, despite being largely ignored by public opinion, has become prominent in all international and regional organizations.

This phenomenon has a long tradition in the EU and has passed through different phases: the Parliamentary Assembly composed of national MPs; the election of the EP and the marginalization of the NPs; the 'second youth' of the NPs since the 1990s; and the acknowledgement of their active 'contribution to the good functioning of the Union', according to Article 12 TEU (O'Brennan and Raunio 2007: 9; see also Raunio in this volume).

Nowadays the interparliamentary cooperation in the EU is performed through:

- the Conference of the Speakers of the EU parliaments, summoned for the first time in 1975, which meets once a year and is entitled to coordinate the interparliamentary activity of the EU;

- the Conference of Community and European Affairs committees of parliaments of the European Union (COSAC), set up in 1989, the only forum on interparliamentary cooperation directly recognized by the Treaties (in the protocol on the role of national parliaments), which meets twice a year in plenary session, twice at the level of Chairpersons, as well as at the level of the *Troika*, composed of the Chairpersons of the EU committees from the parliaments of the three Member States of the Council *Troika*. This is also the most enhanced and structured form of cooperation among EU parliaments, as its rules of procedure are published in the Official Gazette of the EU and it has a permanent secretariat;
- the Joint Parliamentary Meetings (JPMs), Joint Committee Meetings (JCMs), and the Meetings of Sectoral Committees (MSCs), the convening of which depends on the joint initiative of the European Parliament, and the parliament of the EU presidency in the case of JPMs and JCMs, and only on the presiding national parliament for MSCs;
- the participation of MPs, without the right to vote, at the ordinary meetings of the committees of the EP, often on draft legislative acts;
- the meetings of parliamentary officials.

We argue that national legislatures, exploiting the tool of interparliamentary cooperation (in terms of the information and expertise obtained), may contribute to move the European people closer to the EU institutions, although, as we will demonstrate below, at present they are failing to do so. On EU matters, national parliaments have abdicated from performing their 'informative function', and they completely disregard the activity carried out at supranational level. This hypothesis was tested first in the EU context, collecting data on interparliamentary meetings through the interviews of twelve parliamentary officials (2 from the EP and 10 national representatives of parliaments or chambers in Brussels) and using the Interparliamentary EU Information Exchange (IPEX) database. Thus we catalogue the different forms of interparliamentary cooperation in the EU in order to find out who the participants are, what issues are discussed, the frequency of the meetings, and the publicity of the activities. Then we consider two national case studies, France and Italy, chosen not only because of their common history in terms of the process of European integration and the size of their populations, but also because of their differences with regard to parliamentary powers, forms of government, and the perception of interparliamentary cooperation. The analysis aims to 'measure' the rate of success of interparliamentary meetings within the French and the Italian parliaments: namely, whether these meetings and the issues debated are mentioned in parliamentary work, how many times, and for what purpose. We have consulted parliamentary agendas verbatim, resolutions and questions both in the House and in Committees, and we have interviewed nine parliamentary officials of the Italian parliament. The research was undertaken in the period 2007–2010, coinciding with the negotiation and the first implementation of the Treaty of Lisbon, which has enhanced the role of interparliamentary cooperation.[2]

Interparliamentary cooperation in the EU: the increasing of the 'Dialogue' among parliaments

The research has taken into account multi-lateral interparliamentary meetings without considering bilateral meetings between two NPs or conferences between the EP and an NP. Moreover, we have distinguished between interparliamentary dialogue at political level, which involves parliamentarians, and cooperation among civil servants and officials, who act as the 'back office' of interparliamentary activities, although they are also able to condition both the agenda and the results of political cooperation.

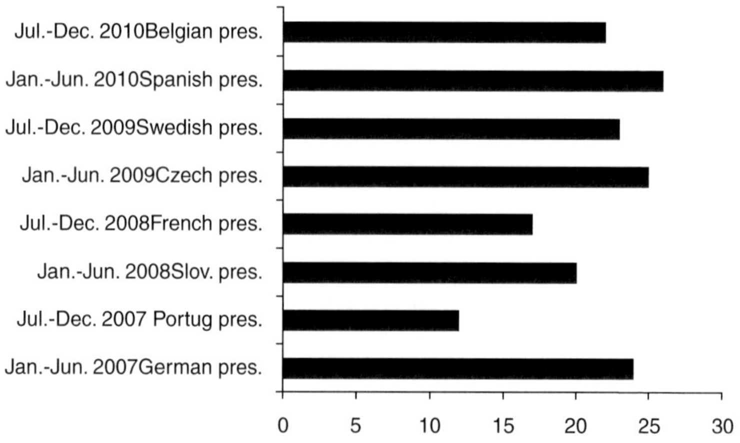

Figure 3.1 Number of multi-lateral interparliamentary meetings per semester (2007–2010)

Note: The figure also includes the multi-lateral meetings of parliamentary officials.

Source: IPEX website (www.ipex.eu) and the EP website, section dedicated to the EP relations with national parliaments (www.europarl.europa.eu).

The empirical analysis reveals that, since 2007, when the negotiation on the Treaty of Lisbon took place, the intensity of interparliamentary cooperation has increased, until it has become, to some extent, a permanent activity of the national parliaments (Figure 3.1).

However, nowadays the problem is the absence of a coherent direction for these parliamentary initiatives, which compromises the effectiveness of the representative claims, and therefore reinforces the frequent criticism about its waste of human and financial resources.

During each semester, most interparliamentary meetings are arranged by the parliament of the EU presidency, a few on the initiative of other NPs of the EU, which are interested in specific topics or legislative acts (for example, road safety), but usually one-third of the meetings are organized or co-organized by the EP, a 'leading actor' in this field, often overarching the role played by NPs.

Even if the activism of the EP seems positive for interparliamentary cooperation, it also has a 'dark side'. Actually, one of the reasons why interparliamentary activity in the EU is often considered ineffective, and therefore neglected (Maurer 2008), is the antagonism between the NPs and the EP. Indeed, outside COSAC, interparliamentary cooperation is led by the EP, which tries to condition the agenda of the meetings and consolidate practices – given the lack of written procedures – favourable to its members (in terms of the composition of the conferences and the allocation of time to the speakers). For example, the rule that one of the four speakers has to be an MEP is applied to the JPMs and the JCMs often does not allow enough time for MPs of all the nationalities to intervene. National parliaments frequently complain about the conduct of the EP, but without any effect; they are disorganized and divided both about the contents of the claims, and how to make them.

Interparliamentary cooperation at political level: figures and tendencies

Interparliamentary cooperation at political level has its linchpin in parliamentary committees because of their specialization in circumscribed matters and because of their size. The conferences of committees, however, can have different *status*; for example, only COSAC has a stable organization and written rules on its functioning.

Article 10 of Protocol no. 1 to the Treaty of Lisbon officially authorized COSAC to make the representative claims – 'to submit any contribution' – that it deems appropriate for the attention of the EP (which is member of COSAC), the Council, and the Commission. Contributions are, effectively, political statements adopted at the end of each plenary session and published in the Official Gazette of the EU as well as on its website. Moreover, with regard to the *expressing function* accomplished by parliamentarians, the agendas, lists of participants and the minutes of the meetings, declarations and letters sent by parliaments to COSAC, as well as the speeches of the guests, are all published on the COSAC website. The secretariat of the conference draws up a biannual report on the specific themes that COSAC has previously debated. Both the reports (14 since 2004) and the questionnaires compiled by national parliaments are then published on the Internet.

The same does not apply to the other forums of interparliamentary cooperation. There are no formally adopted rules of procedure, only practices which can be subject to unforeseen changes and unpredictable adaptations on the part of the EP and the EU presidency.[3] Moreover, the publicity of the meetings depends only on the organizer. Usually, for those convened by the EP audio records, lists of participants and declarations are available on the institutional website, while for those summoned by NPs, this level of 'disclosure' is not so common.

However, all EU political interparliamentary meetings share at least the fact that there are also non-MP components at the conferences. National ministers (normally from the state hosting the session) and Commissioners often address the interparliamentary conferences, and other guests, such as academics or MPs from EU candidate countries, are also invited. There are remarkable differences with regard to the rates of attendance at the meetings: COSAC, JPMs, and JCMs have a higher

Table 3.1 Components and rate of attendance of EU political interparliamentary meetings

	COSAC (plen.)	JPMs	JCMs	MSCs
MPs per Member state	6 (t. 162)	max. 6 (t. 162)	1–2	1–3
MEPs	6	33	max. 33	max. 3
Total components (on average)	168 (plus Ministers, Commissioners, and academics)	max. 195 (Ministers, Commissioners, and academics incl.)	65–90 (Ministers, Commissioners and academics incl.)	35–60 (Ministers and academics included)
Rate of attendance	Very high 90–100%	Quite high 60–70%	Medium 50%	Quite low 30–40%

Source: The EP website, section dedicated to the EP relations with national parliaments (www.europarl.europa.eu) and the websites of the national parliaments holding the presidency.

number of participants than conferences organized by NPs, probably because of the presence of the EP – according to the need for a 'double channel' of parliamentary representation in the EU – and the opportunity to be in contact with other EU institutions. Moreover, within the same category, the number of effective participants can change a great deal over time according to the importance of the issue being debated and its relevance at the national level (Table 3.1).

The representative claims of the EP and the NPs are, in most cases, related to policies in which parliamentary oversight is very weak or where parliaments are, to some extent, marginalized. The analysis underlines, for instance, that interparliamentary meetings prefer to deal with the Common Foreign and Security Policy (CFSP), the coordination of financial and economic policies of the Member States, the Lisbon strategy, and the area of freedom, security, and justice (Figure 3.2). This trend has also been encouraged by the Treaty of Lisbon, which aims to improve the democratic legitimacy of Europol and Eurojust (Article 12 TEU) as well as that of the CFSP.

Even from the perspective of the issues debated, COSAC shows some specificities. Between 2005 and the coming into force of the Treaty of Lisbon in 2009, the activity of COSAC was absorbed by its spontaneous initiative to promote the 'synchronised control' of EU draft legislative

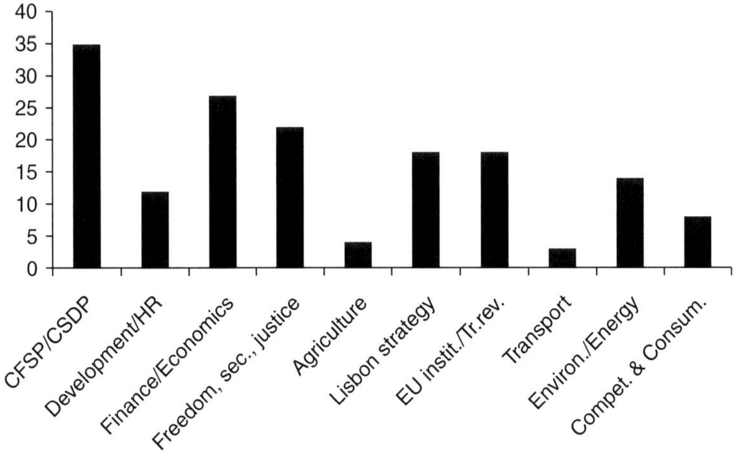

Figure 3.2 Issues debated in the EU political interparliamentary meetings (2007–2010)

Source: IPEX website (www.ipex.eu) and COSAC website (www.cosac.eu)

acts by national parliaments, testing the early warning mechanism (Maurer 2008: 12). In fact, within COSAC, the NPs promoted eight 'subsidiarity checks', to be concluded within eight weeks – according to the Treaties – and whose results were subsequently debated at the following plenary session.

Although COSAC is the driving force of interparliamentary cooperation in the EU, its level of performance as a claim-maker is sometimes very low, and its formalization is, perhaps, double-edged; it is becoming more and more bureaucratic. In the last few years, every plenary session has been devoted to debate on its rules of procedure and structure, instead of giving prominence to issues which actually deal with EU policies and directly concern EU citizens. Moreover, there is no common view of the role of COSAC. For example, the French Senate has tried to make it a third chamber of the EU (next to the EP and the Council), while the EP is clearly interested in COSAC as a non-institutionalized forum of cooperation (Bengtson 2007: 57). Even the mandates of European affairs committees at national level may cause some problems, since they exercise difference functions. Some of them only have advisory powers, such as the Spanish Joint Committee, while others have very strong powers and the full support and recognition of their parliaments for the activities carried out through COSAC, such as the Danish *Minifolketing* (Kiiver 2006: 121).

But the role of COSAC is also challenged by a new tendency. Due to the increase in the EU competences, the NPs and the EP are thinking of making the cooperation between sectoral committees more stable, since the mandate of the European affairs committees and COSAC is becoming wider and wider, and includes all EU policies. They cannot comply properly with such a task. The strengthening of sectoral committees is a turning point also for a new function recognized by national parliaments – that of controlling the activity of Europol – but a major problem lies in the different allocation of competences among the committees of NPs.

Interparliamentary cooperation at administrative level: the key role of parliamentary officials

In general, the role of parliamentary officials is fundamental for any function and/or body of parliaments, but, in particular, the new 'supranational networking function' of parliaments could not be carried out without them. In this sector, officials are not only important for the preliminary work of the chambers (as happens when they help MPs to draft a bill), they are also directly involved in interparliamentary meetings in the EU.

Meetings among parliamentary officials include those of the Permanent Representative of the NPs to the EU, the Interparliamentary EU Information Exchange (IPEX), the European Centre for Parliamentary Research and Documentation (CERDP), and the annual meeting of the Secretaries General.

It is worth mentioning that the NPs felt the need to send their permanent representatives to the EP, in Brussels, in order both to follow and to try to influence its activity and that of the other institutions. These permanent representatives work side by side in the EP and officially meet every Monday morning with the aim of coordinating their agendas. The IPEX, in contrast, is a public web platform created and fostered by the NPs, whose aim is mainly to exchange and share updated information and opinions on EU draft legislative acts and documents. It is one of the most effective tools for the *representative function* of parliaments in the EU as every document approved by an EU legislature can be published on the website by national correspondents – who are parliamentary officials – and thus inform the public and the European and national institutions about its position. The Secretaries General oversee the functioning of the IPEX project and appoint the Board, composed of officials from the financing parliaments (the EP, British, Danish, Finnish, French, Hungarian, Italian, Portuguese, and Slovak legislatures).

Even though these administrative arrangements are of vital importance, one may wonder whether or not the activism of the parliamentary officials is a surrogate for the weakness of political interparliamentary cooperation, but devoid of democratic legitimacy and representativeness and therefore questionable. A *representative claim* made by a democratically elected MP is one thing; a claim proposed by parliamentary bureaucracies is quite another.

The echo at national level: the French and the Italian cases

At national level, the French and the Italian parliaments show a similar attitude, giving a minimal prominence to the interparliamentary activities carried out in the EU context, even though, in 2010, the trend changed slightly. Interparliamentary meetings usually attract little or no media attention and are not debated in the NPs or sounded out in the national public opinion in the Member States, possibly because they can only influence the NPs but are devoid of binding effect. Nowadays, legislatures mainly focus on the oversight of the executive's conduct in EU matters and on the subsidiarity monitoring of EU draft legislative acts, when they are not looking after national interests, which is their principal task. Only on very few occasions have the French and the Italian parliaments, at committee level, mentioned the opinions issued by other parliaments on the same proposal, with the aim of strengthening the legitimacy of their own positions.

Over the years, and notwithstanding the different forms of government and of bicameralism (perfect in Italy and asymmetric in France), the French and the Italian models of parliamentary scrutiny and involvement in EU policies have moved closer and thus are more easily comparable. After the constitutional reform of 2008, the French parliament has been reinforced vis-à-vis the executive, and the approval of resolutions, which was substantially limited before, has become a general rule for orienting the government on EU affairs. Moreover, the former delegations on EU policies have been transformed into standing committees.

Although since the 1990s the Italian legislature has weakened to the government's advantage because of the changes in the political and party systems,[4] it has been able to carve out some leeway in order to condition the executive on EU matters, also thanks to the provisions of the Treaty of Lisbon.

As pointed out with regard to the general attitude of the NPs towards EU affairs (Raunio and Wiberg 2009: 79; Bergman et al. 2003: 175), the role of the Plenum of the Houses in this field is limited in both parliaments: parliamentary committees are usually the protagonists. From 2007 to January 2010, interparliamentary meetings or activities were never mentioned by the Houses of the Italian Chamber of Deputies and Senate. In the French parliament, the analysis reveals that between 2007 (when the thirteenth parliamentary term began) and the entry into force of the Treaty of Lisbon, in December 2009, the results of interparliamentary conferences were debated – more or less in depth – on seven occasions, six by the Plenum of the Senate (in one case, the issue was debated by tabling an oral question to the Minister of Defence) and one by the National Assembly (NA). These debates were mainly coincident with the French presidency of the EU (July–December 2008) and predominantly dealt with interparliamentary cooperation in matters of the CFSP. In 2010, however, the two Houses of the French and Italian parliaments focused on the same issues, adopting motions and resolutions which also cite the outcomes of the interparliamentary meetings on EU economic governance after the financial crisis (res. of November 2 NA; res. no. 6–00043 It. Chamber and res. of 28 October It. Senate) and the setting up, upon the basis of the model of COSAC, of an interparliamentary conference (composed of MEPs and MPs) on the CFSP and the Common Security and Defence Policy (CSDP) (res. no. 86 Fr. Senate; motion no. 1–00423 It. Chamber and motion no. 1–00299 It. Senate).

Although it does not occur upon a regular basis, the debate on interparliamentary cooperation is more frequent in the committees. On average the activity of COSAC is mentioned once a month by the four committees on EU affairs of the two parliaments, and, after each plenary session of COSAC, one of the members of the delegation is appointed as *Rapporteur* to inform his or her colleagues on the committee with regard to what has been done. Sometimes, as occurred in the Italian sixteenth parliamentary term, heated debates have dealt with the issue of the representativeness of the delegation to COSAC, since not all political groups were included, and seats on the EU committees – the same is true of the French parliament – are not equally divided between the majority and opposition.

In the last three years, the parliamentarians of the two legislatures – without specific differences between the lower and the upper chambers – who have participated in JPMs, JCMs, and MSCs, have almost always presented a report of their activity to the colleagues of the appropriate committee (usually those on economic and financial affairs or on EU policies). On some occasions, nonetheless, the Chairman of the committee has only informed the other components that one or more of their colleagues have taken part in an interparliamentary conference without giving any details regarding the contents and the outcomes.

This *informing function* of MPs becomes more evident when the Member States hold the EU presidency, as was the case of the French parliament in 2008. However, when the semester finishes, the creeping unconcern for interparliamentary meetings reappears, a sign that there is no permanent commitment towards these activities, and that the publicity given to the organization of past events is mainly related to the efforts to cut a fine figure during the national presidency.

Although the rate of attendance at the EU interparliamentary meetings is by no means low, unfortunately only a minority of MPs (a few dozen) are involved, and the turnover in the composition of the delegations is quite low. This is a problem particularly for Italian MPs, due to linguistic obstacles (simultaneous translations are always assured, but without knowledge of English or French it is not easy to contribute to the working groups of the conferences), their specific competences, and their *cursus honorum*. The risk is that, as sometimes happens, these meetings are essentially self-referential, since only the people who attend the conference are aware of the issues debated; the other MPs, remaining in the House, might not be informed at all.

Conclusion. Why interparliamentary cooperation is still ineffective in the EU: first explanations

In the previous sections, we have described the theoretical and methodological framework used to assess the performance of interparliamentary cooperation as a tool for representing the people at EU level and for making people aware of what is going on in this context. To this purpose, we have focused, first, on the different kinds of interparliamentary activities developed in the EU, and, second, on their follow-up in two national parliaments, the French and the Italian, both of which are legislatures of two of the founding Member States of the European Community (EC) which have similar populations. The comparison is interesting because of the different attitudes shown by the two countries towards the role of interparliamentary cooperation, and due to their forms of government, parliamentary in Italy and semi-presidential in France. Data have been collected between the years 2007–2010, in other words, from the beginning of the negotiation of the Treaty of Lisbon until one year after the entry into force of this new Treaty.

Due to the shape of the EU legal order as a multilayered constitution (Pernice 2002: 4) and to the principle of democratic representation fulfilled through a 'multi-level parliamentary field' (Crum and Fossum 2009), both national and European, the EP and the national parliaments cannot act 'in solitude' anymore.

Interparliamentary cooperation is not only required by the Treaties, but is also essential to represent European citizens properly, since MPs and MEPs fulfil a complementary role. However, the empirical research shows that one of the problems of interparliamentary activity may be the vertical relations between MEPs and MPs. Sometimes the cooperation is only formal, but the relationship between the EP and the national parliaments is, in fact, antagonistic, with a tendency of the former to 'dominate' the legislatures of the Member States.

Considering, first, the problem of democratic representation through the lens of the 'expressive function' of national parliaments, MPs are not instructed through a binding mandate from their respective parliaments, and thus are not authorized to act upon the basis of a parliamentary mandate and are not held accountable after every mission. Therefore the use of the term of 'parliamentary delegation', as normally employed, is an improper one. Formally, those MPs are not delegated to stand for someone. The features of representation in interparliamentary arenas are those highlighted by Edmund Burke with regard to its 'virtual' nature: the representatives are not delegates, 'but rather trustees who use their best judgment on behalf of those they represent' (Castiglione and Warren 2008: 9). But who are represented by the MPs? Sometimes when they arrive at the interparliamentary meetings, MPs behave as though they were the members of a supranational forum that represents all the people – citizens and residents, even third countries nationals – of the EU Member States.[5] Indeed, most national and EU norms, except those on voting rights, are addressed to both European and third countries citizens, provided that they officially reside in an EU Member State. At other times, especially when EU institutional matters are debated, MPs sponsor national interests. It confirms a point made by Saward (2006), according to whom the electoral factor, the relationship between the representatives and the represented as components of the same electoral district, is not always decisive for assuring representation.

Interparliamentary cooperation as a tool for accomplishing the parliamentary 'informing' and 'expressive' functions (Bagehot 1873) is compromised, above all, by the fact that very few people at national level know about the issues debated or about their potentiality. From this perspective, the fact that the plenary session is rarely involved is significant. Thus citizens remain in the dark about interparliamentary activity and cannot benefit from the chance offered by this channel of representation. Moreover, there is a widespread perception of interparliamentary cooperation as a form of 'parliamentary tourism' because the amount of resources used for the arrangement of conferences and meetings is considered to be disproportionate to the results produced. Certainly the ICT revolution has contributed positively to reduce the costs – as the experience of the IPEX project has demonstrated – and to foster the circulation of information about interparliamentary activity. However, information and communication technologies could be more properly exploited in the future, for example, by organizing interparliamentary videoconferences.

Furthermore, any tendency to make interparliamentary cooperation more bureaucratic, as the key role of parliamentary officials and the focus of the COSAC's activity on its rules of procedure and secretariat seem to reveal, should be avoided. In contrast, the will expressed by most NPs to deal with EU policies, such as CFSP and economic governance (see, for example, the contribution adopted by the XLIV COSAC held in Brussels, 24–26 October 2010), whose democratic control is very weak, should be strongly seconded. In fact, this attempt has already been promoted by the Treaty of Lisbon, which needs to be fully implemented in this regard.

Finally, interparliamentary cooperation should follow a more rational development; the increasing number of interparliamentary meetings is not necessarily accompanied by a higher quality of parliamentary debates and democratic representation in the EU. Instead, the aim to involve a larger number of committees in interparliamentary conferences, which have initially relied only on the committees on EU affairs, according to the COSAC model, is deemed to be fruitful because more MPs will be directly involved in EU issues, increasing the turnover of parliamentary delegations and profiting from a greater variety of expertise and ideas. After the Treaty of Lisbon, the broadening of the EU competences and the higher 'rate' of the parliamentary involvement required might help to reconcile the increasing number of policies managed by the Union with the weak politics of the EU to date (Schmidt 2006).

Notes

1. We use the term supranational according to the meaning described by J. H. H. Weiler, 'Fin-de-siècle Europe: On ideals and ideology in post-Maastricht Europe', in D. Curtin and T. Heukels (eds) *Institutional Dynamics of European Integration* (Dordrecht, Boston, London: Nijhoff Publishers, 1994), 23–41 (31): A transnational regime is 'not simply a neutral arena in which states will seek to maximise their benefits', but an organization where 'a tension between the national self and the collective self" exists.
2. For instance, Article 9 of Protocol no. 1 annexed to this Treaty affirms: 'The EP and national parliaments shall together determine the organization and promotion of effective and regular interparliamentary cooperation within the Union.'
3. These practices, though quite unstable, have been shown in Table 3.1.
4. Indeed, the weakness of the parliament can be perceived both on the side of the legislative function, because the government has intensively used decree laws and legislative decrees – which entitle it to adopt acts having force of law (Art. 76 and 77 It. Const.) – and on the side of the oversight function, because the rules on parliamentary groups and parliamentary committees have not been adapted to the political changes. These changes depended especially on the replacement of the old political parties by new ones (because of the end of the Cold War and political scandals) and on the new electoral law adopted in 1993 (then modified completely in 2005) which caused the bipolarization of the party system and made political competition more conflictual.
5. See the minutes of the XIX (Vienna, 23–24 November 1998) and the XX COSAC (Berlin, 30 May–1 June 1999).

4
The Committee of the Regions and the Upgrading of Subnational Territorial Representation

Simona Piattoni

Introduction: the committee of the regions between consultation and representation

The Committee of the Regions (CoR) was foreseen in the Treaty of Maastricht (1992) and actually created in 1994 to provide the Commission with 'the view from the periphery'. It was conceived as a consultative committee, along the lines of the much older Economic and Social Committee (ESC) that was supposed to feed the opinions of the workers, the employers, and of civil society on EU policy-making. The events leading to the creation of the CoR have been recounted several times (Van der Knaap 1994; Warleigh 1997). The Committee was created under the impulse of the main European associations of regional and local authorities (particularly the Assembly of European Regions [AER] and the Council of European Municipalities and Regions [CEMR]) and thanks to the additional pressure from the most powerful of all European subnational authorities, the German *Länder* and the Spanish regions.[1] The goal of these regions was, originally, to recoup at the European level the powers that they enjoyed at home. The creation of the Single European Market in 1986 and the reform of European Regional Development Policy (ERDP) in 1988 had shifted decision-making powers upwards to central governmental actors. In the case of ERDP, later re-named Cohesion Policy, central governmental actors decided in the Council the amount of funds to be devoted to this policy and the criteria according to which the funds should be allocated, thus de facto disempowering those regional authorities that, domestically, were (in some Member States, at least) mandatorily involved in such decisions (Anderson 1991; Benz 1998, 2000).

Some suggest that behind the decision to create a consultative Committee of Regional and Local Authorities (as the CoR was originally called) lay the attempt of the Commission to create direct links with the subnational authorities (SNAs) of Europe, eluding the gatekeeping powers of the national governments (Hooghe and Keating 1994; Hooghe 1995, 1996; Jeffery 1995). The Commission might have wanted to use direct contacts with regional and local representatives – in some cases, powerful politicians in their own right – to influence the respective national governments and steer their position in favour of proposed European policies. Others venture so far as to argue that the strategy of the Commission was part and parcel of a conscious strategy to create a 'Europe of the Regions' (for a critical view of this position, see Christiansen 1996; Jeffery 1997) by involving them in European level decision-making and trying to obtain greater domestic institutional powers for them. Whether or not the Commission and the SNAs succeeded in these putative goals has been the object of a heated debate (Bache 1999; Pollack 1995; Jeffery 2000; Keating 2008).

Be that as it may, the CoR was founded upon an inherent contradiction: while composed of subnational *political* representatives, it was endowed solely with *consultative* powers. Its task was formally described as contributing a *particular* point of view – that of regional and local authorities – but it was clear that many of its members thought of it as a chamber of political representatives who, at home, often wielded *general* powers (Piattoni 2010b). Next to federal and quasi-federal states like Germany, Belgium, and Spain, at the time of the CoR's creation there were in the Community also unitary states like the UK (at least until the devolution of the late 1990s and early 2000s towards Scotland (1998), Wales (1998), and Northern Ireland (2002)), the Netherlands, Greece, and Portugal, and regionalized states like Italy and France. Therefore, next to powerful subnational representatives who wielded real political power at home, in the CoR sat subnational representatives who did not even have an elective mandate. The contradiction inherent in the creation of a consultative committee composed of political representatives and appointed administrators weakened the Committee and marked the first years of its life (Piattoni 2008).

The situation has since improved. Starting with the Treaties of Amsterdam and Nice, the articles regarding the CoR have been changed to indicate that only *subnational representatives who hold a regional or local authority electoral mandate or are accountable before an elected assembly* can be members of the CoR.[2] No CoR member can now claim not to be a political figure. In time, CoR members have come to emphasize more and more their political, representative role and to de-emphasize their role as consultants. The crowning event, from this point of view, has been the elaboration and release of *The Committee of the Regions' White Paper on Multi-Level Governance* (WPMLG) in June of 2009 (adopted as own-initiative opinion in the eightieth plenary session of 18–19 June 2009, CONST-IV-20). This document offers the CoR's official view on its own role within the EU: a political body that contributes fundamentally to EU multi-level governance.

This chapter will examine the theoretical import of this claim and will explore the tension that still remains unresolved between the two understandings of the role of the CoR: that of a political body, as stated in the WPMLG, and that of a consultative committee, as established in the Treaties. In particular, it will discuss whether the different types of representative claims inherent in these two visions can somehow be reconciled both in theory and in practice. It will argue that, in the EU multi-level governance system, this tension is inevitable and ultimately beneficial to the overall legitimacy of the European Union. Subnational authorities are leading the way in showing how institutional prerogatives enshrined in national constitutions can be transformed to yield a type of representation which is *both* political *and* functional. Next to purely political representation (as provided by the European Parliament) and to purely functional representation (as provided by the ESC and the many pressure groups that gravitate around the Commission), the CoR exemplifies a type of representation which is both political and functional. I will argue that this amounts to an 'upgrading' of the type of representation normally channelled by subnational authorities.

After placing this contribution in the context of the growing literature on the concept of representation, this chapter will discuss the conventional understanding of the CoR as torn between two visions: that of consultative committee and that of representative chamber. Far from constituting a source of institutional weakness, I will argue (2) that, by bridging the notions of representation embedded in these visions, the CoR may try to offer an 'upgraded' type of representation that reinforces the legitimacy of European multi-level governance. In addition to justifying this argument by reference to the WPMLG, I will (3) offer some preliminary evidence drawn from research on the CoR that I conducted in 2008. Originally aimed at investigating the impact of the 2004–2007 enlargements on EU institutions, this research allows me to probe the claims contained in the WPMLG with reference to

CoR members' self-perception.[3] It will emerge that CoR members feel indeed that they should represent not just their particular territory, but all subnational territories regardless of their economic and institutional situation. I additionally speculate that the dual filter through which candidates have to pass in order to become CoR members prompts them to encompass the representation of their own particular territorial point of view into a more general 'view from the periphery'. This induces CoR members to 'upgrade' subnational territorial representation to a higher level of generality and may contribute to the representation of Europe's 'grass roots'. The final section concludes by suggesting that this hybrid or upgraded representation of subnational territories and constituencies might be highly beneficial to EU democracy (4).

The dual representative claim of CoR members

In the understanding of many regional and local representatives, and particularly of its Presidents, the goal of the CoR was to speak for 'the man in the street' and to provide the 'grass roots' of European Union democracy (Schöbel 1997).[4] Because most CoR members were holders of a representative mandate at the regional or local level, it was considered only natural that they should perform this same role at the European level. It was not by chance that the first CoR Presidents were selected from among the most powerful and vocal regional and local authorities of Europe (Piattoni 2008). The letter of the Maastricht Treaty, which established the CoR, however, was very clear: the Committee of the Regions was a *consultative committee* and could not – not even under any stretch of 'federal' imagination – be considered as a 'third' representative chamber alongside the Council and the European Parliament. Too many institutional and legal impediments stood in the way.

The CoR is composed of a selection of regional and local representatives drawn from very different national institutional contexts, domestically endowed with very different institutional powers and ultimately understanding their role in widely different manners. Scholars immediately picked on the many internal divisions and emphasized the weakness of the CoR vis-à-vis other European institutions (Van der Knaap 1994; Christiansen 1996; Warleigh 1999; Hönnige and Kaiser 2003; Scherpereel 2005; Brunazzo and Domorenok 2008). Even those European institutions that had supported its creation – the Commission and the European Parliament – were ultimately sceptical of the attempts of some CoR members to turn it into a third representative chamber: the Commission because, while eager to forge important policy alliances with the peripheral governments of Europe, was cautious not to upset the institutional complexion of the Member States; the Parliament because, while for obvious reasons favourably predisposed towards the injection of greater doses of political/electoral representation in the Community, was somewhat jealous of its role as sole authentic European representative assembly.

Having given up hopes of becoming a third representative chamber, the CoR has with time undergone a remarkable process of institutionalization (Piattoni 2008; Domorenok 2010). Indeed, in times of crisis, such as those following the rejection of the Constitutional Treaty, the CoR has acted as a meeting point for those European institutional and non-institutional actors that still wanted to plan for the future of the Union. Ultimately, the Committee issued its *White Paper on Multi-Level Governance* where it boldly states its own self-perception as a political, representative organ, albeit of a peculiar type.[5] I will here elaborate on the nature of this peculiarity.

The document defines multi-level governance to mean 'coordinated action by the European Union, the Member States and local and regional authorities, based on partnership and aimed at drawing up and implementing EU policies', thus assigning to subnational authorities a key role in EU policy-making. It argues that this notion of multi-level governance 'leads to responsibility being shared between the different tiers of government concerned and is *underpinned by all sources of democratic legitimacy and the representative nature of the different players involved'* (my emphasis). To this end, it suggests that 'each major Community strategic reform should be accompanied by a regional action plan agreed between the European Commission and the Committee of the regions'. It further recommends 'establishing appropriate tools to support participatory democracy', particularly 'reinforcing the partnership practice, both vertically between "local and regional authorities – national government and European Union" and horizontally between "local and regional authorities – civil society" '. The representative, hence political, function of the CoR is thus unequivocally stated.

The same document also recommends that 'the territorial impact analysis should become standard practice through the involvement, upstream of the policy decision, of the various actors concerned in order to understand the economic, social and environmental repercussions on the regions of Community legislative and non-legislative proposals' and that 'experimentation at local and regional level in certain areas of intervention of the European Union, such as the strategy for growth and jobs, the social agenda, integration policy, innovation policy, cohesion policy, sustainable development and civil defense' should be encouraged. It finally proposes 'establishing European territorial pacts capable of bringing together, on a voluntary basis, the different competent tiers of government in order to adapt the implementation of the major political priorities and objectives of the European Union on a partnership basis with the local and regional authorities', that is, it proposes to give a legal dress to existing informal practices. In other words, the WPMLG offers a portrayal of EU governance as being essentially *multi-level*, indicating that the input of SNAs is a fundamental prerequisite for effective and legitimate decision-making.

But how can such an input be provided without grinding EU policy-making to a complete halt (Scharpf 1988)? Yet how simple is it for regional representatives to forgo at the EU level those constitutionally enshrined rights that they enjoy domestically? How can they manage to explain to their constituencies that what they normally do at home cannot be done in Brussels? How can they square their domestic representative mandate to do the interests of their territory and constituency with the higher, but more difficult, European mandate to sustain and implement successfully EU legislation they may or may not benefit from? I will argue that the CoR helps regional and local representatives in this difficult task and that the resulting upgrading of subnational territorial representation may be facilitated by the dual selection filter that they undergo.

CoR members are subjected to a 'double filter' that imparts a particular spin onto their representative function. First, they are selected on the basis of their holding an electoral mandate at home or of being accountable before a representative assembly. Second, they are selected by national governments on the basis of the recommendations issued by national associations of regional and local authorities. By accepting their role as CoR members, subnational representatives accept the idea of representing, in Brussels, not so much their own territory and constituency but all similarly positioned territories and constituencies, and they correspondingly accept the possibility that their territory and constituency will be represented by some other subnational representative at the next round. While their first selection occurs on the basis of their direct linkage with their territory and electoral constituency, their second selection occurs on the basis of their willingness to shed themselves of these particularistic ties and fuse them with those of both similar and different subnational representatives to promote the point of view of all similarly placed SNAs.

What kind of representation do CoR members thus provide: political or functional? The answer is 'both' and testifies to the hybridization of subnational territorial representation performed by the CoR. Subnational representatives in Brussels do not just represent *the functional interests of their territories* nor do they simply reflect *the political orientations of their constituencies*: they represent the interests and preferences of their regional and local communities and, at the same time, contribute to the implementation of policy solutions that hopefully meet those preferences. The expertise that they provide – and for which they might indeed be considered as consultants of sorts – lies in this capacity to translate the resources and preferences of their particular subnational territories and constituencies into policy solutions for the entire EU. The CoR working ethic and partisan affiliation help this otherwise heterogeneous assembly to coordinate its activities and relate to the other EU institutions. In other words, the CoR helps to put into practice multi-level governance and multi-level democracy.

The recent debate has questioned the established conceptual categories of political (electoral) representation and investigated the many other forums, publics, and performers of 'the representative claim' (Rehfeld 2006; Saward 2006). It is now acknowledged that representation may be forthcoming from actors originally charged with different representative mandates or from non-elected officials and that the new types of 'representations' (in the plural, Mansbridge 2003; Rehfeld 2009) may be inherently hybrid (cf. Kröger and Friedrich in this volume). Here I suggest that European integration is encouraging yet another type of hybridization or transformation of representation that had been discarded by the literature based exclusively on national political representation, that between electoral/political and functional representation. This is, I believe, the transformation which the members of the CoR perform.

An additional function that subnational representatives should fulfil is to create bridges between EU institutions and subnational communities, making the former more intelligible to the latter and the latter more relevant for the former. Lack of transparency and a feeling of alienation from EU institutions have been identified as the causes of the EU's questionable legitimacy (White Paper on European Governance 2001). Helping regional and local constituencies understand how 'Europe' is relevant for them – how it helps them restructure industrial and agricultural productions, connect them with other regions and localities, protect their environment, promote higher education, manage migration flows, and so forth – should contribute to improving EU legitimacy. Contrary to national authorities, subnational authorities have an incentive in playing this bridging and ultimately EU-legitimating role.

While national politicians and administrators have an ingrained interest in placing responsibility asymmetrically on Brussels (for tough decisions) and on themselves (for favourable results) because they perceive EU legitimacy as directly competitive with theirs, regional and local authorities derive greater prestige from their action at EU level and can therefore afford to acknowledge merit where merit is due.

One can be obviously sceptical that CoR members indeed manage to upgrade their representative function and that they succeed in bridging the gap between EU institutions and citizens. There are reasons to believe that citizens are not aware of the impact of the Union on their lives despite the activities of subnational governments, and yet they rely on subnational authorities (more than on national political representatives and on their representatives in the European Parliament) to explain to them how European policies impact their day-to-day lives (Eurobarometer 2008: 15). However, in order to assess whether the ambitions of the CoR as expressed in the WPMLG have any substance, we should not ignore how CoR members perceive their role and try to carry it out. This has been one of the focuses of a research project that I carried out in 2008 through 35 semi-structured face-to-face interviews with leading institutional figures within the CoR (the Heads of national representations, the Chairs of the internal commissions, and the Chairs of the party groups) and through a closed-questions questionnaire handed out to all CoR members.[6]

CoR members' self-perception

As recalled above, the CoR has been historically characterized by many internal divisions: between representatives coming from legislative or administrative regions/localities (belonging, that is, to devolved or unitary states); from rich and poor regions/localities; from industrial and agrarian regions/localities; and, ultimately, from old and new Member States. The most significant divide, for our current purposes of assessing the self-perception of CoR members and their contribution to EU democracy, is certainly that between regions belonging to federal and historically devolved states, on the one hand, and unitary or only recently devolved states, on the other, which coincides in large part also with that between representatives from old and new Member States. Looming larger still, however, is the potential fragmentation deriving from the national affiliation of CoR members. This is a common problem that bedevils all EU supranational institutions and one that deserves to be tested for even after more than 15 years of CoR existence.

The greatest variance in institutional powers (and CoR members' self-perception) is observed at the higher levels of subnational government (*Länder*, regions, provinces), whereas local governments are endowed with legislative powers just about everywhere. Clearly, institutional powers can vary considerably also at the local level, but local representatives have almost everywhere a representative mandate and respond to a local representative assembly. Now new members are drawn disproportionately from the lower levels of subnational government,[7] whereas old members come disproportionately from *Länder*, regions and provinces.[8] It follows that the old/new divide impinges upon the type of mandate CoR representatives hold and, consequently, on their self-perception.[9] On the basis of this formal institutional analysis alone, enlargement should have strengthened the self-perception of CoR members as 'political representatives'. However, as it became clear from the face-to-face interviews, the old members of the CoR had in time matured a self-perception as political representatives.

The selection mechanisms of CoR candidates could also be expected to explain the self-perception of CoR members as political representatives rather than expert consultants; the question is, 'representatives of what?' Everywhere, candidates are selected by central governments on the basis of proposals made by national associations of local and regional authorities (often more than one per tier of government).[10] However, in some Member States (e.g. in Ireland) central government really decides quite autonomously, more on the basis of territorial balance and partisan affiliation than on the basis of the recommendations made by local authorities' associations.[11] It is therefore possible that some members may feel themselves to be more representatives of their Member States than of any particular subnational community. However, it is enshrined in the Treaties that CoR members '... shall not be bound by any mandatory instructions. They shall be completely independent in the performance of their duties, in the Union's general interest.'[12] Therefore, a certain independence of opinion and a Treaty-enshrined duty to represent the 'view from the periphery' should bind them as well. The research was consequently also meant to check whether CoR members felt themselves to be more representatives of their regional/local territory/constituency or of their national community.

The data from the questionnaire distributed to all CoR members are particularly telling. Being totally anonymous, the questionnaires may be even more revealing than face-to-face interviews with high-level institutional figures. When asked whether they perceived themselves as being more 'political representatives' or 'expert consultants',

CoR members overwhelmingly (88.0 per cent) replied that they felt they were political representatives. They gave a similar, but attenuated, assessment of the current role of the CoR (69.0 per cent said that it was a political body; 25.5 per cent opted for an advisory body), but they also indicated that, in the future, the CoR should develop into 'something else' (15.0 per cent).

The same self-perception can be evinced from the answers that CoR members gave to the question on which groups they thought they represented most through their mandate at the CoR: 'all European subnational societies', 'the people of their region/locality', 'the people of their electoral constituency', 'their regional/local party', or 'their European political group'. The answers that collected the highest percentage of 'very much' and 'extremely' were 'the people of their region/locality' (80.9 per cent) and 'their European political group' (78.0 per cent), with 'all European subnational societies' coming in third place (65.1 per cent). These results, however partial, seem to suggest that CoR members clearly understand that their task is to represent the interests of their territory and constituency by merging them with those of similarly positioned territories and constituencies and by creating territorial and political cross-European alliances. They are aware that their role is, more generally, to represent all European subnational societies, which would explain their sincere willingness to compromise and build a common front (a point that was often made in face-to-face interviews).

CoR members, then, seem to feel that they are political representatives both because they represent 'the people of their region/locality' (their subnational territory but, by extension, all subnational territories) and because they do so by connecting politically, through the CoR party groups, with the other local/regional representatives (and with members of the European Parliament). In other words, their partisan orientation matters at least as much as their territorial affiliation. This emerged very clearly also from a question that asked what most influenced their vote, whether 'national affiliation', 'CoR party group', 'other EU institutions', 'national government', or 'regional/local government'; 'national affiliation' (69.4 per cent), 'CoR party group' (66.3 per cent), and regional government (65.4 per cent) ranked highest.

Their role as bridge-builders can be evinced from the answers to a question regarding which individuals, groups, or institutions CoR members were most in contact with (the choices being: ordinary citizens, social partners, lobbyists, media, members of the CoR political group, members of their national delegation, members of the CoR commission they worked on, members of the European Parliament, members of the

Commission, members of the ESC). If the answers had indicated that they keep most contacts with social partners and lobbyists, it would have meant that they felt like 'expert consultants' relaying at EU level the needs of the functional groups. If they had underscored their relations with their national delegations and other European institutions, it would have meant that they privileged an inward-looking approach aimed at strengthening their inter-institutional position (probably ancillary to whichever other role they thought they were playing). If they had emphasized their relations with citizens and the media, it would have meant that they felt like 'representatives' and bridge-builders between the EU and the periphery. The categories that were indicated as having the most frequent contacts with them (once a week) were, overwhelmingly, 'ordinary citizens' (83.5 per cent climbing to 96.5 per cent, including also the 'once a month' answers), followed at some distance by 'the media' (47.0 per cent and 86.7 per cent) and 'social partners' (34.5 per cent and 78.6 per cent). High scores (but only on the cumulated score 'once a week' plus 'once a month') were also given to 'members of the national delegation' (72.0 per cent), 'members of the CoR political group' (63.2 per cent), and 'members of the CoR commission they worked in' (45.0 per cent), testifying to the regularity of the work of CoR members within the Committee (whose work routines are organized on a monthly basis), while 'lobbyists' got a cumulated score of 39.2 per cent.

The same idea – that institutional divides were to be downplayed in order to make the subnational dimension relevant for Europe – was often expressed in face-to-face interviews. Heads of national delegations and commissions' and political groups' chairs repeatedly expressed the idea that 'the CoR must speak with one voice in order to be heard'. The need and willingness to strike compromises was, surprisingly, emphasized by all new and old Heads of national representation. This was all the more remarkable since the life of the CoR was initially marked by the attempt of the strongest SNAs – the so-called constitutional or legislative regions – to set themselves apart from the others (e.g. through the Conference of European Regional Legislative Assemblies –[CALRE] and the Conference of European Regions with Legislative Powers –[RegLeg])[13] and to create, within the CoR, two chambers: one for regional authorities and one for local authorities. This institutional divide appeared, at the time of my investigation, considerably toned down and the willingness to help newer and weaker regions and local authorities to strengthen their institutional and political profile both at home and in Brussels was widespread among the older and stronger ones.[14]

It feels safe to conclude that CoR members increasingly perceive themselves as political representatives who must be able to compromise across territorial, economic and institutional divides in order to arrive at strong, unanimous opinions that can have an influence on the decision-making process of the Union (see also Domorenok 2010). CoR members are political representatives in a second way: their political orientation matters at least as much as their national or subnational territorial affiliation. While the CoR's politicization might create in the future new and even deeper divisions, for the moment it helps organize its activities and coordinate its relations with the other European institutions, such as the European Parliament. It also helps overcome the still most dangerous divide: that between institutionally strong and weak subnational authorities, in turn connected to national affiliation. Both results are compatible with the hypothesis put forth in this chapter, that CoR dual filter promotes an 'upgrading' of subnational political representation from that of the specific subnational territory and constituency to all subnational territories and constituencies, and that this might occur along political-party lines.

Conclusion: towards the upgrading of subnational territorial representation

This chapter has argued that the hybrid nature of the Committee of the Regions – a halfway house between a representative assembly and a consultative committee – in reality provides a type of representation that strides across two types – the political and the functional – and delivers a hybrid and perhaps 'upgraded' form of subnational territorial representation. On the one hand, CoR members must be political representatives (or accountable to a directly elected assembly) of a given territory. The inhabitants of their territory and the voters of their constituency constitute the audience towards which they must direct their representative claim upon election or selection (Saward 2010) and also act (in part) as the forums to which they must give account of their action and which can sanction them for their performance at home and in Brussels (Bovens 2007). On the other hand, only few such representatives are selected every five years to sit on the CoR; their selection is performed by national associations of regional and local authorities and by national governments taking into account political, geographical, and institutional considerations.

Upon passing through this second filter, CoR candidates are encouraged to shed their particular territorial affiliation and include in their representative claim all similarly placed territories. The parochial interests of their particular territory are toned down, while the interests connected to the geographical position (and socio-economic profile) of their territory and their partisan coloration are emphasized. The particular institutional powers of each subnational authority will in all likelihood affect the outlook of the chosen candidates in the CoR, but these powers cannot be used to claim a particular role in decision-making (distinct from that of institutionally weaker subnational authorities, as would happen in a 'joint-decision trap' scenario), but rather as a basis for its advisory role as to what can or cannot be done on the ground to implement EU policies. Account must therefore be given also to a second set of selecting agents: national governments and associations of regional and local authorities. In the case of representatives appointed from central government, CoR members will have to be accountable particularly to the latter (and this may explain why some CoR members still feel their national affiliation rather strongly).

The interests that CoR members are allowed to represent in Brussels, then, are based on a complex mix of territorial, functional, and institutional traits that characterize the territory and constituency that they represent (and all similarly placed territories and constituencies). CoR members are also influenced by their political coloration. Both sets of considerations favour the construction of compromises across representatives of widely different subnational authorities and a general upgrading of subnational territorial representation to a sort of categorical representation. Clearly not all regions and localities have the same needs or the same preferences vis-à-vis EU legislation, so that no one solution will fit all. What is represented through the CoR, therefore, are not average, mean, or minimum-common-denominator positions on every issue, but the point of view of 'the periphery', of subnational authorities that want to implement EU policies on the ground while probably trying to respond to the needs and preferences of their constituencies. By trying to find a common position among widely different geographical situations, economic conditions, institutional powers, and political orientations, CoR representatives may indeed succeed in making the concerns of Europe's 'grass roots' relevant for EU policy-making.

The type of democracy to which this highly hybrid type of representation gives rise cannot be immediately compared to any of the existing national models. Other models also attempt to provide representation of interests aligned along different axes (the territorial, the economic, the institutional, and the political), but they do so differently. Federalism (Burgess 2006) works on the assumptions that territorial and economic interests coincide and that they can be mediated through constitutionally enshrined pacts that grant institutional representation to each territory. Compound democracy (Fabbrini 2007) encapsulates territorial and functional divisions within each national institution and entrusts the attainment of equilibriums to the interplay between these institutions (checks and balances). Multi-level governance encourages the 'upgrading' of subnational territorial interests within a political body that is not expected to veto or otherwise obtrude EU policy-making to defend constitutionally entrenched rights but rather convey the preferences of the periphery and contribute to implementing EU policy solutions. In this sense it contributes to the democratic legitimacy of the EU.

Notes

1. I use the term 'subnational' to indicate both regional and local authorities when I do not wish to distinguish between the two.
2. The Treaty of Maastricht (Art. 198a.1 1992) stated that the CoR was to be composed of 'representatives of regional and local bodies' without specifying whether they were elected or appointed. The Treaty of Nice (Art. 263.1 2001) specified that the Committee was to be composed of 'representatives of regional and local bodies who either hold a regional or local authority electoral mandate or are politically accountable to an elected assembly'. The specification is important.
3. When it was carried out, the research was primarily meant to investigate how the CoR had been impacted by the enlargement of 2004–2007 and was part and parcel of a broader assessment of European widening carried out by the Network of Excellence EU-CONSENT (a first assessment of that impact is contained in Best, Christiansen and Settembri 2008; see in particular Piattoni 2008).
4. Pasqual Maragall I Mira, first Vice-President of the CoR, emphasized the role of the Committee as conveying 'the grass-roots concerns', while Dietrich Pause, then Secretary-General of the CoR, saw its role as 'making Europe topical, tangible and accessible to the "man in the street"' (Schöbel 1997: 6).
5. See also the *Consultation Report* Leading up to the *White Paper on Multi-Level Governance – Building Europe in Partnership* (CoR 25/2010). Both can be found at the webpage: http://www.cor.europa.eu/pages/CoRAtWork.
6. We distributed questionnaires to all CoR official members and we got a return rate of roughly 30 per cent – a percentage which held also across the two groups of members (old and new) which were the original targets of the research. The same percentage, however, does not hold across all countries, thus making some voices (particularly those of Cyprus, Italy, Malta, Portugal, Spain and the UK) hardly audible. I am obviously aware of the potential distortion that such uneven sample may impress onto the answers reported in the text. I am confident, however, that the existing evidence can be at least treated as suggestively supportive of the arguments I make in this chapter.
7. LAU 1 (e.g., Cantons, Districts, Dimoi) and LAU 2 (e.g., Cities, Towns, Communities, Villages).

8. NUTS 1 (e.g., States, Länder), NUTS 2 (e.g., Region, Oblasti, Bundesländer) and NUTS 3 (e.g., Provincie, Amter, Nomoi, Kraje, Län).
9. 'Consequently, there are two main models. In federal countries or countries with strong regional systems, such as Germany, Austria, Belgium, Spain or Italy, the representative role of the regions is explicitly described in legislation. In these countries, the national delegations to the CoR are largely made up of regional representatives, whilst local authorities are only marginally represented. However, in countries without regional systems or with weaker regional systems, representatives are mostly or even exclusively local (including Portugal, Greece, Estonia, Latvia, Cyprus, Sweden and Luxembourg)' (The Selection Process 2009: 1).
10. 'Generally speaking, there are two criteria taken into consideration by all countries in the selection procedure: political balance and geographical and territorial balance.... Gender balance is also a priority for increasing numbers of CoR delegations' (The Selection Process 2009: 4).
11. Indeed, in Ireland the relationship between being a local representative and becoming member of the CoR may be reversed: 'Where a member of a local authority is appointed as a member of the CoR but is not a member of a regional authority then on such appointment that member will become, and be and hold office as, a member of the relevant regional authority' (The Selection Process 2009: 31).
12. This provision is contained in all Treaties since Maastricht; now it is in Art. 300 (4), Part Six 'Institutional and Financial Provisions' – Title I 'Institutional Provisions' – Chapter 3 'The Union's Advisory Bodies' of the Treaty on the Functioning of the European Union – TFEU.
13. For CALRE , see: http://www.calrenet.eu; for RegLeg see http://www.regleg.eu/.
14. Some scholars are deeply sceptical of this development and rather argue that the stronger regions, by now, play an individual game in Brussels, accessing and lobbying directly the Commission, without bothering any more to work through either the CoR or the CALRE. This may well be, but I still have on record the interviews with the Heads of national delegations coming from strong regions claiming that they had understood that the CoR has to 'speak with one voice' if it wants to have an impact on EU policy-making. And that they understood the difficulties of the newer and weaker members and they supported their efforts to play a more forceful role both domestically and in Brussels.

5
Whom Do They Represent? Mixed Modes of Representation in EU-Based CSOs

Håkan Johansson

Introduction

The European Union (EU) has become increasingly interested in the role of civil society organizations (CSOs) as a link between political institutions and citizens across Europe (European Commission 2001; Sanchez-Salgado 2007, Smismans 2006). New discourses have emerged on citizens' involvement and the establishment of new forms of civic participation beyond representative democracy. New ideas have been explored on how citizens can become more active in decision-making as a means to revitalize democracy, and even to create a 'European civil society'. EU institutions have made 'civil dialogue' and 'participatory democracy' into a key objective, aiming at an open, transparent, and regular dialogue with citizens, representative associations, and organized civil society. The 2007 Lisbon Treaty (Art. 8 B) introduced the Citizens' Initiative – providing the possibility for one million citizens from a number of Member States to call on the Commission to present new policy proposals, a provision meant to diminish the distance between European citizens and Brussels decision-makers. The European Parliament has installed a model of a Citizen's Agora, bringing together citizens, civil society representatives, and elected politicians to debate key challenges for the EU.

These changes draw attention to the role CSOs play in the EU political system. Great hopes are placed on them as actors who will mediate the views, opinions, and preferences of citizens at national and local levels. Politicians expect them to become a means to regain citizens' trust and avoid having the EU become a project for the elite and not for the citizens of Europe. Scholars have, however, noticed a conspicuous absence of a representation discourse in the EU's official talk on civil society (Trenz 2009a: 37). The Commission has only made a few general remarks that with participation follows responsibility, and that CSOs should be representative of the concerns of their membership or their constituency (Kohler-Koch 2007a). This is surprising, as politicians tend to be highly conspicuous to CSOs and their spokespersons/leaders: Whom do you represent? How can we be sure that you have a mandate to speak for this group? To whom are you accountable (Jordan and van Tuijl 2006)?

This paper analyses the development of a network of CSOs operating at EU level, the European anti-poverty network (hereafter EAPN). EAPN was founded in 1990 and aims to/claims to represent 'the poor' and 'socially excluded' in Brussels.[1] It defines itself as '...an independent network of non-governmental organizations...and groups involved in the fight against poverty and social exclusion in the Member States of the European Union' (www.eapn.org), and has become a key actor in recent EU strategies to combat poverty and social exclusion (Daly 2008). It is composed of 26 national networks of NGOs, voluntary organizations, and grass-roots groups and 23 European organizations, but indirectly adheres to a much wider constituency in terms of several hundreds of national, regional, and local anti-poverty organizations or even the greater number of approximately 78 million people living in poverty across Europe. Based on interviews, document studies, and observations, the paper analyses the following questions: How has EAPN defined its constituency? Has it changed over the years? What forms of internal authorization and accountability can members exercise to hold representatives responsible?

The first part of the paper discusses Pitkin's (1967) key understanding of political representation, and reflects on its relevance for studies of CSOs. The following sections of the paper analyse how debates on representation have evolved within EAPN: the origins of the networks, its membership structure, internal decision-making structures, and innovative ways in which EAPN has sought to represent people experiencing poverty before the final section concludes.

CSOs and political representation

A common view of political representation is that it denotes a form of political action in which a person or group acts in the place of another or others with a certain kind of authorization to do so (Castiglione and

Warren 2008; Urbinati and Warren 2008). Political representation then implies the existence of a relation between 'a representative' and 'a represented', even though this relation sometimes can be of a symbolic nature. This relationship can be untangled by using the different views of political representation as developed by Hannah Pitkin in her seminal essay from the late 1960s (Pitkin 1967). The following discussion will reflect on the relevance of these in relation to the constitution of 'representatives' and 'represented' in CSOs, above all those operating at EU level (Guo and Musso 2006; Mendonca 2008).

The notion of a constituency generally refers to a voting district or a geographical entity that separates those having a voice in political affairs from those who do not (Rehfeld 2005). Such a definition is only partly relevant for studies of how CSOs interact with their members/beneficiaries. The most straightforward way to define a CSO's constituency is naturally to look for formal members. These could be considered as the inner 'core' of an organization's constituency and can – at least in theory – become involved in the organization's policy formulation, the authorization of the association's leaders, and the ways by which these are held responsible for actions (Halpin 2006: 921). A CSO's constituency could also include looser forms of 'membership'. Individuals or organizations can act as 'supporters' or 'contributors' to a CSO. They might lack formal membership privileges, but could be considered a part of a wider constituency since they support the organization's general vision and mission. However, CSOs may adopt other constituency-building strategies. They might speak not only for their members, but also for the wider community, set of beneficiaries, or even ideas and values. Many well-known CSOs, such as Greenpeace, operate according to such a standard. They tend to be value-driven and hold an ambition to primarily change the world order, rather than directly acting on behalf of the interests of their members (Halpin 2006). Scholars have noticed that CSOs, above all those acting at the international level, tend to define their constituencies highly flexibly. For instance, thanks to technological advances and the fact that they operate across borders, they can rather quickly mobilize a large number of supporters, or even members, which makes it difficult to fully grasp their base (Charnovitz 2006: 36). Moreover, many networks claim to have a large number of members, yet one might raise doubts as to whether some of these members are actually aware of the fact that they are counted as members in a network.

A key aspect of political representation concerns *substantive representation*. Pitkin (1967: 145) defined this term as whether a representative should follow the wants of the constituents and be bound by the types of mandates given to him (as a delegate), or whether he could act freely according to his own spirit, as long as it benefited the welfare and desires of his constituency (as a trustee). These notions help us untangle the relationship between CSO leaders and members. Previous research indicates a certain gap between leaders' actions and the wants of the members (Grant 2003, 2005), and there are good reasons to believe that CSOs operating in Brussels follow a similar logic. Geographical distances might hamper the contact between leaders and members, and above all for CSOs with members in many Member States. Language and cultural barriers can make it more difficult for members to identify with what is taking place at EU level. Arguably, representatives who aim to act according to a delegate-model might find it difficult to interact with members and to gain clear instructions on what activities to pursue. Barriers of this kind might hence push leaders to act according to a 'trustee model' (see Rodekamp in this volume).

The relationship between 'a representative' and 'a represented' can also be assessed as a form of *formal representation*, that is, authorization and accountability. The first-mentioned notion refers to the ways by which those represented (for example, voters or members) give representatives (for example elected officials or leaders of CSOs) a grant of authority to act in their name (Pitkin 1967: 43). The last-mentioned notion refers to all the ways by which voters/members hold the representatives responsible for their actions. Even though these notions are best suited for analysing electoral representation, they can be used to analyse the democratic credibility of CSOs. In a large survey of membership-based organizations, Clarence et al. (2005: 130) found that a large proportion of the organizations had an internal decision-making body and/or venues that members could attend to make their voices heard vis-à-vis leaders. Warleigh's study (2001) of CSOs operating in Brussels came up with corresponding conclusions. He noticed that many Brussels-based CSOs had internal assembly meetings (annual or biannual) that functioned as the main decision-making forum. Despite these opportunities, decision-making activities were centralized, and members seemed to have limited direct influence over the affairs and activities. Most decisions were rather taken by an executive committee or specialized policy committees (ibid.).

In her original codification of representations, Pitkin also developed notions such as *descriptive* and *symbolic representation*. Descriptive representation refers to the extent to which a representative mirrors the characteristics of its constituents, that is, whether the representative looks like the represented or shares similar experiences (Mansbridge 1999, 2003). For many CSOs this aspect of representation is of greatest importance. We can find ample examples of detailed regulation of both membership and leadership, for example within the disability movement, women's movement and civil rights movement (Young 2000). Although it is difficult to identify a direct EU dimension to these issues/debates, some EU-based CSOs are certainly challenged by the fact that participating in EU politics tends to require extensive knowledge and experience on the part of the person representing the organizations. They face a situation in which they need to consider whether 'poor' and 'homeless people' can and/or should represent themselves in Brussels, or if their cause is better handled by the professional advocates.

There are other ways through which CSO leaders might earn legitimacy and trust from their constituencies. The concept of *symbolic representation* draws attention to the fact that representatives might have strong legitimacy without being formally elected (formal representation) or without sharing any similarity (descriptive representation). Some scholars maintain that symbolic representation is the most important when analysing the relationship between CSOs and their wider constituency (Peruzotti 2006). CSOs are not political parties and should hence not be assessed according to the same standards. This might be debated, but an organization's legitimacy might depend on its ability to communicate with society in general, to present the views and perspectives of the people it claims to represent, rather than formalistic means of internal decision-making. CSOs that have less ability and/or ambition to secure internal decision-making structures might hence seek symbolic representation, for example to reach out in media and to participate in public debate in combination with extensive information within the organization.

Mobilizing support for a network representing poor people

The following section will provide a historical background to the establishment of EAPN and an analysis of how the network defined its constituency during its initial years. (For a general discussion on the Commission's consultations regimes, see Kröger in this volume). In contrast to what one might have expected, the European Community was in charge of a series of poverty programmes from 1974 until the early 1990s (Bauer 2002). These involved CSOs and researchers from different Member States, and provided them with financial means to develop their activities and reasons to cooperate across borders. During the time of the second Poverty Programme (1984–1986), Jacques Delors became president of the European Commission, and he immediately expressed an ambition to strengthen 'the social dimension' of the Community and to a greater extent involve different stakeholders in the process (Ross 1995).

Delors' ambitions encouraged the Commission to look for partners also in other policy areas, an endeavour that turned out to be difficult as 'homeless people', 'poor people', 'disabled people', 'women's groups', or different 'ethnic groups' lacked representation at EU level. It was equally difficult to identify possible national partners, for instance national peak organizations or large federations of CSOs that represented/claimed to represent marginal groups (Harvey 1993: 190).

The situation challenged the Commission to develop a much more entrepreneurial role in relation to the representation of marginalized groups. Its ambition to form a European-wide network of anti-poverty organizations materialized in the late 1980s, as the Commission invited interested national CSOs to discuss 'the poverty issue' (ibid.). A broad range of stakeholders turned up at the first meeting (researchers, professionals, and representatives of local and national organizations) (Harvey and Kiernan 1991), and participants got the impression that the establishment of a European network working against poverty was sanctioned by Delors personally and high up on his agenda.

The Commission encouraged representatives of national CSOs to set up a provisional working group with representatives from several European countries. It was expected to '...build an anti-poverty network in the European Community, based on a process of consultation at national level...' and '...to consider proposals for a more permanent structure for the European anti-poverty initiative....' (Harvey 1990: 1). A large part of the working group's activities was hence to identify national organizations working with poverty issues and to enter into discussions with them if they were interested in joining a European network (Harvey 1991).

The formal establishment of EAPN took place in autumn 1990, and CSOs from most Member States had managed to send a delegation to the assembly meeting (except for Germany) (EAPN 1991). National delegates came to the meeting with a mandate to speak and vote for their national anti-poverty networks. One can naturally question how solid their mandate was, but the national delegations were anyhow defined as *the* national representatives at EU level. During this inaugural meeting, EAPN made its first attempts to define its constituency and decided that the network would allow '...voluntary anti-poverty groups whose explicit and main purpose is the empowering of people and communities facing poverty and social exclusion, and whose actions aim at strengthening the autonomy of these people...' (see Harvey 1991 for original EAPN statutes). Membership was defined in a fairly broad manner *as long as* the member was directly involved in the fight against poverty, that is, as a kind of normative condition for membership. Members could then either be informal groups or formal organizations, groups established as non-profit associations or cooperatives, formal and informal local networks and wider federative organizations, but not public organizations.

This definition caused some debate as some delegates asked for more 'descriptive representation', that is, EAPN should be a network for and by people experiencing poverty (EAPN 1991: 9). These concerns reflected general tensions with regard to how best to represent poor people and the great mix of actors that had come together to try to form a European network. Some national delegations mainly consisted of persons with a 'professional/expert profile' who came from larger national organizations and were used to working with public authorities and administrations (e.g. the Portuguese and French delegations). Other national delegations were dominated by people with personal experience of living in poverty and came from grass-root activists (e.g. the Belgian and Dutch delegations) (communication with national representatives, see Johansson 2010).

A Multilayered membership structure

The previous section analysed how EAPN started to define its constituency and allowed a wide mix of organizations to enter the network. Today, the network consists of 26 national networks and can hence be pictured as 'an organization of organizations', 'a network of networks' or 'an umbrella organization'. This implies that other organizations construct the network's main membership type (and not individuals) and EAPN has also restricted its membership to one formal member per country. This way of building a network at EU level has certain implications, e.g. EAPN can take an active stance in forming members.

We notice that almost all EU Member States are represented in the network (see Table 5.1). Although the network lacks members in Latvia and Estonia it includes organizations from Norway. Its membership coverage illustrates an ambition to secure geographical representation, partly due to external pressure from EU institutions. The Commission expects umbrella networks, such as EAPN, to have a member in each Member

Table 5.1 EAPN membership

National EAPN networks (in chronological order)
Belgium (1990), Ireland (1990), Spain (1990), Greece (1990), France (1990), the UK (1990), Portugal (1990), Denmark (1990), the Netherlands (1990), Italy (1990), Luxembourg (1991), Germany (1994), Finland (1995), Austria (1995), Sweden (1998), Bulgaria (2003), Hungary (2004), Malta (2004), Czech republic (2004), Cyprus (2005), Norway (2005), Lithuania (2006), Poland (2007), Slovakia (2007), Romania (2008), Slovenia (2009)

Source: www.eapn.org, accessed 20 December 2010.

State. This is spelled out as a prerequisite for substantial EU funding, both when it comes to gain and to maintain funding. Certainly it is also a matter of legitimacy. A network with members all over Europe can naturally gain higher legitimacy, in relation to politicians and other CSOs.

EAPN's ambition to build geographical representation has, however, resulted in some complexities. National organizations have been sceptical about acting within the framework of an EU-based network of CSOs, which has been questioned, for example, by German organizations. They challenged EAPN's independence from the Commission and, among other things, argued that one could better represent 'poor people' from their national basis (see correspondence between representatives of German organizations and EAPN in Harvey 1991). EAPN has also experienced 'difficulties' in finding national organizations that had or could have an interest in becoming a representative at EU level, for example, when EAPN tried to establish a Swedish EAPN network (Johansson 2010). Recent EU enlargements have also pushed EAPN to look for members in Eastern Member States. This expansion caused some internal anxiety within the network as to what kind of organizations *and* people one got involved with (ibid.). This illustrates how the network takes an active stance in creating or at least establishing members, an activity that raises doubts about the network's representativeness.

EAPN also consists of a fairly large number of international CSOs or EU-based networks. Organizations such as ATD Fourth World, Caritas Europa, EMMAÜS International, Eurochild, EURODIACONIA, Salvation Army, Red Cross, and so on are all members of EAPN. Possibly this could lead to a conflict of interest over which type of issues the network is actually representing. EAPN has, however, limited the formal status of these international organizations and EU-based networks, as they hold limited voting power in the networks' internal decision-making structure (see www.eapn.org).

The discussion above indicates the formal membership structure of EAPN. However, to fully understand its multilayered structure one needs to unpack it somewhat further (see Table 5.2). Being a network of organizations, national networks consist of other organizations (national, regional, and local). Internal documentation indicates that the 26 national networks have almost 1,600 members (EAPN 2005). Some national networks have a large number of member organizations (Portugal, the UK, and Ireland), while other national networks have less than 25 member organizations (Germany, France, Italy) and mainly consist of peak organizations at national level (ibid.)

These figures originate from EAPN and must be read cautiously, for example, concerning the counting of regional and local organizations. Nonetheless, these different national profiles raise relevant questions

Table 5.2 Profile of national networks

Country	National (umbrella) organizations	Regional and local organizations	Total
Austria	33	5	*38*
Belgium	65	–	*65*
Bulgaria	15	–	*36*
Cyprus	16	–	*16*
Czech Republic	14	–	*14*
Denmark	–	10	*10*
Finland	30	2	*32*
France	28	2	*30*
Germany	14	–	*14*
Greece	24	2	*26*
Hungary	33	46	*79*
Ireland	38	178	*216*
Italy	–	10	*10*
Luxembourg	2	11	*13*
Malta	53	–	*53*
Netherlands	5	25	*30*
Norway	9	12	*21*
Portugal	–	–	*478*
Slovakia	25	–	*25*
Spain	15	16	*31*
Sweden	15	23	*38*
United Kingdom	54	255	*309*
Total	*498*	*587*	*1584*

Source: EAPN (2005) and own calculations from www.eapn.org, accessed 20 December 2010.

with regard to EAPN's constituency. Membership numbers can be used to portray the network in a 'good manner'. The 'representation' of more than 1,500 organizations across Europe can impress political actors, make the network more credible, and raise the network's symbolic legitimacy vis-à-vis existing members and the wider constituency the network adheres to. However, figures of this kind need to be critically examined, above all as the network has made few attempts to regulate national networks' internal affairs. National networks differ considerably. Some are acting as one coherent national organization (for example, the Portuguese network), while others are constituted as coalitions of national organizations with a loose coupling to other domestic organizations.

The fact that EAPN primarily has tried to secure geographical representation has hence provided national networks with a great degree of freedom to govern membership profiles, internal decision-making procedures, and decision-making bodies. Even though national networks are EAPN's main constituency, their representativeness is largely unknown. Whom do national networks represent? Can we be sure that they have a mandate to speak for poor and socially excluded groups in a national context? To what extent can national, regional, and local members hold the leaders of national networks accountable? Arguably, a complete analysis of patterns of authorization and accountability in EU-based networks needs to operate at different levels, but this is far beyond the scope of this chapter.

Patterns of authorization and accountability

EAPN's decision-making structure, that is, channels for members and representatives of national networks to participate in the networks' decision-making process, can be portrayed in Figure 5.1 (see below).

The general assembly meetings (held annually) constitute EAPN's main democratic arena, and at these representatives of national networks and European organizations come together to debate general policy positions (each assembly meeting includes a general declaration) and matters of general importance for the network (for example, acceptance of new members and election of leaders for the network) (EAPN 2009e). National representatives can write comments in advance or take the floor to discuss proposals coming from leaders. An executive committee, elected by the general assembly, formally leads EAPN. Its role is to develop, promote, and manage the work of the organization. It is comprised of one representative from each national

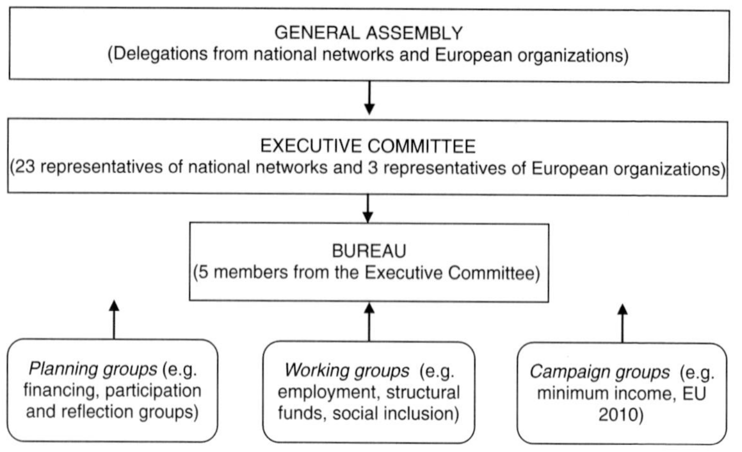

Figure 5.1 EAPN organizational chart
Source: www.eapn.org, accessed 20 December 2010.

network and three representatives from the European organizations (EAPN 2009d).

These structures suggest that national networks – and their delegates – have at least a formal mandate to hold leaders accountable. However, EAPN's direct leadership is located at the bureau, which consists of the networks' president and vice-presidents. Despite what one would have anticipated, the election of the bureau takes place behind closed doors as members of the (newly) elected executive committee decide on who will lead the network. The bureau is expected to have a sound gender, north/south, and east/west balance and also consider differences between different types of organizations within the network.

A few comments are relevant. The establishment of its decision-making structure did not come about without debate. One of the issues discussed is the relative strength of different national networks, that is, how would one calculate the number of delegates each national network could send to the general assembly meetings? An interesting debate took place at the time during which EAPN was founded. The initial model for calculating delegates (developed by the provisional working group before the formal establishment of the network) followed the same principle as the European Community: national networks would receive delegates according to the size of the population in each country. Delegates from Southern European countries objected to this proposal, and claimed that it would be a misrepresentation of poor people if countries like Portugal, Ireland, and Greece had the same number of delegates as countries like Belgium, the Netherlands, and Denmark (EAPN 1993). Because the problem of poverty was so much higher in these less industrialized countries, they had to have a higher proportion of 'seats' in the general assembly.

This suggests contradictory views on how to calculate the strength of each national network: the size of the population in each country or the size of poverty as a national and societal problem. The model chosen (ibid.) turned out to be a compromise, as Southern European national networks got a slightly higher proportion of the seats at the assembly meetings than Northern European countries of the same size. Even though EAPN now includes national networks coming from countries with a much higher poverty rate than some of the Southern European countries had in the beginning of the 1990s, the balancing of votes has remained unchanged. New members gain seats according to the size of the population and not according to the size of the 'problem'.

In addition to these formal assembly meetings, interaction between network leaders and representatives of national networks takes place in working, planning, and campaign groups. These constitute a channel through which representatives of national networks can participate in EAPN's internal affairs and influence its policy positions. However, instead of being an arena for internal deliberation and discussion, these working groups have become EAPN's production units. The arrows in Figure 5.1, indicating that it is a 'bottom-up' process, need to be interpreted carefully. The working groups on employment, social inclusion, and structural funds follow and monitor EU's policy development, write analyses and prepare position papers. Each group has approximately 15 to 20 members and hence participation is restricted to a few national representatives. Those who participate are expected to have high competence with regard to EU policies in each respective field (EAPN 2003a). Obviously, professionalization and expert orientation is a delicate issue for any CSO. The production of technical, handy, and policy-relevant information can raise EAPN's legitimacy among external actors (for example, the Commission), but might increase the distance to the concerns of members and the wider constituency one represents.

EAPN hence has a democratic structure that builds on members' formal involvement. Yet apart from annual general assembly meetings, it appears as if members have limited direct influence on EAPN's affairs and activities. Most decisions seem to be taken by the executive committee or specialized policy committees. Even if we find clear evidence that members can hold the leaders and spokespersons accountable, their relative influence over the networks' positions and operations then seems to be fairly limited, and particularly if we think of EAPN's membership in the form of local, regional, and national organizations or even the wider constituency of people experiencing poverty. Although the delegate and the trustee models are two extreme ideal types, EAPN's leaders have a fairly high degree of discretion to act on behalf of their members and the wider constituency.

Can 'Poor People' be the representatives in the network?

The previous discussion pictures key aspects of representations within EAPN. However, there has been a continuous debate within the network about whether one should give more power to national networks and shift the decision-making structure so that people experiencing poverty could be better included in EAPN's activities (EAPN 1991). Factions in favour of more direct participation of people experiencing poverty had difficulties making 'their voice' heard within the network, but gained unexpected support as the Belgian government in 2001 invited EAPN to take part in organizing annual 'people experiencing poverty meetings', that is, meetings for and by poor people themselves in the very heart of Brussels (EAPN 2003b: 7).

However, the executive committee hesitated as to whether EAPN would participate in such an event (EAPN 2001a), even though the issue of the participation of poor people was intensively debated at general assembly meetings during the same time (EAPN 2000; EAPN 2001b). Members of the executive committee argued that such meetings could stigmatize and exploit poor people and serve as a method to strengthen the position and legitimacy of decision makers.

The invitation challenged EAPN in other respects as well. Considering that the network previously had not built on a broad participation of people experiencing poverty (see above), the proposal was hence an opportunity *as well as* a risk for the network. If EAPN could prove to mobilize people experiencing poverty, it would strengthen its legitimacy. A mobilization failure would similarly question whom the network really represented. Such concerns must be understood in relation to wide differences among national networks. Some national networks consisted to a large degree of large umbrella organizations and/or service providers, and had potentially great difficulties in mobilizing poor people within their own ranks, while other national networks were comprised of user or grass-roots organizations. Possibly some key people might have felt uncomfortable with directly involving those experiencing poverty in the networks' affairs. To speak for members is sometimes easier than letting members speak for themselves, as one does not know what they will say. Based on these concerns, EAPN decided not to support the first 'people experiencing poverty' meeting (autumn 2000), but soon changed its mind and has since been highly involved in following 'people experiencing poverty' meetings (EAPN 2002).

What then is a 'people experiencing poverty' meeting and how does it relate to our general analysis of representation? Such a meeting takes place each spring in Brussels, and one can easily conclude that it is a contrast-rich event. EAPN, the Belgian government, and the spring presidency jointly organize these meetings. EAPN is very much in charge of arranging them, particularly when it comes to mobilizing national delegations of people experiencing poverty to participate. Each national EAPN network sends a delegation of people who – at least in theory – should have (or have had) personal experience of living in poverty. Several national politicians and Commission representatives attend meetings together with a large number of CSOs. Moreover, debates and interventions follow a special logic. National delegates are actually those who are speaking and presenting their views on how it is to live in poverty (EAPN 2003b; EAPN 2007a; EAPN 2009a).

EAPN's involvement in these meetings has fuelled the internal debate on differences between national networks: whether it is national networks that represent people experiencing poverty or larger CSOs without any connection to the daily lives of poor people. Communication with network members and observations at people experiencing poverty meetings suggest even internal ranking procedures (Johansson 2010). National delegations are scrutinized to determine if they consist of people who are actually poor and not of people who are working with poor people. They are also scrutinized to see whether they have managed to bring 'new' poor people to meetings or whether one has managed only to mobilize persons who have already attended previous people experiencing poverty meetings. Arguably, these efforts could be interpreted as an essentialist drive among some members of EAPN, that is, the views and opinions of poor people can only be truly presented by poor people themselves.

There is, however, no formal connection between what takes place at these people experiencing poverty meetings and EAPN's internal activities. The participants at the people experiencing poverty meetings are not 'members' of EAPN – even though they might be working for or be a beneficiary of any of the national networks and/or organizations. They have hence limited possibility to influence EAPN's positions or hold the leaders responsible in any way. Nonetheless, EAPN has acted very strategically to secure its position as the main CSO working with the people experiencing poverty meetings. One takes part in the planning process and has more or less been handed the right/obligation to find poor people who are actually willing – and capable – of travelling to Brussels and taking part in a three-day meeting, including expressing their views and opinions on national and local poverty policies. Coordinators from national EAPN networks handle such 'recruitment' processes. EAPN has also initiated capacity-promoting activities to help delegates understand EU policies (EAPN 2007b). These operations add to the general picture of a network that defines its constituency in a fairly flexible manner. It aims to speak not only for its formal members, but also for a wider constituency of 'poor people'.

It would, however, be an exaggeration to conclude that EAPN's involvement in these meetings is only for strategic purposes. During recent years, the network has started to change its internal working orders. All national networks are encouraged to arrange people experiencing poverty meetings, certainly as a way to broaden their base, but also to change the ways by which the people represented can have 'a say' with regard to the national networks' activities (EAPN 2009b). Similar innovations are currently implemented in the networks' main organizational units. The executive committee is partly reformed and one has decided to initiate a greater contact between committee members and people experiencing poverty from different countries. They will meet on a regular basis to discuss EAPN's policy positions and the development in different localities across Europe (EAPN 2009c). Whether this will lead to a greater possibility of 'the represented group' to become 'the representative' needs further empirical investigation. Nonetheless, these internal changes signify that EAPN is continuously seeking new ways to constitute and interact with its constituency.

Conclusions

The previous analysis has pictured EAPN's membership structure, internal decision-making structures and ways by which EAPN has sought to represent people experiencing poverty. These discussions not only give us some insight into the relationship between EAPN, its members, and the greater set of beneficiaries included in a wider definition of its constituency, but we also see that EAPN embodies several overlapping and even conflicting modes of representation.

The first of these identifies EAPN as a *representative of organizations working against poverty and social exclusion*. Formal members (national networks and European organizations) have possibilities to raise their voices, take part in recurring elections of leaders and spokespersons and hence exercise some control over the networks' activities and positions. Ideally, EAPN's leaders – for example its president and vice-presidents – would act then according to the mandate they have received, and if they diverge too much from the decided program, members have the possibility of electing new leaders at a following assembly meeting. Members' possibilities of holding leaders accountable are, however, circumscribed by the unclear ways that the bureau is elected. Moreover, although the network has managed to secure a solid geographical representation across the EU, what takes place within national EAPN networks is largely unknown territory – not only for us but also for EAPN leaders. This raises doubts concerning what mandate national representatives enter into the debate and discussion at EU level. Are they formally elected or are they participating based on other grounds? Are national organizations counted as members by EAPN actually aware of the fact that they are considered part of an EU-based organization against poverty? These are issues we obviously cannot answer here. Nonetheless, we recognize that a complete analysis of representation within EAPN – and in similar networks – needs to operate at different levels: between representatives and represented at EU, national, and possibly even local levels.

EAPN could also be considered as *an advocate against poverty and social exclusion*. In spite of the fact that EAPN follows some – at least basic – principles of membership democracy, it is also acting as an interest group or a lobbying organization. Over the years this mode of representation has grown more significant. The network is a frequent producer of reports, position papers, newsletters, and press releases on issues relating to poverty and social exclusion. It participates in recurring events at EU level and has – for two decades now – acted as a key stakeholder in the debate on poverty and social inclusion policies at EU level. This suggests that EAPN not only aims to represent members as part of a primary constituency, but also seeks to act as a representative of 'the fight against poverty and social exclusion'. Although members can exercise their voice at assembly meetings, major decisions tend to be taken in its expert committees and working groups. Few people are directly involved in the networks' activities (working groups and meetings) and in spite of its extensive membership basis (at least if one includes all national, regional, and local organizations) there is a high consistency regarding who participates and acts as representative.

The last mode pictures EAPN as *a representative of people experiencing poverty*. The idea (and ideal) that EAPN would be an arena for participation of people actually living in poverty was intensively debated when EAPN was established and has been used by people within EAPN to make distinctions between national networks (and even individuals). Some national networks are considered as expert and lobbying oriented, while others are portrayed as made up of users or people with a direct and personal experience of living in poverty. The former are categorically seen as representatives of service providers or interest organizations, and the latter as part of a grass-roots organization or a user organization.

This mode of representation lost some of its significance as the network transformed more into an interest group, but has recently become more significant. The network has become one of the key proponents of the so-called 'people experiencing poverty' meetings and has also started to change some of its internal decision-making structures to directly involve people experiencing poverty. This could be considered an innovative approach, but raises some reservations. At best, the network seeks ways to introduce the perspectives of poor people into its internal operations and the general debate on poverty and social exclusion at EU level. The views, stories, and experiences of people experiencing poverty could be seen as a part of a deliberative process in which different perspectives are brought together, a process considered by some as especially important in order to include the perspectives of marginal groups into the policy-making process (for example, Young 2000). At worst, the people involved end up in a 'hostage situation', in which other actors use their experiences to push their agenda in a certain direction.

These modes make it difficult to fully grasp the ways by which representation is constituted in the EAPN. We find combinations of the 'mandate' and 'trustee' models and a complex conceptualization of its constituency, ranging from other organizations working against poverty and social exclusion, self-assumed ambitions to act as a representative in the fight against poverty and even aspirations to become a representative made up of people experiencing poverty themselves. Whether this chameleon feature is typical for EAPN only, or also applicable to other networks of CSOs working at EU level, is certainly an issue that needs further empirical research, but considering that many EU-based networks of CSOs share EAPN's organizational structure – for example the European Disability Forum, the European Women's Lobby, and the European network against Racism – it is plausible to assume that we would find similar combinations of representation in these.

Note

1. The paper draws on a study of the 'The History of the EAPN Network'. The project is funded by the Swedish Council for Working Life and Social Research (2005–2009) AU: CHANGE OKAY? and is part of a larger project on 'The EU, an opportunity structure for Swedish civil society organizations'.

6
Representing Their Members? Civil Society Organizations and the EU's External Dimension

Meike Rodekamp

Introduction: CSOs' representative role

In the debate on how to solve the alleged democratic deficit of the European Union (EU), Civil Society Organizations (CSOs)[1] have come to be seen as a potential remedy. They are said to channel citizens' interests and concerns to policy-makers, thereby functioning as transmission belts between the citizenry and political institutions (Steffek and Nanz 2008: 8) and contributing to the EU's input legitimacy. This requires that political choices be derived 'directly or indirectly, from the *authentic preferences* of citizens' (Scharpf 1997: 19; emphasis in original). CSOs are supposed to have a role in guaranteeing that governance is not only *for* but also *by* the people. They are seen as a complement to the territorially fragmented interest representation of government representatives (Warren 2001: 83).

However, some scholars have expressed doubt about the intermediary function of CSOs. They have pointed out that CSOs are not intrinsically democratic, or, according to Robert Michels' famous iron law of oligarchy, even inherently undemocratic (Barber 1950; Finer 1974; McLaverty 2002). CSOs, so the criticism goes, have become professionalized and detached from their membership base. CSOs operating close to the decision-making centres of the EU and other international organizations especially have been accused of being elite-driven and efficiency – rather than member-oriented (Warleigh 2000; Peeters 2003: 12). Consequently, the internal structure of CSOs has come into the focus (Saurugger 2008). Scholarly endeavours to develop criteria for CSOs' democratic governance testify to this trend (Steffek et al. 2010a; Wiercx 2010).

The European Commission shares the view of CSOs as representatives,[2] stating that they have an 'important role in giving voice to the concerns of citizens'. But it also argues that '(w)ith better involvement comes greater responsibility' (European Commission 2001: 15). CSOs seeking to contribute to EU policy-making should follow the principles of good governance, including representativeness. They must reveal which interests they represent and how inclusive that representation is (European Commission 2002b:17). The Commission has expressed its preference for consulting with European federations as opposed to individual organizations. If CSOs are seen as legitimizing agents by the Commission, this is especially so for allegedly representative federations (Greenwood 2010; see also Kröger in this volume). Unfortunately, among those who consider CSOs as representatives and those who question this role, very few have presented empirical results to substantiate their claims (but see Steffek et al. 2010b). To what extent do Brussels CSOs actually speak for their members? The present chapter contributes to filling this gap in the literature by providing an explorative study of CSOs' performance in representing their members. Besides the question of whether CSOs actually exert influence on political decisions, adequate member representation seems crucial in order for CSOs to fulfil the expected democratizing function in the EU context.

The representative qualities of CSOs active at the grass-roots or national level have frequently been explored (Bolduc 1980; Cnaan 1991; Swindell 2000; Guo and Musso 2007; Liston 2009). Bozzini (2007) has provided a study of national CSOs in ten European countries and the extent to which they represent their members. However, this kind of evidence is largely missing for EU level CSOs (but see Johansson in this volume). Notable exceptions are also the contributions of Warleigh (2001) and Sudbery (2003), who have studied the role of Brussels-based CSOs in contributing to political socialization and the creation of a European public sphere. Both find that CSOs have limited engagement with individual supporters. In light of these results, I suggest exploring the first level of the transmission belt, namely the relationship between EU CSOs and their immediate member organizations.[3] If the chain of communication at this level is dysfunctional, the links to lower organizational levels are also unlikely to work.

Recently a connection has been made between civil society and the concept of representation, offering a valuable analytical frame for the question of member representation in CSOs. Pitkin (1967: 2, 2004) already pointed out that representation is not limited to representative government. Current contributions dealing with political representation call for a 'wider, broader, closer, deeper' (Taylor 2010) understanding of the concept. Scholars studying representation have incorporated the representative function of civil society into their work (Mansbridge 2003; Saward 2006, 2009; Castiglione and Warren 2008; Stoffel 2008; Taylor 2010) and authors researching CSOs have started to frame their role in terms of representation (Lavalle et al. 2005; Trenz 2009a).

The focus in this chapter is on the 'performative function' of CSOs in contributing to the EU's legitimacy. In this view, CSOs represent by aggregating citizens' preferences (Kohler-Koch 2008: 9, 11). Organizational representativeness refers to the question whom the individual group represents (Kohler-Koch 2008: 13; Smismans in this volume). That CSOs actually fulfil their representative claims is often implicitly assumed. Yet a lack of organizational representativeness implies a fundamental criticism of the assumption that associations mirror societal interests. While the question is relevant to CSOs' role in EU democracy, it is equally important from an inner-organizational point of view and with regard to the question whether CSOs comply with their self-set standards of speaking for their members.

The remainder of this chapter is structured as follows: section two is dedicated to the research strategy and case selection. Section three reports the empirical results, and section four summarizes and discusses the findings.

Research strategy, case selection, and methods

Research strategy

CSO representativeness can be defined in different ways, for example, as geographical representativeness to which the Commission attaches importance. Annex 2 shows that the sampled CSOs are represented in many European countries. In the subsequent analysis, representativeness is understood as the extent to which CSOs speak for their members. This is the Commission's postulation but also the standard set by CSOs themselves, many of whom publicly claim to speak for their members. To analyse CSO representativeness as it is understood here, elements of formalistic, participatory, and substantive representation are combined (Pitkin 1967; Loewenberg and Kim 1978).

Formalistic representation refers to the formal organizational arrangements governing the relationship between leaders and constituents. It is comprised of two aspects: authorization and accountability (Pitkin 1967). Authorization refers to the process of election. Therefore, the concept of accountability appears more suitable for analysing the relationship between hired (and not elected) staff and member organizations in professional CSOs. This relationship is often only vaguely defined by formal provisions, such as CSOs' statutes.

Accountability refers to a relationship between power-wielders and 'accountability-holders' (Piewitt et al. 2010: 3). It implies that the former have the right to measure the latter against a set of standards, to assess whether they have fulfilled their responsibilities and to impose sanctions if not (Grant and Keohane 2005: 29). The representatives have to answer to the represented for what they do and be responsive to their wishes (Pitkin 1967: 55, 113). Central to this is, among others things, the existence of complaint procedures: structured channels through which members can voice criticism when they disagree with (in)actions of office-holders and ways of resolving conflicts. Examples in this case are juries, ombudsmen, and informal complaints to the leadership.

In the sampled CSOs, the importance of member accountability among the various accountability relationships in which CSOs are engaged is considered (Piewitt et al. 2010). Subsequently, the occurrence of internal conflicts is explored and whether complaint mechanisms are available in such cases. Do CSOs have procedures in place through which members can voice complaints and hold their officers to account?

The concept of participatory representation was not among Pitkin's dimensions of representation but is especially suitable for analysing CSOs. It is given 'when there is a direct, unmediated, and participatory relationship between an organization and its constituents' (Guo and Musso 2007: 312). This dimension of representation requires that organizations maintain a variety of communication and participation channels with their constituents to ensure receptiveness to their demands (Loewenberg and Kim 1978: 38). Communication is a crucial element of member representation because CSOs' representative power depends on their ability to communicate their members' interests. Organized communication between members and those who speak for them is thus a precondition for 'representative communication' (Warren 2001: 84). It is investigated via which channels and how frequently CSOs communicate with their members and how satisfied officers and members are with their mutual communication. To assess participation, the study asks how often members are consulted for feedback and whether they take part in decision-making and organizational activities.

Substantive representation is defined as acting 'in the interest of the represented, in a manner responsive to them' (Pitkin 1967: 209). It raises the question to what extent the orientation of the representative is in line with the interests of the constituents (Peterson 1970: 64), referring to the capacity of officers to represent the preferences of constituents. It is frequently measured by the extent to which CSO leaders and constituents agree on specific policy issues (Guo and Musso 2007: 312). In this study, another way is pursued and the satisfaction of members with their representation at the EU level in general is scrutinized.

A major controversy has arisen from the definition of substantive representation: the distinction between the delegate and the trustee model of representation. While in the case of the former 'power is legitimate only when it is authorized by the legitimating consent of those who delegate it', in the latter view officials do what *they* believe is best for their constituents' welfare (Grant and Keohane 2005: 32). In this context, the distinction will serve as an analytical tool to identify different models of representation in the sampled CSOs. While the models are usually discussed in the framework of substantive representation, in this context the analysis of participatory representation is better able to reflect towards which model CSOs tend. Therefore this aspect will be considered in the section on participatory representation.

Rather than defining standards for what CSOs should achieve in terms of organizational representativeness, the purpose of this explorative study is to find out how CSOs perform in the three dimensions identified.

Case selection and research methods

The primary selection criterion for the CSOs subject to this analysis was their level of access to EU institutions, determined by their presence in Brussels and involvement in partnerships and consultations with the European Commission and the Council. In terms of policy relevance it is especially salient to investigate whether groups that have the best institutional access are still linked to their constituencies because they are most likely to influence EU policies. Second, the chapter concentrates on EU CSOs with organizational members (so-called 'umbrella organizations'). They regroup the major CSOs and CSO federations working in a specific policy field and have taken on a leading role among CSOs in Brussels. For them the issue of representation seems especially pertinent because their primary membership base is clearly defined and they explicitly claim to speak for their members.

CSOs active in the EU's external dimension, namely in Trade Policy and in Security and Defence Policy, will serve as the case study. These policy fields are considered to be state-dominated and thus constitute a hard case for civil society participation (Broscheid and Coen 2007: 355–6; Bexell et al. 2010: 96).

The sampled CSOs were studied by carrying out two sets of semi-structured interviews. The first set was conducted with 13 CSOs active in the EU's external dimension (see Annex 2).[4] Three of them, BusinessEurope, WIDE, and EPLO, were selected for closer scrutiny. For each of them, ten member organizations were interviewed (thus a total of 30) (see Annex 1). The aim of the selection process was to achieve a balance between large and small, as well as Brussels- and non-Brussels-based, members. In the end, the availability of organizations for an interview was also decisive. The interviews were complemented with information provided on CSOs' websites and in their statutes.

BusinessEurope is the main horizontal business association at the EU level, regrouping 41 European industrial and employers' federations. It claims to represent a total of 20 million European companies. Its main goal is to ensure that companies' interests are defended vis-à-vis the EU institutions. BusinessEurope was established in 1958 as the *Union des Industries de la Communauté européenne (UNICE)*. It is a social partner in the European Social Dialogue. Women in Development Europe (WIDE) is a network of 13 national platforms working on women and development issues. Since 1985, WIDE has advocated for women's economic, social, and political empowerment in international forums. The European Peacebuilding Liaison Office (EPLO), founded in 2001, is the platform of European peacebuilding organizations. Its members are 26 individual organizations, networks of organizations, and think tanks. EPLO's goal is to promote peacebuilding policies among EU decision-makers. Most of the member organizations of the three CSOs are based in European capitals. About one-third maintain a branch office in Brussels.

Results

The following sections report the results for the elements of formalistic, participatory and substantive representation as discussed above.

Formalistic representation: member accountability

Presented with different accountability channels, all CSO representatives who provided an answer to this question (12) responded that they felt accountable to their members. Many officers confirmed the existence of additional accountability relationships: to beneficiaries (4); nature/future generations (2); donors (2); the general public (1); or the line manager (1). Yet member accountability seems to be the common overriding principle for the majority of CSOs interviewed.

Most CSO representatives reported to have been confronted with situations of internal conflict. Disagreements may arise between members and the Brussels officers or among members. The former are more relevant with regard to the question of whether EU CSOs speak for their members. Not surprisingly they were reported less frequently in the interviews with CSO staff. One interviewee explained that members were not always satisfied with the way she and her colleagues worked: 'People are often critical and ... say: "we weren't consulted about this. ..." They actually were but just didn't read their e-mails.' The interviewee did not consider these conflicts to be very serious though: 'I think this is just the nature of working in a member[-based] organization. Members are always unhappy. It's their job to be unhappy.' Another officer reported that members had expressed concern about the too pro-European stand taken by the staff.

With regard to complaint procedures, some officers said that the goal was to act by consensus and conflicts were dealt with on an individual basis. However, most representatives, especially those of larger umbrellas, claimed that complaints were referred to specific bodies of the organizational hierarchy. In large organizations with more complex decision-making structures, the more severe the complaint, the more high-ranking is the body that takes on the responsibility for solving it. Formal complaint procedures, such as juries, play a subordinate role in the CSOs interviewed. Regarding the three CSOs under closer scrutiny, the interviewees at BusinessEurope, WIDE, and EPLO all claimed that members could complain to specific organizational bodies.

Turning to member organizations, about half responded that they had experienced internal conflicts. They largely confirmed the preference for informal complaint-making. Most BusinessEurope members confirmed their staff's answer that they could make complaints to certain organizational bodies. However, WIDE and EPLO members usually mentioned bilateral conversations rather than the bodies which their Brussels officers indicated to be responsible. At WIDE, three members did not know at all to whom they could voice criticism. Hence, some members are not familiar with the possibilities for complaint-making at their CSO and thus will not hold their EU officers accountable via these channels.

Participatory representation: member participation

How well members are represented by their Brussels-based umbrella organization is strongly determined by the extent to which they can participate at the EU level. Therefore the intensity of interaction between the Brussels offices and member organizations is explored, as well as the latter's involvement in long- and short-term decision-making and in organizational activities.

The CSOs interviewed rely on a wide variety of communication channels. All organizations that provided an answer to this question (12) communicate with their members via e-mail, phone, newsletters, personal meetings, and sometimes additional means, such as Skype conferences. The representatives of member organizations largely confirmed this. All 30 claimed to communicate via e-mail and face-to-face meetings with the Brussels staff. Many mentioned phone contact and internal newsletters. When asked to rank these channels, the majority (17) said that face-to-face contact was most important. This included Brussels- as well as non-Brussels-based members. However, the frequency of face-to-face meetings varies considerably from biannual General Assemblies to daily chats in the elevator. The opportunities for making use of this important communication channel are distributed rather unevenly among members, to the disadvantage of those without a Brussels office and without funding for regular flights to Brussels.

Regarding the frequency of interaction, most of the umbrellas are in touch with their members on a daily basis. Two organizations claimed to communicate weekly with their members and only one 'infrequently'. BusinessEurope, WIDE, and EPLO were among the CSOs who indicated they had daily member contact. When confronting their members with the same question, only one-third confirmed this (see Figure 6.1). All others answered that they were in touch less frequently, often only weekly or every two weeks.

At BusinessEurope, the correspondence between the responses of the Brussels representative and the members is rather high. At EPLO and WIDE, however, there are large disparities between members. Daily contact is not the rule for most of them. At WIDE, none of the 10 out of 12 members interviewed confirmed the staff's answer of daily contact. Therefore, while one cannot consider the answers of the Brussels representatives to be false as they might be in touch with different members each time, they are only true for a small number of members. This is an indicator of inequalities between members in terms of the frequency with which they are consulted.

Finally, both EU staff and member organizations were asked about their satisfaction with the communication. Out of the 13 Brussels officers, about half claimed to be generally satisfied with member

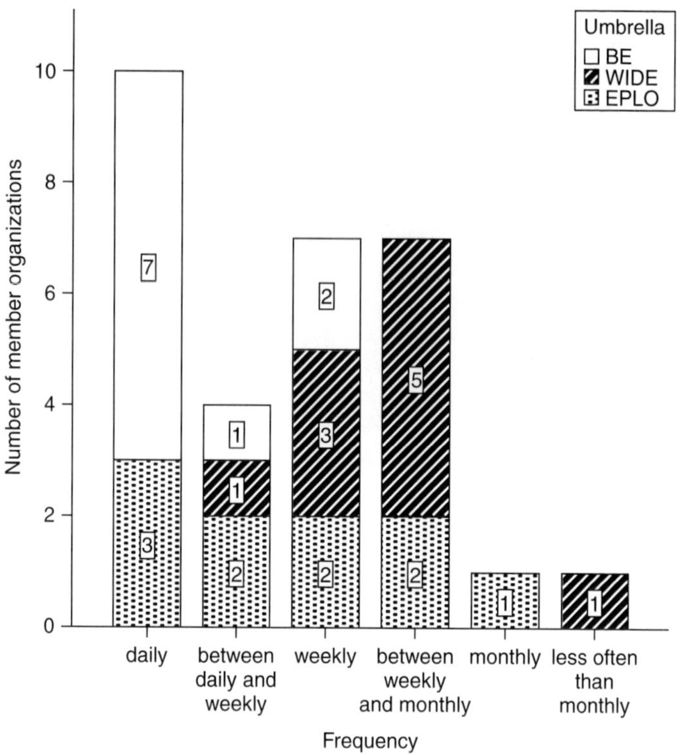

Figure 6.1 Frequency of interaction[a]

Note: [a]All figures and tables are my own presentations.

communication. The other half would like to receive more feedback from members. One representative replied ambiguously, explaining that some members were very active while others were not.

Turning to the member organizations, three-fifths claimed to be generally satisfied with the communication with their EU level office (see Figure 6.2). Many members put forward reasons for their dissatisfaction. The most frequent criticism was that the Brussels officers send out too much information for members to process (8). Furthermore, members complained that they received important information too late (4). One explained that 'the timing of the communication ... is not always the best. It is hard to respond to a paper in a very short time span. Sometimes when we make up our minds about something ... it is too late. ...' One interviewee suggested that this might be due to the

Commission's and not the umbrella's way of working, a dilemma that has been reported elsewhere (Kohler-Koch and Buth 2011). Two non-Brussels-based members offered the criticism that the language of documents distributed to members was too technocratic: 'The language… is Brussels-language, a kind of technocratic, made-up language that I don't always understand and that usually takes three pages for what could be said in one'. A few Brussels-based member organizations also raised this issue, thus demonstrating their awareness of the problem. They did not consider themselves to be affected, however, because they were familiar with the 'Brussels talk'.

The results display a mismatch between the amount and kind of information distributed by the EU offices and the 'absorption capacity' of members. While the Brussels staff would often prefer to receive more feedback, members display a lack of capacity in terms of time and knowledge. The problem seems to be especially severe for non-Brussels-based members with insufficient resources. The information distributed by the Brussels offices does not always match member organizations' needs in terms of conciseness and timeliness. However, not all members

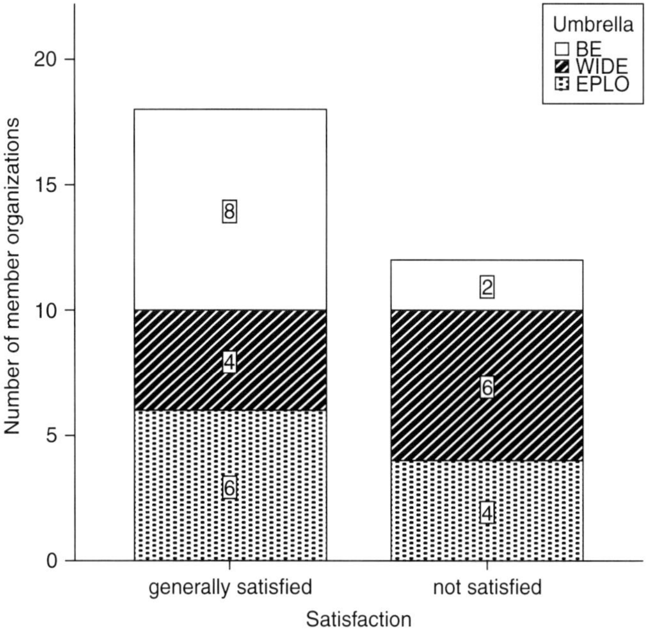

Figure 6.2 Satisfaction with communication

are disadvantaged by the communication style of the EU offices. More than half are satisfied.

Turning to the participation of members in decision-making, all EU CSOs claimed that they involved their members in strategic decision-making. This was confirmed by all member organizations with the exception of two EPLO members (see Figure 6.3). One of them said that although her organization took part in the General Assembly, she did not always feel that this was the place where strategic decisions were made. Moreover, the long-term strategic objectives of the organization were not always clear to her. The other member representative saw the cause for the lack of participation rather in the priority-setting and limited resources of her own organization.

Turning to operational decision-making, only about half of the CSOs interviewed claimed to involve their members.[5] The representatives of BusinessEurope and WIDE reported that they did not consult their members on operational issues while EPLO claimed that it did.

Indeed, more EPLO members than BusinessEurope and WIDE members responded that they were involved in operational questions (see Figure 6.4). However, even at BusinessEurope and WIDE some members claimed to participate in short-term decision-making. It seems that

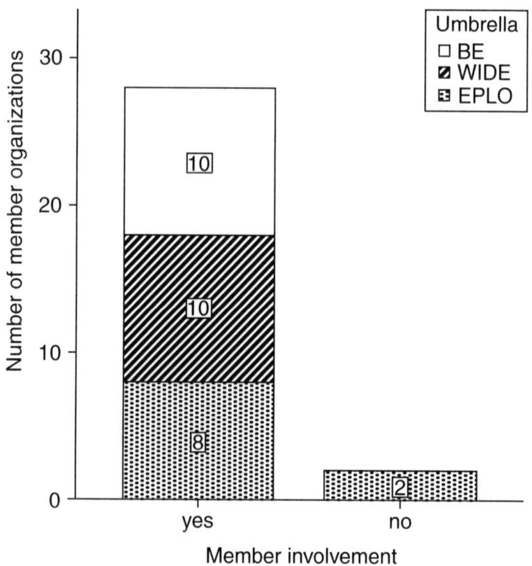

Figure 6.3 Member involvement in strategic decision-making

they attach more importance to their involvement than the Brussels secretariat does. Interestingly, almost all members who claimed to take part in operational decision-making at BusinessEurope belong to the 'big five' of the umbrella: the biggest member federations from large, old Member States. At EPLO, the members not participating in the day-to-day decision-making are non-Brussels-based. While many members pointed out that they did not wish to be involved in operational decisions, some emphasized that they would like to participate more if they had the necessary resources.

The Brussels staff of BusinessEurope and WIDE seems to be more autonomous from their members in the day-to-day management of the organization than the EPLO office. This is in line with statements made by some EPLO members who perceive the Brussels office to be 'on a very short leash' of member organizations. This suggests that EPLO tends towards a delegate model of representation while the leadership styles at BusinessEurope and WIDE rather resemble the trustee model.

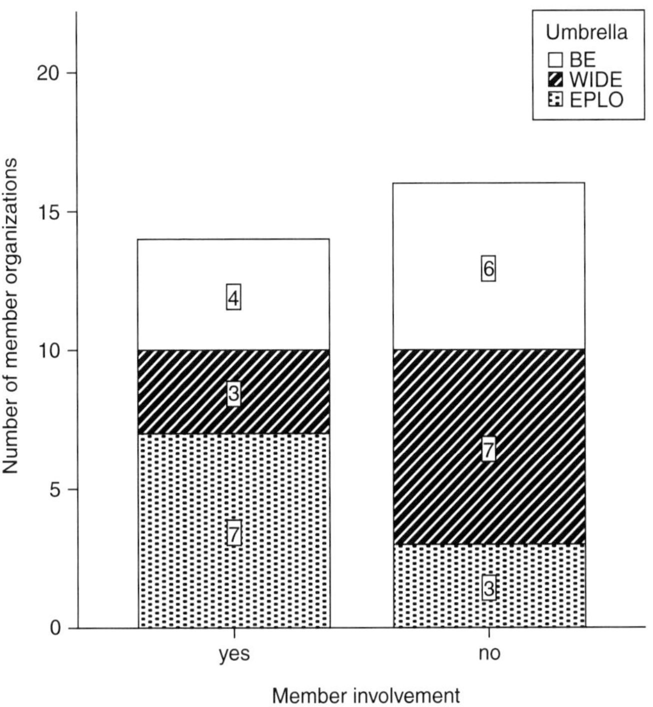

Figure 6.4 Member involvement in operational decision-making

Table 6.1 Member involvement as seen by Brussels staff

Function	Help provide services to public	Policy-making	Project/ Campaign implementation	Fundraising	Evaluation
BusinessEur.		X	X	X	
EuroComm.		X	X		X
ESF		X	X		X
ETUC		X	X		X
FoEE		X	X	X	X
Solidar	X	X	X	X	X
WIDE		X	X	X	X
EN.CPS		X	X	X	X
EPLO		X	X	X	X
NP		X	X	X	
PDCI	X	X	X	X	X
Pax Christi		X	X		
QCEA		X	X	X	X

The second aspect investigated here is the involvement of members in the activities of the EU level offices, namely in helping to provide services to the general public, policy-making, project/campaign implementation, fundraising, and the evaluation of organizational activities. All CSOs interviewed claimed to engage their members in the crucial functions of policy-making and project or campaign implementation (see Table 6.1). Only two organizations involve their members in the provision of services to the general public.[6] Many CSOs encourage their members to take part in fundraising[7] and most also in the evaluation of activities. Evaluations are conducted to assess whether policy goals have been met and how satisfied members are with the CSOs' work. About half of the CSOs involving their members in evaluations have formal processes or surveys in place that analyse member satisfaction on a regular basis. The remaining organizations stated that evaluations were a constant process throughout all organizational activities. The results show that all CSOs involve their members in the central function of policy-making. The general interest groups also engage their members in fundraising. While most organizations claim to involve their members in the evaluation of organizational activities, only about half have formal processes in place.

Turning to the members' responses, the answers are to some extent confirmed. Table 6.2 shows the number of members that responded positively to the involvement in the different organizational activities.

Table 6.2 Member involvement as seen by member organizations

Function	Help provide services to public	Policy-making	Project/ Campaign implementation.	Fundraising	Evaluation
BusinessEur.	5	10	9	2	8
WIDE	5	8	4	3	5
EPLO	1	9	7	6	9

Almost all claimed to be involved in policy-making. With regard to implementation, many members of BusinessEurope and EPLO also responded positively. At WIDE, many members are not involved in functions in which the Brussels representative claimed they were, such as implementation and evaluation. Interestingly, some members reported to take part in functions in which the Brussels office claimed they did not, such as the provision of services at WIDE and the provision of services and evaluation at BusinessEurope. Member organizations seem to participate rather intensely in most cases, but in some instances involvement appears to be limited to a small number of members, with the others being passive.

Substantive representation: member satisfaction

Finally, the general satisfaction of member organizations with their representation at the EU level is explored: do members feel that the Brussels officers generally act in their interest by representing them substantively? And, if not, what could be improved? Most members indicated that the representation of their interests within the EU level organization was very good or good (see Figure 6.5). Only four members did not feel adequately represented. None said that interest representation was poor. Generally this results in a rather positive image of the members' satisfaction with their EU level representation.

When inquiring how their interest representation could be improved, one-third of member organizations said that it was their responsibility to implement changes if they wanted to be better represented. They would have to shift their focus towards issues debated at the EU level or they would have to get more engaged in their umbrella organization. Some CSOs explained that they lacked the resources to be better represented. However, in most cases members did not intend to make changes in order to be better represented. Only a few interviewees put forth suggestions for improvement which were targeted at the Brussels

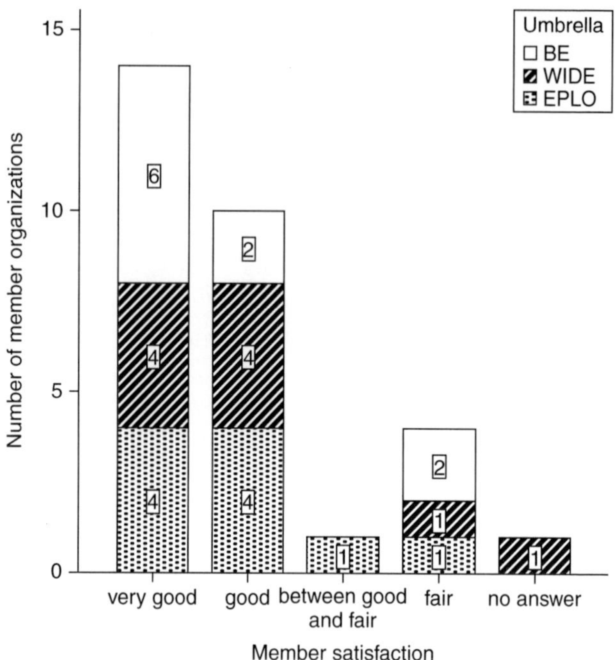

Figure 6.5 Member satisfaction with interest representation

secretariats or the organization as a whole. The proposals are, however, rather diverse and do not reveal general organizational deficiencies. In sum, the majority of members are satisfied with the overall representation of their interests in the EU CSOs. When they are not so well represented this is often because the EU is only one of their focal points and they also engage at the national and international level.

Summary and conclusion

With regard to the element of formalistic representation considered here – member accountability – the findings reveal that the relationship to members is the dominant accountability channel for the CSOs interviewed. And yet when it comes to holding the Brussels officers responsible, hardly any organization has formal complaint procedures in place. While the majority of CSO members know at least which body to turn to in order to voice criticism, a small number is not at all aware of complaint mechanisms at their umbrella. Regarding participatory representation, most CSOs are often in touch with members, but not to the same extent with all of them. Communication is seen critically by some members who consider information to be excessive and sometimes belated. All CSOs involve their members in strategic decision-making. Members with the necessary resources are also involved in operational decision-making. Whether CSOs involve their members in daily business also depends on whether they prefer a trustee or a delegate style of representation. All CSOs involve their members in policy-making and implementation. Concerning substantive representation, this study yields very positive results. Most members are satisfied with their representation at the EU level.

The findings reveal differences in the three dimensions of representation analysed. Most strikingly, shortcomings in formalistic and participatory representation are accompanied by positive assessments of substantive representation. This means that while members do not necessarily participate intensely, they are content with the advocacy positions taken in their name and feel that their views are reflected. This raises the question of whether adequate member representation can be realized without member participation. It can be argued that lower levels of participation serve the effectiveness but harm the equality of representation. On the one hand, the results show that members are central in policy-making and most members are satisfied with their representation. There is no evidence of a general detachment of Brussels offices from their membership bases. Advocacy positions of Brussels-based CSOs appear to be based on their constituencies' views. Thus, while EU umbrellas may not involve individual supporters, as Warleigh (2001) and Sudbery (2003) have shown, they do speak for those most of them claim to represent, namely their immediate member organizations.

CSO officers require a certain amount of participation to guide them in their policy work. The demand for more member feedback expressed in the interviews proves this. Yet moderate levels of participation by a small but active minority have the positive effect of counteracting the trade-off between member communication and effectiveness and might serve all those involved, at least at first glance. Partial member consultation allows officers to react more quickly in the fast-paced EU context. The active members, usually large organizations from large Member States, can drive and shape CSO-policy according to their priorities. Finally, members with fewer resources are happy to receive the service of being represented without extensive involvement as long as they agree with the general policy direction, which the majority of CSOs studied here do. The effectiveness of representation is thus ensured.

On the other hand, this study shows that the extent to which members are involved depends, above all, on their resources and whether they are based in Brussels. It must be noted that member organizations that are ill-equipped in terms of funding, personnel, and expertise cannot even develop an opinion on EU issues in the first place. Their alignment with the position of the active members might not be a question of convenience but of necessity. Differing degrees of participation are inevitable. But if members are excluded from participation because they do not understand the information received or notoriously obtain it too late, it seems that Brussels-based CSOs need to make more efforts to bridge the gap between members with different amounts of resources and ensure that all those wanting to participate are given the opportunity to do so.

Democratic representation is perceived as the means to safeguard political equality (Friedrich and Kröger in this volume). If CSOs actually want to be the voice of their constituents, they have to ensure that all members are part of the choir. Otherwise it could be suspected that the diversity suggested by the geographic comprehensiveness of CSOs' membership (see Annex 2) is spurious. If members do not participate on an equal footing, equality of representation is not warranted and the position taken by EU CSOs is not a fair reflection of their members' views. Whether the first level of interest intermediation analysed here functions or not is thus a question of the standards applied. This study has shown that in the CSOs reviewed, effectiveness of representation might be guaranteed, but equality of representation is not.

The limitation of this study is that it merely considers the level of representation between CSO offices in Brussels and their direct member organizations. It thus cannot confirm or refute the claim that the European Trade Union Confederation (ETUC) speaks for 16 million trade unionists,[8] for example. It can only assess the representation of immediate members. Additional research should pursue the transmission belt further down to the levels between national organizations and the individual citizens and study the question of representation throughout. Furthermore, due to the explorative character of this contribution it can only provide a snapshot of representation within EU CSOs. Future investigations could explore internal structures quantitatively and put some of the results of this chapter to the test.

Annex 1 List of member organizations interviewed

	BusinessEurope	
	Member organization	**Location**
1	Bundesvereinigung der Deutschen Arbeitgeberverbände e.V. (BDA)	Berlin/Brussels
2	Confederación Española de Organizaciones Empresariales (CEOE)	Madrid/ Brussels
3	Confederazione Generale dell' Industria Italiana (CONFINDUSTRIA)	Rome/Brussels
4	Estonian Employers' Confederation (ETTK)	Tallinn
5	Irish Business and Employers Confederation (IBEC)	Dublin/ Brussels
6	Employers and Industrialists Federation Cyprus (OEB)	Nicosia
7	Hellenic Federation of Enterprises (SEV)	Athens/ Brussels
8	Republikova Unia Zamestnavatelov (RUZ)	Bratislava
9	Svenskt Näringsliv	Stockholm/ Brussels
10	Vereniging VNO-NCW	The Hague/ Brussels

	European Peacebuilding Liaison Office (EPLO)	
	Member organization	**Location**
1	Crisis Management Initiative (CMI)	Helsinki/ Brussels
2	Fundación para las Relaciones Internacionales y el Diálogo Exterior (FRIDE)	Madrid
3	International alert	London/ Brussels
4	Kvinna till Kvinna	Johanneshov (Stockholm)
5	Life and Peace Institute (LPI)	Stockholm
6	Plattfom Zivile Konfliktbearbeitung	Berlin
7	Quaker Council for European Affairs (QCEA)	Brussels
8	Saferworld	London/ Nairobi/ Brussels
9	Search for Common Ground (SFCG)	Washington/ Brussels
10	Toledo International Centre for Peace (Toledo)	Madrid

Continued

Annex 1 Continued

	Women in Development Europe (WIDE)	
	Member organization	**Location**
1	Bulgarian Gender Research Foundation (BGRF)	Sofia
2	Grupo Mujeres y Desarrollo – Spanish Platform (CONGDE)	Madrid
3	Finnish Women in Development (FinnWID)	Helsinki
4	Gender and Development in Practice (GADIP)	Gothenburg
5	Gender And Development Network UK (GADN)	London
6	Karat Coalition (Karat)	Warsaw
7	Women and Development (K.U.L.U.)	Copenhagen
8	Le Monde selon les Femmes	Brussels
9	WIDE Austria	Vienna
10	WIDE Switzerland	Bern

Annex 2 CSOs and Member Organizations in Europe: Numbers and Geographic Distribution

Country Code\ EU CSO	AD	AL	AT	BE	BG	CH	CS	CY	CZ	DE	DK	EE	ES	FI	FR	GE	GR	HR	HU	IE	IS	IT	LI	LT	LU	LV
BusinessEurope			1	1	1	2		1	1	2	2	1	1	1	1		1	1	1	1	2	1		1	1	1
ESF				19		1				2	1			1	2					1						
ETUC	1		1	3	2	2		3	1	1	3	2	4	3	5		2	1	6	1	2	3	1	3	2	1
EuroCommerce			2	1		1		1	1	2	1	1	3	1	4		4		2	1	2	2		1	1	1
FoEE			1	2	1	1		1	1	1	1	1	1	1	1			1	1	1		1		1	1	1
Solidar			2	2		1				3	1		4	3	6							6				
WIDE			1	1	1	1					1		1	1						1						
EN.CPS			2							2			1	1	1	1						2				
EPLO				7		2	1	1		1			1	2	1					1						
NP			1			1				2			1		1							1				
PDCI		1			1		2		1										1					1		
Pax Christi			1	2		1		1							2	1		2		2		1			1	
QCEA				1		1				1	1				1					1					1	
	1	**1**	**12**	**28**	**6**	**14**	**3**	**8**	**5**	**17**	**11**	**5**	**18**	**14**	**25**	**2**	**7**	**5**	**11**	**10**	**6**	**17**	**1**	**7**	**7**	**4**

	MC	MD	ME	MK	MT	NL	NO	PL	PO	RO	RU	SE	SI	SK	SM	TR	UK	Total of MOs in Europe	Country Total
BusinessEurope			1		1	1	1	1	2	1		1	1	1	1	2	1	41	34
ESF												1					2	30 (excl. corporate members)	9
ETUC	1				2	3	3	2	2	4		3	1	1	2	4	1	82	36
EuroCommerce					1	3	1	2	2	1		1	1	1			1	46	29
FoEE				1	1	1	1	1				1		1			1	28	27
Solidar						1	1					1					3	34	13
WIDE						1		1				1					1	13 (excl. individ. members)	12
EN.CPS		2				1	2			1				1			1	18	13
EPLO						1	1					2					3	26	13
NP						3	1			1				1				13	10
PDCI								1		1				1				10	9
Pax Christi						1		2	1		4	1		1			1	25	17
QCEA						1	1					1					1	11	11
	1	2	1	1	5	17	12	10	7	9	4	13	3	8	3	6	16		

Notes

1. The term 'civil society organization' is applied here as opposed to other denominations, such as interest or lobby groups or non-governmental organizations, to account for the wide variety of non-state actors active at the EU. While the terms 'interest' and 'lobby group' are often associated with the representation of the special interests of professional or business associations, the term non-governmental organization is usually applied to organizations acting in the public interest. CSO in this chapter denotes a non-governmental, non-profit organization that has a clearly stated purpose, legal personality and pursues its goals through political advocacy and in non-violent ways (cf. Steffek et al. 2010). This comprises 'classical' NGOs, but also social partners, charities and religious groups. This broad definition also corresponds to the European Commission's use of the term. Business associations are included in this definition as they are non-profit at least at the EU level and are usually registered as *associations sans but lucratif (asbl)* in Belgium.
2. The Commission also ascribes other functions beyond citizen representation to CSOs (see Kohler-Koch 2007b).
3. In this chapter, the term 'member organization' is used for any full member of the EU level CSOs subject to this study. The lists of full members were obtained from the CSOs' websites. Members are legally independent organizations.
4. The interviews were conducted in the framework of the Research Project 'Legitimation and Participation in International Organizations' at the Collaborative Research Center 597 'Transformations of the State', University of Bremen, funded by the Deutsche Forschungsgemeinschaft (DFG).
5. Where members are involved, operational decisions are, for example, taken by the Steering Committee, in which some member organizations are represented. Where members are not involved, short-term decisions are usually made by the advocacy office.
6. The low number is due to the fact that most Brussels-based CSOs focus on advocacy.
7. Most of them are general interest organizations unable to cover their expenses through membership fees and therefore dependent on donors.
8. Interview with a representative of ETUC.

Part II

The Politics of Claims-Making

7

The Plural Representative Space: How Mass Media and National Parliaments Stimulate Pluralism through Competition

Pieter de Wilde

Introduction

Perhaps the most (in) famous claim in EU politics is Margaret Thatcher's statement, 'I want my money back'. The former UK Prime Minister made this claim in the context of negotiations on the EU multi-annual budget at the time of the EU Fontainebleau summit, in 1984. The claim was widely reported by mass media throughout Europe, and has resonated in EU budget negotiations ever since. It has strengthened an understanding of EU budget negotiations as highly contentious intergovernmental battles concerning Member States' net-contributions (Laffan 1997, 2000; Lindner 2006; Rant and Mrak 2010). Literally, the claim makes no sense as Mrs. Thatcher had no personal money invested in the EU. Yet it is clear to all observers that she was in fact not talking about her own money, nor would she personally like to receive funds from the EU. Rather, she made an argument for the reduction of financial contributions of the United Kingdom to the EU budget. The statement presented her – the claimant – as a representative of the UK – the constituency – in the public sphere, and is thus an example of an elected official engaging in a practice referred to as representative claims-making (Saward 2010: 88).

Theory about political representation has recently drawn attention to this practice of representative claims-making. The argument is that representation ought to be understood as a dynamic interrelationship among representatives and between representatives and represented, which is constituted through discourse in the public sphere (Hendriks 2009; Pollak et al. 2009; Rehfeld 2006; Saward 2006, 2009; Taylor 2010). That is, representation should not be solely understood as a static relationship between elected politicians and voters, constituted through periodic elections. Instead, a dynamic understanding of representation is necessary in light of two trends facing Western democracies (see Kröger and Friedrich in this volume). First, growing international interdependencies as a result of globalization problematize the principle of territorial representation on which nation-state democracy is founded. Decisions made by representatives of nation-states now carry consequences for people in other nation-states, even though they have no say in who is representing them. Secondly, elected politicians are losing their monopoly on representation as trust in political parties is declining throughout the West (Katz and Mair 1995). The two trends increasingly lead to blurred channels of representation and prominent roles for non-elected representatives in politics. A prime example is U2 singer Bono claiming to represent 'Africa' in his 'Making Poverty History' campaign (Saward 2009).

Claimants aiming to present themselves as representatives need a platform to reach out to a wider audience. In today's 'mediatized' democracies (Altheide 2004; Bennett and Entman 2001), this platform is first and foremost the mass media. Yet mass media are not the only important public spheres where representative claims-making takes place. Following Nancy Fraser (1992), we may distinguish between 'weak' and 'strong' public spheres. A weak public sphere refers to a general arena for discussion on political issues without direct influence on collective decision-making, such as the mass media. In contrast, a strong public sphere, such as a parliament, is an arena for communication while at the same time being directly involved in decision-making processes (Eriksen 2007). Both mass media and parliaments have their own operating logics which may affect representative claims-making (Pollak et al. 2009: 23). These effects concern who is doing the claiming and who is claimed to be represented.

From the perspective of EU studies, the challenge in the study of representative claims-making is now twofold. First, based on the theoretical work of Saward and others, a mapping of the EU representative space as constituted by claims is necessary in order to enrich our understanding of EU representative politics beyond the election of the national and European parliaments. Secondly, lessons from such empirical exercises should be drawn to improve upon the theory of representative claims-making as, so far, empirical studies of representative claims-making remain scarce. The aim of this chapter is to contribute to this dynamic understanding of representation by conducting an in-depth empirical case study of how weak and strong public spheres – mass media and parliaments – affect the practice of representative claims-making in the EU. Following this introduction (1), the chapter sets out to theorize the effects of different operating logics of mass media and parliaments on the practice of representative claims-making in the EU (2). The chapter continues with an analysis of how these operating logics affect the claimants by mapping empirically who is doing the act of claims-making in both public spheres (3). Then it analyses how these two different public spheres affect who is claimed to be represented (4) before the final section concludes (5).

The chapter investigates this question in the case of EU budget negotiations. It does so through a comparative study of claims-making in the media and parliaments of the Netherlands, Denmark, and Ireland in the three most recent multi-annual budget negotiations. The EU budget affects a plurality of constituencies in the EU, multiple levels of government, and has consequences for people living outside the EU (Laffan 1997; Lindner 2006). It is a package deal of all EU revenues and expenditures. Expenditures include funds for farmers (Common Agricultural Policy) and poorer regions (Structural Funds), as well as EU administrative costs, development funds, and nature preservation policy. The question of revenues concerns taxpayers throughout the EU as well as the balance between richer, net-contributing Member States, and poorer, net-recipient Member States. The EU budget thus provides an interesting case for the study of representative claims-making as it potentially concerns multiple representatives and multiple constituencies in a continuously developing representative space.

Representative claims-making in mass media and parliaments

This chapter aims to look at acts of representation in the public sphere – or 'representative claims' (Saward 2006, 2009) – through which the EU's representative space is shaped and altered in public discourse (Trenz 2009b). Just like electoral rules affect the representative outcome and functioning of elections, so do operating logics of different public spheres affect representative claims-making. Thus, understanding public spheres as arenas where representation is constantly reshaped and reproduced directs our attention to ways in which the operating logics of different public spheres affect this practice (Pollak et al. 2009: 23).

Two primary EU public spheres in which representative claims-making unfolds are mass media and national parliaments (Eriksen and Fossum 2002; Fraser 1992). Mass media have come to dominate political communication in Western societies, transforming modern politics into mediated politics (Altheide 2004; Bennett and Entman 2001). A range of different representatives have incentives to make the news with their claims on EU issues. This is so not only because trust in political parties in Europe has been declining, but also because the unclear and continuously developing political system of the EU forces both national and European politicians to seek legitimacy through reaching out to the public (Morgan 2005). Yet journalists and editors shaping mass media operate under a media logic, which includes criteria for establishing news value. This makes them non-neutral transmitters of representative claims. It is well known that media particularly report on personalized conflict (Galtung and Ruge 1965). Also, quality journalists often aim to present 'both sides of the story', thus providing a platform for a plurality of representatives (Donsbach and Patterson 2004). In short, mass media provide a competitive space, both in terms of which representatives make the news and in terms of emphasizing conflict between them. The parliamentary public sphere is also characterized by an operating logic of institutionalized competition. Here different political parties compete for office and policies with the ever-looming prospect of the next elections. This stimulates interparty competition (King 1976; Schumpeter 1976). Thus, in the parliamentary arena, different political parties engage with each other in debate testing out the validity of arguments and cueing voters as to their primary interests and opinions. In the parliamentary democracies of EU Member States, government is elected or appointed by a majority of parliament. Parliamentary debate then takes the form of competition between government and their backbenchers on the one hand, and opposition parties on the other. In the language of representative claims-making, elected party politicians in parliament have an incentive to present themselves as prime representatives of certain constituencies and challenge similar claims made by other parties.

This chapter therefore places a focus on competition at the centre of the study of representative claims-making in the EU. Although mass media and parliaments have very different operating logics as public spheres, each in their own way is characterized by institutionalized competition where political actors compete with each other to present themselves to the wider audience as legitimate representatives. The main research question of how operating logics of mass media and parliaments affect representative claims-making is thus specified, based on this brief theorizing of these logics. The aim of investigation is to empirically analyse how competition – institutionalized in the operating logics of both mass media and parliaments – affects who is claiming to represent whom in EU public spheres. To start, this chapter continues with the question of who claims to represent whom on relevant EU issues in mass media and parliaments and how often. In terms of amounts of claims, this will consequently allow for the comparison of how prominent different claimants are and to what extent claimants engage in addressing the interests of multiple constituencies. Furthermore, it will allow for the analysis of how prominent different constituencies feature in representative claims and whether they are claimed to be represented by multiple claimants or are rather monopolized by a single claimant.

The case of EU budget negotiations: data and method

The EU may be considered an ideal laboratory for studying patterns in representative claims-making for several reasons. First, the EU itself as a composite polity is characterized by three channels of representation (Bartolini 2005; Lord and Pollak 2010; Norris 1997). In the first channel of representation, citizens directly elect the European Parliament, which acts as a co-legislator with the Council of Ministers and to some extent controls the European Commission. In the second channel, citizens elect national parliaments which control the Member State governments who collectively constitute the Council of Ministers, the European Council, and Intergovernmental Conferences. In the third channel, citizens are represented by interest groups, social movements, and NGOs which informally influence EU decision-making. Secondly, the EU as a polity itself remains constantly under development. It is as of yet unclear and contested what kind of polity the EU is and what it will become in the future. As a result, there are multiple competing representatives in need of legitimating themselves (Morgan 2005). These representatives have a continuous incentive to establish a publically acknowledged role for themselves.

EU budget negotiations involve representatives from all three channels. The European Commission has the sole right of initiative and interest groups such as farmers' associations have an opportunity to influence the drafting of the proposals. Then, the different components of the financial perspectives are negotiated in the relevant Council of Ministers leading up to a unanimous decision on the whole package in the European Council. As the decision rests on unanimity, every national parliament has an opportunity to effectively control their government's action in the Council. Finally, following the Council decision, the package is renegotiated between the Council, the European Parliament, and the Commission resulting in an Inter Institutional Agreement. The periodic re-negotiation of the budget, the involvement of a broad range of legislative actors from all three channels of representation, and the broad effects on multiple contributing and recipient constituencies make the EU budget a highly interesting case for studying representative claims-making (Laffan 1997; Lindner 2006).

In order to isolate and contextualize patterns in competitive representative claims-making, the present study conducts a comparative case study (Lijphart 1971; Yin 2003). In order to control for country-specific characteristics that might affect representative claims on the EU budget, this study includes data from the Netherlands, Denmark, and Ireland. These three countries resemble a net-contributing country (Netherlands), a country receiving more or less as much from EU funds as it contributes (Denmark), and a net-recipient country (Ireland). To isolate possible operating logics, both plenary parliamentary debates and newspaper articles are included. Finally, to minimize idiosyncrasies caused by unique events, data is collected from three different budget negotiations. This includes the three most recent negotiations on the financial perspectives of 'Delors II' (negotiated between February 1992 and December 1992), 'Agenda 2000' (July 1997–March 1993), and 'Financial Perspectives 2007–2013' (February 2004–December 2005). Comparing the differences between newspaper coverage and plenary parliamentary debates, the inclusion of three countries and three budget negotiations function as controls in the cross-institutional comparison.

Taking into account the operationalization of a representative claim by Saward (2006), this study builds on the empirically tested method of claims-making analysis (Koopmans 2002; Koopmans and Statham 1999) as a specific form of qualitative content analysis. A claim is defined as a unit of strategic or communicative action in the public sphere '...which articulate[s] political demands, decisions, implementations, calls to action, proposals, criticisms, or physical attacks, which, actually or potentially, affect the interests or integrity of the claimants and/or other collective actors in a policy field' (Statham 2005: 12). The archetypical claim would be a verbal act concerning some political good that could be loosely translated as 'I (do not) want ...'. However, the definition above is far more inclusive, including claims such as meetings of the European Council, protests by farmers, resolutions tabled by parliaments, and critical comments by journalists. In textual terms, a claim can be as short as a few words or as elaborate as several paragraphs, as long as it is made by the same claimant(s) making a single argument on a single topic related to the EU budget.

Coded variables of claims include WHERE and WHEN, WHO makes a claim, on WHAT, HOW, addressing WHOM, for/against WHOSE interests, and WHY. Of particular importance for the present analysis are the claimant variables ('WHO') and constituency variables ('WHOSE interests'). It should be noted here that although all claims are made by a claimant in a particular time and space, not all claims are representative claims in the sense that they include an explicitly stated constituency. Only representative claims, including an explicitly stated constituency potentially affected by the claim, are included in the analysis.

The newspapers included in the sampling are *NRC Handelsblad, Trouw,* and *Algemeen Dagblad* for the Netherlands; *Berlingske Tidene, Politikken,* and *B.T.* for Denmark; and *Irish Times* and *Irish Independent* for Ireland. This study thus incorporates both quality and sensation-oriented newspapers of different political signature in all three countries. As differences between quality and sensation outlets are larger than between different media – for example, TV and newspapers – this sample is arguably representative of national media (Semetko et al. 2001). Newspaper articles and plenary debates were sampled from digitalized archives using the search string 'European budget', or 'EC/EU budget', or 'Delors II/Agenda 2000/financial perspectives', with the exception of plenary debates from 1992 in the Netherlands and Denmark which were manually selected from the physical archives of the *Tweede Kamer* and *Folketinget.* For The Netherlands and Denmark, every fourth newspaper article in chronological order and all plenary debates were selected for coding. Sampling for Ireland was twice as restrictive to cope with a larger amount of available material. In total, 462 newspaper articles and 133 parliamentary debates were coded, resulting in 4,435 claims.[1] Of these, 2,129 (48 per cent) contained explicit references to constituencies and are thus defined as representative claims.

Findings

Tables 7.1 and 7.2 provide an overview of representative claims made in the media and parliaments, respectively, during EU budget negotiations. In the discussion of the data provided in tables 7.1 and 7.2, attention will first be drawn to the presence of different claimants – or representatives – in both the media and in parliament. Secondly, the

Table 7.1 Percentages of representative claims in the media, N = 1059

		Constituency									
		Nation	**EU**	**European Commission**	**Other Member State(s)**	**Countries outside the EU**	**Organized business**	**Farmers**	**Citizens / tax payers**	**Other**	**Total**
Claimant	National politicians	6.2	2.8	.1	2.4	1.1	.7	1.6	1.6	.9	17.5
	EU	2.0	3.7	.5	6.6	2.0	.5	1.6	.7	1.5	19.0
	European Commission	3.5	3.6	.3	4.1	2.2	.9	2.5	1.0	.9	18.9
	Other Member States	1.5	3.5	.1	14.1	.7	.1	1.7	1.2	.1	22.9
	Countries outside the EU					.6					.6
	Organized business	.1		.1			.3				.5
	Journalist	1.9	1.4	.3	1.6	.3	.4	1.0	1.5	.8	9.0
	Farmers	.7						4.0	.1		4.7
	Citizens / tax payers		.2						.3		.5
	Other	1.9	.7	.2	.9	.4	.1	.6	.9	.8	6.5
	Total	17.8	15.9	1.5	29.6	7.2	2.9	13.0	7.2	5.0	100.0

Table 7.2 Percentages of representative claims in parliament, N = 1070

		Constituency									
		Nation	**EU**	**European Commission**	**Other Member State(s)**	**Country(ies) outside the EU**	**Organized business**	**Farmers**	**Citizens / tax payers**	**Other**	**Total**
Claimant Affiliation	Radical Left	2.0	.6	.1	.2	.3	.1	.9	1.5	1.0	6.7
	Green	.6	.8		.3	4.2		1.0	1.4	.4	8.7
	Social democrat	2.9	1.4		2.3	4.7		3.5	1.4	1.6	17.9
	Progressive liberal	.8	.4		.6	.9		.4	.3	.3	3.7
	Liberal	2.9	1.4	.1	.7	2.0		3.3	.8	.2	11.4
	Christian democrat	4.2	1.3		1.3	.9	.1	4.1	1.7	2.3	15.9
	Conservatives	9.2	2.7	.0	3.2	1.0	.7	5.6	.8	1.7	25.0
	Radical right	1.2	.5		.9	3.0		1.6	2.9	.8	10.7
	Total	23.8	9.0	.2	9.4	17.0	1.0	20.3	10.9	8.4	100.0

presence of constituencies – or represented – in both public spheres will be discussed. This descriptive discussion will be related to the central question of this chapter: how is representative claims-making affected by the operating logics structuring mass media and parliaments?

Claimants

Interestingly, the most prominent representatives in the media (29.6 per cent of all representative claims; Table 7.1) are those representing other Member States. Typically, such representatives are government executives, such as Prime Ministers, Finance Ministers, or Presidents. For example, discussing the ratification process of the Maastricht Treaty, the *Irish Independent* reported that, 'Spanish Premier Felipe Gonzalez was a major driving force behind the planning for the [Cohesion] fund and his government feels that Spain has not received its proper share of EC [European Community] aid in the past' (Downing 1992). We find similar claims in Danish news, as exemplified by a claim reported in *Berlingske Tidene*: 'Countries like Germany and Sweden, which pay considerably more to the EU than they get back, are at this moment fighting with all they have got to restrict the EU budget'[2] (Kragh 2004). As these examples underline, EU budget negotiations were often portrayed as struggles between different Member State governments (cf. De Wilde 2010). Mass media focus on members of the executive as representative claimants because they are considered to be among the most important decision-makers (Koopmans and Erbe 2004). They do this especially when executives engage in personalized conflict, such as when Prime Ministers and Presidents of Member States engage in direct conflict with each other. This so far reinforces the image of EU budget negotiations as intergovernmental conflicts about net-contributions. Yet the data presented here provide a more plural picture. Besides governments of other Member States, prominent roles in the news were performed by the EU (European Council, rotating Presidency, European Parliament) (19.0 per cent of representative claims) and the European Commission as key initiator of the negotiations (18.9 per cent). For example, Commission President Delors claimed to represent poorer Member States in particular when presenting Delors II: 'Delors wants to take into account differences in welfare within the EC. He demands a larger share of GDP from Member States. Obligatory VAT contributions from EC capitals can then be reduced. Poorer Member States, where a larger share of income is consumed than in rich countries, will profit from this' (Aben 1992). The national government would typically be quoted in response to the claims of EU officials and other Member State governments (17.5 per cent of representative claims in the media), in particular concerning the 'national interest':

> 'What is on the table now is unacceptable for the Netherlands,' argued Balkenende after yesterday's government meeting. The government wants a significantly lower contribution to Europe than foreseen in the compromise tabled by Juncker, the Prime Minister of Luxembourg. 'These proposals are unthinkable. They mean no significant improvement of the Dutch net-contribution,' the Prime Minister stated. (*Trouw* 2005)

The national government regularly performs a dual representative role in the media. It defends the national interest in EU framework while at the same time defending the EU interest against domestic critics. In other words, media pick up on the 'two-level game' (Putnam 1988) – national and European – on which national governments are operating in EU framework. The Irish Prime Minister Bertie Ahern took the effort to write a letter to the *Irish Independent* representing the EU in Ireland, explaining how he and other European executives represented their nation-states in the EU: 'These [EU budget] negotiations involve 25 Governments strongly pursuing their specific national interests while at the same time seeking to shape an overall agreement which will better promote those national interests than any Member State could do acting alone. That is what the European Union is about' (Ahern 2005). Finally, a smaller but still significant role was played by journalists (9.0 per cent) and farmers' associations (4.7 per cent). Typically, journalists would take issue in op-eds with what in their eyes appears as irrational or unjust results from ad hoc intergovernmental negotiations. For example, Danish journalist Ole Bang Nielsen (1998) argued in favour of a more just distribution of EU funds:

> In 2006, the New Member States will receive 14 per cent of the EU budget, including agricultural funds. As the Enlargement will at least include Poland, Hungary and the Czech Republic with 58 million inhabitants, it is comparable to the 1980s enlargement with Spain, Portugal and Greece. There are today 59 million inhabitants in these three 'poor' Member States, but they receive 30 per cent of EU funds. Candidate countries will not realistically have any influence on this biased distribution of EU funds....

In short, a plurality of claimants is featured in mass media. The fact that media home in on domestic and European contestation about the EU budget leads them to present a range of actors claiming to represent certain constituencies. Thus the mass media operating logic of news value criteria, including an interest in (personalized) conflict, can be argued to bring about a plural representative space in newspaper coverage of EU budget negotiations.

Although other claimants dominate, a similar picture emerges in the parliamentary debates (Table 7.2). When looking at the prominence of different party families, it is unsurprising to find the largest political parties of the mainstream centre (Conservatives, Christian Democrats, Liberals, and Social Democrats) to be making most claims. Together, these mainstream parties are responsible for 73.9 per cent of representative claims made in parliament. This reflects their dominance in both parliament and government. A significant share of these claims is made by government officials outlining their strategy in EU negotiations. For instance, Irish Prime Minister Bertie Ahern argued how he represented Irish agricultural interests:

> From the outset we have availed of every opportunity to highlight the serious repercussions the [EU budget] reform proposals would have for Irish industry. Beet has long been a valuable cash crop for Irish farmers, as well as playing a significant role in the tillage cycle. Some 3,700 beet growers and producers, whose representatives I met last week, and the 1,000 people employed in the processing sector could be wiped out if the [European] Commission goes ahead with the proposals in this regard. (Dáil Éireann 2005a)

Claiming to represent the interests of farmers in the Irish parliament might be considered a no-brainer, since Irish farmers receive large amounts of EU funds, contributing to Ireland's status as a net-recipient country. Yet, government – opposition dynamics would even in such cases bring members of the opposition to challenge government by representing alternative interests. In the heat of discussions on Agenda 2000, where major Irish agricultural interests were at stake, Trevor Sargent, TD of the Green Party, challenged the government as follows: 'The Santer proposals will further widen the link between the primary producer, the farmer, and the consumer and it is time consumers were much more involved in this debate' (Dáil Éireann 1997). Similarly, the Dutch government's efforts to reduce Dutch net-contributions were challenged in parliament. For example, Leoni Sipkes of the Green Left party (GroenLinks) argued:

> It appears that [Finance] Minister Zalm calculated the Dutch contribution too high by approximately 2 billion [Guilders]. The Minister

> denies this vehemently. In light of all the embarrassing government behaviour concerning contributions, I would like to ask the Prime Minister to supply us with a clear letter on this issue, so we may know what we are talking about. (Tweede Kamer 1997)

Government and opposition representatives in parliament thus went into debate concerning both which constituencies ought to be represented and what exactly their stakes were in the EU budget. In other words, the operating logics of parliaments that stimulate interparty conflict – especially conflict between members of the ruling government and those of the opposition – brought about a plural representative space in national parliamentary debates on the EU budget. The findings clearly show a plurality of different political parties engaging in representative claims-making on this issue. This stands in stark contrast to the traditional perception of EU budget negotiations as intergovernmental conflicts between Member States, where each Member State is representing the 'national interest'.

Constituencies

The reputation of other Member State governments as representatives in the news directly translates in prominence of other Member States as the most important constituency. Close to one-third of representative claims in newspapers (29.6 per cent) portrayed other Member States as the main interested party in EU budget negotiations of which half (14.1 per cent) were made by other Member State representatives themselves. A few examples of this have been given above. Additional prominent constituencies include the nation as a collective and unitary group of people (17.8 per cent), often represented as either net-contributor or net-recipient of EU funds. Although these claims were most often made by executive actors, Members of Parliament regularly engaged the budget debate in the media as well. Either they would be quoted by journalists, or they would send in a letter, as Tom Behnke, MF of the Danish Progress Party (Fremskridspartiet), did in 1992:

> A welfare tax that Danish society must pay because we are rich. According to the 'Delors II' plans, Danish contributions will rise by 30 per cent to 12 billion Kroner per year. The state has two possibilities for paying this tax. The first is to raise taxes in Denmark, to the detriment of all Danish. The second is to cut in public welfare provisions. This would weaken Danish social security, to the detriment of the weakest in Danish society. (Behnke 1992)

The EU (15.9 per cent) was regularly represented in claims in terms of whether the budget was in the EU's general interest and how budget negotiations, national contributions, and the possibility of an EU tax impacted the stability and legitimacy of the EU as polity. Successive Commission Presidents all defended proposed increases in the EU budget as being in the wider EU interest:

> Mr. Barroso maps out ambitious plans in two of the EU's 'growth areas': increased co-operation in home affairs and in beefing up Europe's presence on the world stage. Presenting his plans to the European Parliament, the new Commission president said the EU could not deliver unless it was given the money to do so, a warning shot to countries like Germany, Britain and France, which want tight curbs on its next budget. (*Irish Times* 2005)

Yet it is not so that representatives only claim to represent their 'formal' constituency. National politicians regularly claimed to represent the EU interest and EU officials claimed to represent national interests. Illustrative is a conflict between the Dutch Social Democrats (PvdA) in government and their MEP representative, Piet Dankert, during the negotiations on Agenda 2000. Dankert discussed criticism from his national colleagues after having challenged the Dutch negotiating strategy as not being in the national interest: 'In contrast to members of the *Tweede Kamer*, we [MEPs] allegedly would not be willing to defend the interests of the Netherlands. State secretary Patijn [European Affairs] dares to ask who we think we are representing' (Dankert 1997).

Farmers – being the primary recipients of the funds in the EU's Common Agricultural Policy, which takes around 40 per cent of the EU budget – are prominently represented by a variety of claimants, not least by themselves and their own professional organizations. Also in net-contributing countries like the Netherlands, farmers made the news defending their own interests:

> A substantial dispossession of income for both crop and livestock farmers. That is the direct consequence of European Commission plans for agricultural policy as they were presented yesterday, according to agricultural association *LTO Nederland*. Price reductions in milk, wheat and meat will only partially be compensated and that is unacceptable to the farmers' association. (*Trouw* 1998)

Just as the operating logics of mass media appear to stimulate a plural representative space when it comes to claimants, so do they stimulate a plural representative space when it comes to represented constituencies. It is not the case that a single constituency – farmers, for example – dominate the debates. Rather, Table 7.1 clearly shows how a whole range of constituencies are claimed to be represented, in newspaper coverage of EU budget negotiations, by multiple claimants.

In Parliament, the interests of other Member States were represented less than in the media, though still present in the debates (9.4 per cent). For instance, the interests of the new Eastern European Member States were claimed to be represented by Noel Treacy, Minister of European Affairs for the governing Conservative party (Fianna Fáil):

> The enlarged European Union needs a [budget] deal now. This is of particular interest to the new Member States which rely on cohesion funding to help drive their individual domestic economies forward. This point was brought home to me at many meetings of the cohesion countries where I represented Ireland, to underline our continuing commitment to the principles of economic solidarity which lie at the heart of the European Union. (Dáil Éireann 2005b)

Most represented in parliament were the interests of the nation (23.8 per cent) and farmers (20.3 per cent), but also those of countries outside the EU (17 per cent) and citizens and taxpayers (10.9 per cent). Although rarely the recipient of direct EU funds, countries outside the EU are often argued – by leftist parties in particular – to be negatively affected by the EU's CAP which limits their possibilities to export agricultural products to the EU (cf. Karimi MP in Tweede Kamer 2005). Furthermore, the second budget under study – Agenda 2000 – was specifically presented by the Commission as preparing the EU for Eastern enlargement, including funds to help bring candidate countries into the EU. In terms of differences among political party families, the national interest is most often claimed to be represented by centre-right parties (Conservatives 9.2 per cent; Christian Democrats 4.2 per cent of representative claims in parliament) whereas radical right parties present themselves as the primary defender of the taxpayer's interests (2.9 per cent of representative claims in parliament). The latter would typically field in an argument to reduce EU funds.

To conclude, the operating logics of both mass media and parliaments appear to stimulate a competitive representative space, where multiple constituencies are claimed to be represented by multiple claimants. Elected and appointed politicians continue to perform an important role when it comes to representative claims-making, not only because they frequently feature in the news and feature exclusively in parliamentary debates as discussed above, but also because they claim to represent a wide range of different constituencies, both in the media and in parliament. To some extent the constituencies represented may not be surprising as national politicians claim to represent the national interest and EU officials claim to represent the EU interest, or when right-wing parties defend the interests of farmers and taxpayers while left-wing parties defend the interests of Third World countries. Yet the data have also shown representatives to engage with each other. They do so in particular by discrediting the representative claims of other representatives in various ways. The result is a highly plural representative space where elected and appointed politicians perform a vital role in claiming to represent a multitude of constituencies and no constituency is monopolized by a single representative.

Conclusion

Building on a dynamic understanding of representative claims-making developed in political theory recently, this chapter has empirically investigated how operating logics of public spheres affect this practice of claims-making in the EU. Based on a case study of EU budget negotiations, the main finding is that competition institutionalized in the public spheres of mass media and parliaments leads to a plural representative space. The inclusion of three countries and three budget periods as control variables in the research design lends additional credibility to this conclusion as the findings appear robust across time and space. Although mass media and parliaments have very different operating logics, each in their own way stimulate competition between representatives. As a result of this competition, political actors engage with each other trying to present themselves as legitimate representatives. The resulting pluralist representative space can be observed in both a plurality of claimants and of constituents present in public spheres. With regard to EU studies and our knowledge about EU budget negotiations in particular, this chapter demonstrates how representation in the EU is more plural than is often presumed (Laffan 2000; Rant and Mrak 2010). With regard to political theory on representation, this chapter shows the importance of incorporating the operating logics of public spheres for our understanding of the practice of representative claims-making. Neither mass media nor parliaments are 'neutral' transmitters of representative claims. Rather, they each in their own way stimulate competition between claimants with clear effects on representation.

There are very clear differences between the media and parliaments with regard to the claimants present in these respective public spheres. Media present a platform for a plurality of claimants, of which a large proportion consists of other Member States' governments, EU officials, and non-elected representatives. In contrast, parliamentary debates only field Members of Parliament and Ministers, where the mainstream parties are dominant given their larger share of parliamentary seats and government positions. A difference of constituencies is also noticeable, but it is much less pronounced than the difference in claimants. Representative claims in the media feature other Member States, the nation, and the EU as most prominent constituencies. In parliament, the nation, farmers, and countries outside the EU are the three most often claimed constituencies. Together, this points to how dynamics of competition that structure both mass media and parliamentary public spheres stimulate pluralism in representation. Though characterized by very different operating logics, both mass media and parliaments stimulate competition. Through news value criteria emphasizing (personalized) conflict and the prospect of the next election respectively, both the weak public sphere of the mass media and the strong public sphere of parliaments stimulate competition in representative claims-making during EU budget negotiations in their own ways.

This empirical study draws attention to an aspect of representative claims-making that has so far been under-appreciated in the theoretical literature. The inherent competitiveness of claims-making has not received due attention (cf. Jentges in this volume). Both claimants and constituencies compete for presence in public spheres. Even if different dynamics of news value criteria and partisan conflict underlie this competition, the result is very similar: a plurality of claimants is featured trying to bring their message across to potential constituencies. As illustrated by the examples of representative claims about the EU budget in this chapter, claimants often combine a defence or challenge concerning a particular constituency's interests with a challenge to other claimants' conduct as representatives. Furthermore, this competition results in constituencies becoming contested by multiple claimants. This study does not find important constituencies to be monopolized by one or few claimants. Rather, intensive representative claims-making concerning a particular constituency coincides with multiple claimants defending, challenging, and reinterpreting the interests in question. We may therefore tentatively conclude that it is particularly this competitive nature of representative claims-making, stimulated by operating logics in both mass media and parliamentary public spheres, that ensures a plural representative space in the EU.

Notes

1. The codebook, the heuristic ATLAS.ti files and the SPSS database can be obtained from the author upon request.
2. All translations from Dutch and Danish into English by the author. Original quotes available upon request.

8

A Media Perspective on Political Representation: Online Claims-Making and Audience Formation in 2009 EP Election Campaigns

Asimina Michailidou and Hans-Jörg Trenz

Introduction

Mass media play a crucial, though frequently neglected, role in the social construction of political representation. Media touch the core meaning of political representation, in Hanna Pitkin's famous words: the making present of something which is nevertheless not literally present (Pitkin 1967: 144). Most importantly, mass media do not only create a notion of presence of the absent, they are also the field of contestation about the meaning of 'presence' and its wider implications (Hall 1997). In modern, anonymous mass politics the relationships between decision-making actors and the constituency of those who are potentially affected by these decisions is usually mediated. The performance of political agents is re-presented by media discourse and as such constructs the political reality that becomes salient to a broader audience, from which the 'principal' of representative politics is constituted. Mass media can therefore be said to build a 'representative relationship' between those who 'perform' in the political arena and those who interpret and evaluate the performance from the balcony. The principal-agent relationship of political representation is thus reproduced in the relationship of mass media and politics.

As we are going to argue in the course of this chapter, the notion of a media audience of political representation also broadens the principal-agent relationship, since the audiences and the constituents of representative politics are rarely identical and frequently fluctuate. The group that a political agent speaks for (the constituency) might not be identical with the group that is addressed by representative politics (the audience), but also the group of people that actually pays attention to representative politics might differ from those who are addressed by the political agents. At the same time, in the era of global, digital political mediation, we can no longer rely on a unitary representation of the political spectacle to a territorially confined and socially integrated audience. Through online social networking, interactive journalism, and micro-blogging (Web 2.0), the layers of this mediation process are infinitely multiplied (cf. Castiglione and Warren 2008). How is political representation mediated in a transnational political context? How do constituents and audiences respond to representative claims raised by transnational actors and institutions (such as the European Parliament)? Does the focus of political legitimacy shift from national to transnational context? And how do online media in the Web 2.0 age re-configure the act of representation among political agents, various constituents, and audiences?

To answer these questions, we propose an analytical model which simultaneously captures the respondent to a representative claim (counter-claimant), the topic, the target, the frame, and the justification of a claim made in the online public sphere. In the first part of this chapter, we discuss the conceptual and theoretical grounding of the notion of 'mediated political representation', which we locate in the triadic configuration of the communicative act of representation among representative, constituents, and audiences (cf. Saward 2010) (Section 2). We then proceed to present our analytical framework, methodology, and case selection, where we focus on online debates concerning the 2009 European Parliamentary elections (Section 3). The subsequent section presents our findings, resulting from coded 'representative-claims' found in professional news media (online versions of newspapers, TV channels, news platforms), and user-driven media (political blogs, social media) concerning the representativeness of the EU polity (Section 4). At the end of our chapter we revisit the concept of representation as a triadic communicative act and discuss how our focus on audience reception and participation casts new light on the dynamics of representative claims-making and its transnationalizing potential (Section 5).

Mediated political representation

The audience: a third part in political representation

If at the heart of political representation as a communicative act is the constitution of a relationship between principal and agent (constituency), research has to turn to the creative processes through which constituencies are imagined and how such images are amplified and find public resonance. Andrew Rehfeld proposes, at this point, to ground a 'general theory of political representation' on the notion of the audience which accepts a representative claim (Rehfeld 2006). Re-focusing attention on the role of the audience as recipient of political representation claims allows us to spell out the general conditions for societal recognition and acceptance of representative claims-making. The audience becomes decisive as the wider resonance body of representative claims-making, which accepts a claim as being representative for something or not. The process of representative claims-making thus needs to be studied in relation to its capacities to create wider societal resonance and reception, which requires an analytical shift from the narrow institutional account of formal representation bound to elections to a more sociological understanding of the various ways of enacting political representation in practice beyond its normative prescription.

Michael Saward's theory of representative claims-making (Saward 2006, 2010) offers such an explanatory framework by focusing on the dynamic and performative aspects of political representation. The latter is no longer conceptualized as a dual relationship between represented and representative but as a triadic configuration of constant exchange between political agents (claimants), various constituents, and an audience. Linking to some of the core themes of classical sociology, the representative claim is ultimately about the social attribution of meaning and about role ascriptions in social life. It is about reputation and charisma, about recognition and the building of social trust through symbols as well as through discourse.[1]

This new approach also implies an epistemic change in studying political representation which is no longer assessed in relation to the character of the representative, its compliance with normative rules and standards, and its authorization by a given constituency. Representative claims-making focuses instead on the act of representation, which, as Saward (2006: 299) aptly calls it, leads to the constitution of constituencies. Constituencies and political communities are thus not only underlying, and as such authorizing, the representative act, but also being constituted by it. It is not the people who select their representatives, but equally so the representatives who actively create and offer the type of symbols and images of what is to be represented (Saward 2006: 301). The represented does not exist independently of the representative act but because of it.

Processes of public claims-making in front of an audience and consequent acceptance or rejection by the audience produce political representation (Saward 2010: 67; see also Jentges in this volume). By bringing in the notion of the audience, representation is no longer seen as a direct relationship between the principal and the agent but as a mediated relationship. The audience is the 'third part' (Pollak et al. 2009: 14), that is, it is not identical with the constituent the political agent claims to stand for, but rather the unknown and not calculable receiver of the representative claim. Due to the presence of the audience, representative claims-making is therefore less strategic than contingent; as the constituents, the audience also can be addressed by the claimant, but frequently audiences are also formed as anonymous bystanders of public communication creating non-calculable effects of public resonance.

How, then, does the audience of representative claims-making come into existence? We can argue that an audience of political representation comes into existence by way of being addressed and/or by way of paying attention to representative claims-making.[2] Consequently, the existence of an audience depends on ongoing debate and contestation about political representation. But how can this audience exist before being addressed and before paying attention? Warner (2002) resolves this paradox by arguing that the audience as an addressable object is conjured into being in order to enable public discourse. The decisive point here is that those who become engaged in public discourse have a certain representation of the audience in mind, a confidence in its listening and reading capacities and its capacities of comprehension.

In conceiving political representation as a triadic and mediated configuration between political agents, constituents, and the audience, we, therefore, argue against the approach of the audience as the confined constituency of political representation that can be socially and territorially confined and to which only acts of 'acceptance' or 'recognition' of representative claims can be attributed (Rehfeld 2006). The relevant audience is neither supplied by the formal or legal context of political representation nor can it be objectively identified and statistically described by the media analyst (Saward 2010: 27). What rather counts is contestation that invokes, brings into being, but also constantly transforms the audience. In most cases the audience of political representation is not identical with those who are strategically addressed by the representative claimant. The sender of the representative message might, for instance, address his claim to his particular constituents (e.g. the electorate) but this message might also be received by bystanders who are not part of the formal constituency and whose reactions might impact on the acceptance of the claim. In this role as the wider resonance body of representative claims, the audience will ideally encompass the addressee/constituents but, when things go wrong, might also completely miss them.

In real life, the representative rarely meets the same audience she is supposed to represent (i.e. her constituents in legal terms, or the exact number of say 232,456 voters who are entitled to elect her). Moreover, media audiences are considerably larger than the communities of legal constituents. In international politics, also the world public plays an increasing role as a resonance body of representative claims-making, not only for civil society but also for state actors having to justify state action in the international arena (Meyer et al. 1997). In an insightful contribution, Carolyn Hendriks speaks of contemporary representative politics as a 'democratic soup' in which mixed meanings of political representation are attributed across multiple sites and with reference to plural and cross-territorial constituencies (Hendriks 2009). In European and international politics, the audience-constituency difference matters frequently. For instance, the German Minister of Finance claiming to represent German interests addresses a French audience and asks for understanding of its proposed measures in monetary policies (intended foreign audience). Or, the nationalist party, X, proposes harsh measures to defend the integrity of the nation, but its overtly racist programme outrages a wider European audience (actual foreign audience). In the latter case, the active audience might even strive for a broadening of the representative relationship and claim to be taken into consideration as a relevant constituency. See, for example, the case of the Haider debate, discussed in Risse 2010; Haider claims to represent Austria in Europe (constituents) but other Europeans might pay attention (the audience) and believe that he also (badly) represents Europe.

Representation as a mediated relationship

Further developing our understanding of the audience as the third part in political representation, we argue that there is a fundamental link between representation, the public sphere, and the mass media. As a publicly constituted exchange, political representation is filtered through the media. The more complex the political community and system of governance, the more layers of such mediated (filtered) representation we have. Furthermore, because the representative act takes place in the public sphere, it does not only concern the dual relationship between the represented and the representative, but is 'triadic' in configuration, a constant exchange between political agents (claimants), constituents, and audiences.

In the case of contemporary polities, the media underpin the political public sphere. They may not be the only mediators, but are certainly the most influential in terms of filtering, shaping, and re-structuring representative claims. Mass media 're-present' the political spectacle to a wider audience. In the pre-Internet era, newspapers and television provided the key filter between political claimants and constituents/audiences, with the roles of communicators and receptors clearly defined. While constituents have always had the opportunity to judge the quality of representation through voting and demonstrating, their reflections and arguments on the efficacy of the political system representing them found their way into public discourse mostly in a controlled and nearly always indirect manner (i.e. newspapers publishing a select amount of readers' letters on political matters; journalists reporting on citizens' views, with the occasional citizen interviewed live; or TV channels hosting carefully planned 'live audience' debates). In other words, the voice of constituents and audiences only appeared in the political public sphere intermittently and largely not spontaneously.

In the era of interactive public communications, exemplified by such online functions as social networking, blogging, micro-blogging, public file-sharing (Web 2.0), however, audiences and constituents can respond to a political claimant's representative claim spontaneously, within the same media frame (article, broadcast) on a grander scale than ever before. These communication functions have enabled constituents and audiences to take the place of political claimants by projecting their own representative claims in the public sphere. Not only this, but political claimants' statements are now open to public interpretation, a re-framing and rejection not only of traditional mediators (journalists, political actors, intellectuals) but also of every 'average Joe/Joan' with Internet access. The layers of mediation of a representative claim are thus infinitely multiplied. Certainly, the scope of mediated political representations has followed the transnationalization of decision-making (global/transnational audiences), and goes hand-in-hand with the diffusion of informal structures of democratic representation (e-governance, e-consultation, global-scale networking of organizations), as well as with the trend for 'tailor-made' representation of specific interest or issue-focused political communities (customized news contents, specialized communities online) (see Buss et al. 2006; Chadwick and Howard 2009).

Introducing the component 'Audience' in representative claims-making analysis

In mapping the representative claim, Saward (2010: 35 ff.) has mainly focused on the strategic and performative aspects of representative claims-making, but less so on its intermediation and resonance with the audience. This is what a media approach brings into the study of political representation: the claims-making approach, originally developed and tested out by social movement and media research (Koopmans and Statham 1999; Tarrow 1989), emphasizes precisely these informal channels (outside of the legal process of elections) through which social actors mobilize outside the formal arenas of political representation. It thus allows us to explore the *making of* political representation.

This approach facilitates the understanding of the context conditions for the acceptance of representative claims-making. In the media, the representative claim is filtered through and (re)moulded, thus becoming a media construct. In many cases, a 'representative claim' does not become such until a journalist ascribes a 'representative role' to the actor making the claim. Moreover, the media can also play the role of representatives themselves. A journalist can claim to speak 'in the name of the public', or a journalist can claim to represent the public interest, questioning the representative performance of public actors or bringing to the fore the performance of actors who might not want to be visible (e.g. when journalists question what kind of general interest is or should be re-presented by financial managers). In this respect, representative claims-making concerns the building of broader discursive coalitions with the media, where the aim is to set a 'moral agenda' that resonates with a wider audience.

An instance of political claims-making is defined as a unit of communicative action in the public sphere that can be put forward by individual or collective actors. In more detail, a claim consists of *'public acts which articulate political demands, decisions, implementations, calls to action, proposals, criticisms, or physical attacks, which, actually or potentially, affect the interests or integrity of the claimants and/or other collective actors in a policy field'* (Statham 2005: 12, my emphasis). Of relevance here is the particular form of articulating a concern (the claims-making act), that is, the way of presenting this concern to somebody else (the social relationship) and the justifications provided to support the demands (the argumentative strategy).

This 'grammar' of claims-making has been applied in political representation analysis in order to capture how representatives enact their right to represent and request constituents' support in the public sphere. The same claims-making grammar offers the basis for capturing the reception of representative claims by audiences and journalists, as it can be used to analyse the counter-claims publicly expressed in reaction to the representative claims of political actors.

In the following sections we turn to the implementation of our analytical model in the case of the EU polity and present findings from the analysis of the 2009 EP election online debates in 12 Member States and at trans-European level.

Representative claims-making and the EU polity: the case of the 2009 EP elections

The question of the representative function of the media, in relation to the enhancement of a European democracy, becomes particularly relevant in the context of EP election campaigns, that is, in a period when the representatives of the citizens of Europe towards the EU are elected (approved) by the electorates. The institutional and constitutional set-up of the EU and, more specifically, the context of EP elections, provides the background for a particular form of representative claims-making that is about the allocation of popular sovereignty on an emerging transnational polity (Trenz 2010). Furthermore, there is a principled uncertainty with regard to who can claim to be representative in the EU context and how these claims can be addressed to and received by the audience (Crum and Fossum 2009). The context of EP elections is used not only by the candidates but by all kind of other actors (political parties, civic groups and associations, journalists and citizens) to raise representative claims in relation to the EU. It is the moment in which media representations of the EU play a decisive role and public communication about the contours of European integration (its institutional and constitutional set-up and future project) is stimulated.

In this context, we focus on the 'representative claim' as an evaluative statement that carries an opinion about the legitimacy of the EU polity (Michailidou et al. 2010). The coding scheme we have used simultaneously recorded political actors who generated the evaluative statement (such as citizen; journalist; politician), as well as the object of political representation, that is, the dimension(s) of the EU polity evaluated for their legitimacy (see Trenz and de Wilde 2009; de Wilde et al. 2011). More specifically, we distinguish:

(a) The actor: this is the agent who makes a claim or counter-claim on the political legitimacy of the EU in the context of the EP elections (this can be either a national or transnational European contestant, and either an institutional actor, a representative of political parties, or a citizen);

(b) The framing of claims-making, which concerns the context within which claims and counter-claims appear, that is, the journalistic frames applied to contextualize news stories or analyses concerning the EU elections;

(c) The evaluations and justifications of EU evaluations made by an actor: these include the object of political representation (which can be the principle of EU integration, the institutional/constitutional infrastructure of the EU or the future project of EU integration; the verb or the adjectives that indicate a positive or a negative evaluation of legitimacy; and the justifications or underlying criteria of evaluations (the different notions of the common good on which a representative relationship is built and publicly justified).

To identify legitimacy evaluations of the EU, we further distinguished between polity contestation and policy contestation. For the purpose of our study, only positive or negative evaluations of the polity dimensions of the EU were considered relevant for the representation of the political system of the EU.[3] The basic grammar of 'representing' EU legitimacy was, therefore, formulated as follows:

Object of evaluation	**Evaluation**	**Criteria of worthiness**
The European Union European integration Europe	is affirmed is denounced	as efficient/inefficient as transparent/ opaque as democratic/ undemocratic

We further recognize that there can be different degrees of contesting EU legitimacy, either in a principled, categorical, and unconditional way or as a qualified judgement that only focuses on particular aspects of European integration or takes a balanced view on assets and drawbacks. We therefore distinguish whether an evaluative statement assesses the principle of European integration, the institutional and constitutional design of the EU, or the project of integration in terms of future development (de Wilde et al. 2011). The type of legitimacy contestations underlying our analysis can, in this sense, be understood as 'framing claims', which Saward (2006: 307) defines as concerning the basic constituency character of the political system of the EU.

Methods

Our study has specifically focused on the most recent EP elections, which took place in June 2009. We applied a mixed-methods design, which combines the measurement of online platforms of communication (how? where?) with the content of public communication (what? by whom?). This was done through the combination of a qualitative content analysis of public messages (message level of analysis) with a quantitative profiling of the selected websites in the same coding scheme (thread level of analysis). In the resulting coding model (de Wilde et al. 2011), evaluative statements concerning EU legitimacy were identified and categorized in a standardized manner, filtering out transnationalizing trends of public opinion formation but also crucial qualitative variations at the national level.

In order to demarcate the European elections' online public sphere, we first investigated where and to what extent online public debates were mobilized in relation to the 2009 EP elections. In this context we identified the main online outlets for circulation of EU news and opinions. Subsequently, we mapped the profile of sites where opinions on the EU were presented, directly or indirectly, outside institutionally funded, supported, and controlled forums. This included an assessment of the websites' salience in the online public sphere, as well as the websites' quantitative news-making capacity (amount of coverage of the EU elections).

After identifying and evaluating the web spaces that have the potential to focus attention of the mass electorate on EU elections, we measured participation in terms of who contests what kind of topics in these debates. We further compared participants and contents of online debates across different media formats and countries. This concerns the presence of EU, foreign, and domestic actors, of state and non-state actors, of news on domestic, foreign, or European issues. We then analysed the particular group dynamics unfolding in EU polity contestations online by examining the forms of interaction between the core communicators (bloggers, journalists) and their audiences. This includes also a qualitative assessment of whether the main traits of online communication are met (free access, free speech, adherence to the online codes of conduct).

The third step in our research was to measure public opinion formation, in terms of justifications given in contesting EU issues and the general evaluations of the EU and of European integration. Here we look at how political contestation confers legitimacy with regard to the

EU political entity and political community. Is the EU supported or rejected? Is there a difference in evaluation between journalists and users? How are EU evaluations justified? What are the specific common good references through which the EU/European integration is seen as legitimate/illegitimate? (See Table 8.1 below).

In order to create a representative map of the EU elections web sphere, we looked for EU debates in all publicly available (where no paid subscription is required) online outlets encompassing debates that took place during the last three weeks of the EP election campaign in May–June 2009, as well as the first few days following the elections. Our sample comprised of only the most popular web spaces per country and at trans-European level.[4] In total, we included 36 professional journalism websites and 24 independent blogs of national scope, while at the European/transnational level we included one professional journalism website and two blogs. In addition, Facebook groups focused on the EU elections and two Twitter threads with EU election-related hashtags were included as representative of social networking communications popular with younger audiences.[5]

Besides the criterion of popularity, and in order to be able to measure impact in terms of inclusion, web spaces were selected based on their potential to open an interactive space between proponents and users. In most cases this referred to the widespread practice of publicly

Table 8.1 The contours of the EU online public sphere

Level of analysis	Operationalization	Measurement (qualitative and quantitative variables)
Publicity	Salience	• Website profiles (centralization/decentralization of media ownership) • Website visibility and salience of EU news within it (focalization/fragmentation of audiences)
	News-making capacity	• Quantity of EU elections coverage (number of threads)
Participation	Inclusion	• Range of actors • Scope of actors
	Community-building	• Framing of debates • Manners of interaction
Public opinion formation	Expressions of EU regime support/opposition in online EU debates	• Evaluations of EU legitimacy • Regimes of justifications

available user feedback and comments on articles or blog entries. If this commenting option was not available, a website needed to host at least an online debate forum in order to be selected. In total, our website monitoring through RSS feeds resulted in the 'clipping' (selection) of 4,815 articles. We have used a multi-stage, random (probability) sampling design to select 50 articles per country (25 for Belgium, as only the French-speaking websites were included in the monitoring). This resulted in 638 threads drawn for further analysis, in which a total of 1,128 EU polity messages were identified and coded.[6]

The grammar of EU legitimacy contestation during the 2009 EP election campaign

Actors

The EP elections e-sphere is dominated by the voice of a category of actors that is largely absent in offline media, namely citizens (Figure 8.1).[7] They are the unquestionable protagonists of the evaluative debates concerning the project of European integration in its principle, present, and future forms. Of the 1,128 evaluative messages coded, 63 per cent were generated by citizens (709 messages). On the other hand, party actors were a distant second-most visible group of contributors in the EU evaluative discourse, with 309 messages attributable to this category. Party actors also did not play an active role (i.e. presence) in mainstream online coverage and debates of the EP election campaigning. Rather, and in contrast to citizens' evaluations of EU legitimacy, their EU representative claims are only in a minority of cases (124 out of 309 messages identified) directly transmitted; the rest are merely attributed to them by third parties (either journalists/bloggers or citizens). For citizens, the percentage of directly transmitted evaluations stands at 85 per cent (605 out of 709 messages found with citizens as their originators).

EP election online debates are thus not so much dominated by representative claims of political agents, who stand for elections, but by counter-claims of citizens, who critically debate the legitimacy of the EU and of their representatives. The inextricable link between citizens and counter-representative action in the EU elections e-sphere was verified independent of country of origin, type of website, and actor scope. Online news media empower the constituents, who are given voice to challenge political representation, and not necessarily the elected representatives who need to campaign to defend their mandates

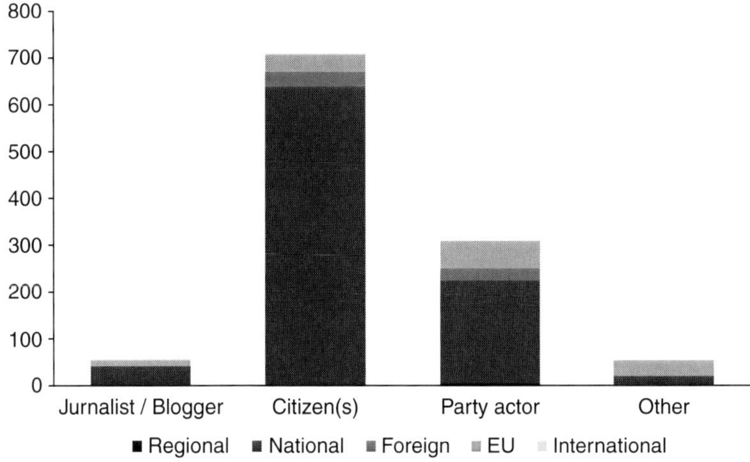

Figure 8.1 Number of evaluations per actor category and scope
Source: Michailidou and Trenz; Data source: Euroscepticism project.

in the election. Furthermore, analysis of the actors' scope, that is, the geographic capacity in which a participant contributes to the online debate, shows that nearly all online discussions about the EP elections remain a national affair. Transnationalization of EU debates can be observed only within the trans-European websites and social networking groups, where the highest number of non-national actors was identified. The political space within which political representation is contested remains nationally confined (Figure 8.1).

To some extent this observation reflects the linguistic barriers among the peoples of the EU, in that consumption of online news or participation in relevant online debates requires knowledge of the language used by that news website/blog. Hence the vast majority of citizens raising their voice in EU debates were nationals of the same country as the blog or news website on which they left their comments. However, this nationally confined scope of participation in online debates does not only hold for citizens but also for partisan or governmental actors. The studied online news media rarely hosted views or reported on actions of EU level or foreign actors. In addition, candidates or other official representatives hardly ever participated in online debates directly. Rather, their messages were carried forward to the public through journalists/ bloggers, as we discuss in the following section. Online news media (be they professional journalism websites or blogs) thus display a clear tendency to replicate the national public sphere as a reference point for political representation.

Framing of representative claims-making

In addition to being the most represented group of actors in the 2009 EU election e-sphere, citizens were also the most proactive in terms of directly presenting their views on the EU polity. Out of 715 messages with citizens as their originators, 611 were directly transmitted (self-representation), unlike those generated by political actors, which were mostly attributed to them by third parties (either journalists/bloggers or citizens). Of the 308 messages identified as having originated from party actors, 124 were directly transmitted (40 per cent of all party-actor generated messages).This indicates that in the case of online debates concerning the elections, party actors rely on filtered representation of their claims (Figure 8.2).

Further scouring our data for trends in (self) representation of the underlying political community and its perception of legitimacy of the EU, we find a clear trend across all countries to discuss the EP elections predominantly in relation to domestic topics and debates. Of the 638 trends coded in total, 367 (57.5 per cent) were classified under the category of 'domestic politics' in terms of the main topic introduced

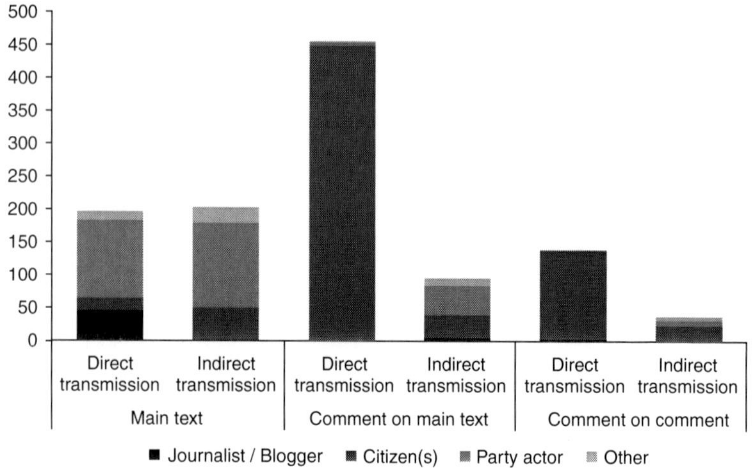

Figure 8.2 Number of evaluations per actor category, type of transmission and location in text

Source: Michailidou and Trenz; Data source: Euroscepticism project.

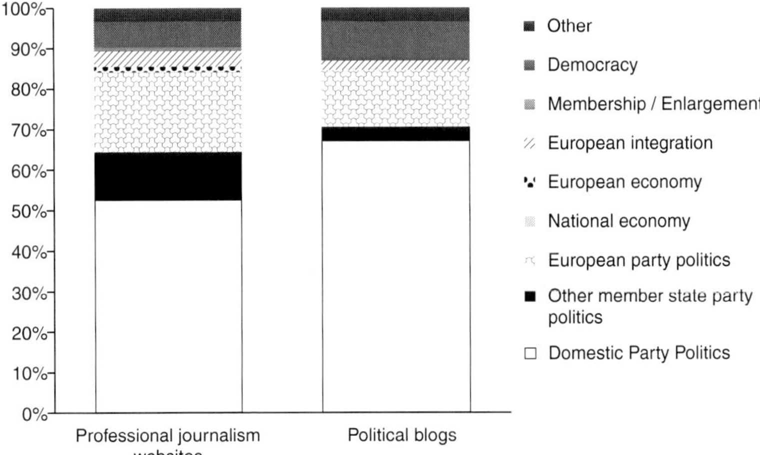

Figure 8.3 Topics of threads (framing) within which EU evaluations were found

Source: Michailidou and Trenz; Data source: Euroscepticism project.

by the central article/blog entry of each thread. Thus the framing of the debates indicates that, with very few exceptions, online debates represent national constituencies that relate to national politics and do not introduce a notion of a multi-level, federal, or cosmopolitan polity as a reference point of democratic politics.

This observation is in line with the traditional role ascription of professional journalism as the key medium of the national public sphere. Political blogs also frame EU election issues in the context of national politics or political debates, but this is hardly surprising given the overall 'niche' focus of political blogs, both in terms of scope and addressed/targeted audiences (Figure 8.3).[8]

EU polity evaluations and opinion justifications

When examining the content of the analysed online debates, negative evaluations of the EU polity dominated, with 817 of all messages coded containing at least one dimension of negative evaluation. In particular the EU's current institutional/constitutional set-up received most negative evaluations across all countries and at trans-EU level (60 per cent of all cases contained a negative evaluation of this dimension; 648 cases). Attributes such as 'the Brussels dictatorship', '(political) monster', and

Figure 8.4 Proportional distribution of evaluations of the current EU political/constitutional set-up, per source type

Source: Michailidou and Trenz; Data source: Euroscepticism project.

'elitist government' regularly featured in the evaluations of the current EU polity set-up across countries. Negative evaluations prevailed irrespective of the source/platform hosting the EU debate, as well as irrespective of the actor's position (i.e. acting in his/her capacity as journalist, citizens, political, or NGO actor) and scope (national, transnational, foreign/non-EU) (Figure 8.4).

The prevalence of negative views expressed in assessment of the EU's legitimacy, in combination with the relative homogeneity of actors participating in EU election e-debates (mostly citizens), points to the emergence of an ad hoc community online, which comes together above all in order to express discomfort with the current state of EU affairs. This trend was consistent across all countries. Moreover, the type of evaluations is independent of the type of news source. Despite the more plural range of topics and opinions hosted in the main articles of professional journalism threads, the majority of EU evaluations in these threads was 'current EU polity-negative', coinciding with the majority of EU evaluations in the selected blogs, which are certainly more partisan and subjective in tone and audience orientation.

We can further observe homogeneity in the type of justification that is underlying the polity evaluation: democracy is the most frequently used category to contextualize/justify an evaluation of the EU polity across the Europhile/Eurosceptic spectrum, with 422 evaluations (55 per cent) out of a total of 762 justified (68 per cent of all messages coded) on the basis of democratic principles/governance.

This finding is unaffected by the type of actor formulating the evaluation and the type of source where messages are found. It is also independent of countries and country groups. The following contributions selected from different sources of our data set exemplify typical justifications of an (negative) EU polity evaluation based on the concept of democracy:

> ...The notion of any EU country's (I refuse to use the EU jargon of 'state') laws being made by it's own commissioner and 26 others who perhaps know little of that country's language, heritage and mentality...is ridiculous at best. The Dutch, French and Irish made their opinions clear on the Constitution/Lisbon. Germans, Austrians and Brits also demand that the EU be given less rather than more power. Sadly,...the un-elected commission refuses to listen and has the audacity to encourage us to vote in a 'democratic' EU election where one German vote has only 1/16th the democratic clout of a voter from Luxembourg. Welcome to post-democratic Europe! [*sic*] (user 'Johannestannes' in Mardell 2009).
>
> the Commission doesn't want to democratize, it is the government of experts against democracy....The problem is that this technical Europe has forged very liberal policies that go against the European model that they are supposed to promote. (Nouvelobs.com 2009)[9]
>
> My opinion is that the EU should become more democratic....And at this stage, Members of the European Parliament don't have enough power. Too much is being decided by unelected people.[10] (Nu.nl 2009)

The predominantly critical attitude of participants in online debates across all countries examined, combined with the tendency to evaluate EU legitimacy in negative terms and to express a concern with democracy, point to the possibility of the emergence of an online community of dissatisfied citizens. Yet EU online debates remain episodic and fragmented and the heterogeneous group of users do not constitute a media audience in the classical sense. Online audiences rather represent a segment of the national public sphere; the single users go online to express and share their dissatisfaction, sometimes seek out like-minded, national websites where they can air their views, but they do not necessarily perceive themselves as part of an emerging EU constituency. Our model of mediated political representation as a triadic configuration is thus useful to accentuate some of the particularities of the EU representative system, which in relation to EP election campaigning generates a fragmented audience of dissatisfied citizens, but not the imaginary of an underlying constituency.

Discussion

Responding to recent debates in political theory, which have called for a re-conceptualization of the so-called standard account of political representation in order to factor in the challenges facing contemporary democracies (transnationalization, specialization, diversification of decision-making and political community-building processes), we have proposed a media approach of political representation. In our analytical model, the latter is understood as a dynamic communicative process within a triadic configuration that encompasses not only the political claimants and their constituents, but also audiences. As this communicative act of political representation takes place in the public sphere, it is filtered and shaped by the media environment, which in turn is subject to the same trends of transnationalization, specialization, and diversification insofar as audiences, media content, and user empowerment are concerned. In this context, we have focused our attention on how political representation unfolds in the public sphere vis à vis European political institutions. Our analytical model has been tested on a case that epitomizes the transformation of contemporary democratic governance in terms of transnationalization, specialization, and diversification: the EU polity.

Through the simultaneous study of online media content on the 2009 EU elections in 12 Member States and at trans-European level, we have found that the content of representative claims concerning the EU polity remains anchored in national constituencies, traditional institutions of decision-making, and mostly 'simple political egalitarianism' (Castiglione and Warren 2008), rooted in principles of representative democratic governance. Nevertheless, in terms of who constitutes a representative (claimant) in the EU elections e-sphere, we find, on par with the above-mentioned trends, a turn from formal institutional representatives to what can be classified as 'voice representation' (ibid.) – individuals acting in their capacity mostly as constituents (electorates), but also as affected third parts (non-constituent audiences). These 'voices' often claim to represent the wider 'we, the people of X EU country', but more importantly claim the non-representativeness of the EU as a democratically legitimate polity. Their focus is not so much to declare their right to publicly represent themselves and/or their fellow country people or a specific group of constituents, but to refute the EU polity's right to claim representation *of* them.

In the 2009 EU election e-sphere constituency is constructed on the basis of geographical borders and/or principles of democratic governance, and the EU polity is found to meet neither of these requirements. Representative claims made on this basis are thus not conducive to the formation of an EU constituency. Diversified audiences develop a critical attitude towards the EU and share a similar concern with democracy, yet do not act as being represented by the same polity. Overall, the limited framing of topics and narrow scope of actors in EU election debates certainly raises questions with regard to the ability of online media to re-present a constituency of democratic politics that is different from the community of co-national citizens and, therefore, to enable audiences to reach beyond the boundaries of nationally framed political debates. The issue that arises and merits further conceptual and empirical investigation is how a process of democratic government can be established at EU level, if the plural audiences, which make themselves available as the recipients, and often counter-claimants, of the representative claims raised by EU actors and institutions, for the time being rebut the role attributed to them as the constituents of such a transnational democratic polity.

Notes

1. See Jentges 2010, who reconstructs the sociological core of a political theory of representation.
2. See Dewey 1927: 16f., on his conceptualization of the public as a consequential effect of a discourse that deals with collective problems and its possible solutions.
3. This means that an evaluation must generalize beyond the critique of particular policies or decisions and beyond the performance of particular actors (politics).
4. Popularity is measured by visitor numbers and influence within the blogosphere, using the top 100 websites per country listings on Alexa.com (Alexa Internet, 2011) and blog aggregator lists, such as Wikio (Wikio.com, 2011). For Facebook threads, popularity was determined by the number of members subscribed to a group, while for Twitter threads we identified the hashtags linked with the EU elections, and selected all threads ascribed to them. All but four of the professional journalism websites and four independent blogs were in the Alexa Country top 100 websites lists, while the majority of the independent blogs were in the top 500 websites in their country.
5. Hashtags are a 'Twitter community creation', invented by users to easily group tweets and/or add extra data.
6. We used Krippendorff's alpha to measure inter-coder reliability before, during and at the end of the coding week (eight coders involved). All variables had a score between 0.7 and 1, with the exception of the EU Polity evaluation dimensions, where the score was 0.62. Although this is slightly

below the usually recommended minimum measurement of alpha (0.667), we have accepted it as a valid and reliable score, due to the complexity of the EU polity evaluation dimensions (seven values).

There was no correlation between the extent of coverage of the 2009 EP elections by an online news outlet or blog and the intensity of debate (number of comments per article). Rather, the factors affecting the amount of comments posted varied across countries and ranged from the level of 'maturity' of Web 2.0 functions (i.e., the amount of time that Web 2.0 functions have been widely available in a country) to a country's culture of public debate. At any rate, country-specific analysis of the data suggests that online debating behaviour is the result of a combination of sociopolitical and technological factors, for which further research is required.

7. All actors making a claim in their capacity as private individuals, without making use of their political or other public identity, were automatically coded as citizens.
8. Chi-square tests and symmetric measures did not confirm a strong and significant link between the actors' scope and type of source (cross-tabulation controlled for country group; also cross-tabulation of actors' scope and country, controlled by type of source).
9. '...la Commission ne veut pas se démocratiser, c'est le gouvernement des experts contre la démocratie... Le problème c'est que cette Europe technique a développé des politiques très libérales qui affaiblissent le modèle européen qu'elles sont censées porter' (Crespy and Fimin 2011: 92).
10. 'Ik vind dat Brussel democratischer moet... En op dit moment hebben Europarlementariërs te weinig macht, teveel wordt geregeld door mensen die niet gekozen zijn.' (de Wilde et al. 2011: 160).

9

Unelected Representatives in the Europolitical Field: CSOs between Berlin and Brussels

Erik Jentges

Introduction

If it is true that the voice of Europe's citizenry is raised by civil society organizations (CSOs), then those actors who become active on European policy issues are representatives of European citizens.[1] But they are unelected actors – the mechanisms through which CSOs can become representatives are not based on voting. When assuming that CSO are representatives, most of the underlying assumptions of democratic political theory need to be revised (cf. Saward 2006 and the Introduction to this volume by Kröger and Friedrich). It is, for example, largely taken for granted in democratic theories that political representation is constructed bottom-up by citizens who articulate their political will. My understanding is that representation also emerges from the intermediary position. Representatives of CSOs depend on recognition by policy-makers from 'above' and by supporters from 'below'. They have to create and stage performances as representatives to gain acceptance.

I approach the subject via the political activities and the political communication of CSOs in order to trace their representative claims-making. My observations are embedded in a larger theoretical framework that integrates elements from Bourdieu's political sociology and Elias's figurational sociology in order to explain the relational dynamics of making representative claims. As a consequence, interdependencies and power relations become relevant. My case studies cover German CSOs from the policy fields of consumer protection and organized religion; two fields that differ tremendously regarding the Europeanization of core policy issues. The EU has a big say on consumer affairs, but no competencies regarding religious matters and state – church relations. In both policy fields, however, the European dimension has become more relevant, either because EU legislation changes national policies or because actors became active on the European level in order to protect their national status quo and fend off the EU's influence.

This chapter is structured as follows: I approach political representation by illustrating how representative claims as units of communication construct, form, and affect the settings of representatives within triadic figurations (2). The following section focuses on the representatives who become active in the europolitical field and connect national and European policy-making arenas (3). I then turn to case studies on German CSOs in two policy fields, religion and consumer protection (4). In the conclusion, the role of rites of institution, performances, and biographies of representatives are discussed (5).

Representative claims and figurations

Saward's ideas on political representation open up a promising path because he focuses on performative aspects and looks at specific units of communication that he calls representative claims (2006). They pertain to political matters and are relevant to the construction of authority and authenticity for both elected and unelected representatives. The short form of a claims reads like this: 'A maker of representations (M) puts forward a subject (S) which stands for an object (O) which is related to a referent (R) and is offered to an audience (A).' (Saward 2006: 302). These five elements stand in an interesting relation to each other.

Anyone can be a maker of representative claims. A claim can be made by a politician about himself, for example during a press conference. It can also be a comment by a journalist on TV about that politician. And CSO activists can make claims about that politician. Likewise, a politician may refer to a CSO as representing the interests of consumers, believers, musicians, and so on, assuming that interestees for the issues in the real world actually exist. Identifying and analysing representative claims is thus a complex matter. For example, according to Saward's definition, makers may or may not stand in as the subject. While the subject identifies who is representing, the object refers to who or what is represented. In the grammar of representative claims, subject and object are also symbolical entities, while makers, referents, and audiences can best be imagined as real-world people.

A crucial element is the linkage between subject and object. At what point do the churches represent 'the Christians'? Does an environmental CSO actually represent 'the environment'? How do such claims gain acceptance?

Bourdieu's political sociology offers some help. For him, it is not unimportant who the maker is. The maker establishes the link between subject, object, and referents by attaching his or her personal authority and reputation to the claim: 'the speech of the spokesperson is an authorized speech that owes its authority to the fact that the person who speaks it draws his authority from the group which authorizes him to speak in its name. When the spokesperson speaks, it is a group that speaks through him, but one that exists as a group through that speech and its speaker' (Bourdieu 2005: 60). Speakers can fuse subject and object in 'felicitous performances' (Alexander 2009: 67). In other words, makers need to literally embody and incorporate the subject and portray themselves as personification of the objects that are represented. When speakers are perceived to stand behind their arguments, the chances increase that audiences recognize and accept the claims as legitimate.

The concept of figuration is an extension of the idea of embodiment and incorporation and builds a bridge towards contextual and relational analysis of interdependencies. According to Elias, figurations are dynamic and open patterns of relations between interdependent individuals.[2] Individuals create figurations and they are part of them with 'their whole selves, the totality of their dealings in their relationship with each other' (Elias 1978: 130). It means that those working in a CSO form a figuration of interdependent individual actors who together constitute the organization as a collective actor. In order to understand the dynamics of claims-making that can lead to a CSO becoming accepted as a representative, we should thus not neglect the biographies of the activists.

As representation often presupposes the existence of collective actors, we have to be aware that CSOs themselves are embedded in larger and more complex figurations within issue networks or policy communities. Our analysis has to be sensitive towards networks of interdependent social relations with fluctuating power balances within the internal environment of a CSO between leaders, office staff, activists, members, and supporters, and within a CSO's external environment where elected decision-makers, bureaucrats of governmental agencies, other CSOs, and business actors populate the political field. Interactions can be based on cooperation or on confrontation. Some are staged in front of audiences, others are kept secret.

From the perspective of a CSO, it is useful to distinguish between at least two kinds of audiences. When we assume CSOs to be in an intermediary position, they link their internal environment with their external environment. They link the 'below' with the 'above'. To contextualize the making of representative claims as an activity of performance that is enacted within figurations has consequences for the theory of political representation, because now the general notion of political representation as a dual relationship between representative and represented has to be opened up to include a third position. Reduced to a simplified formalistic model, representatives find themselves embedded in triadic figurations with their constituency on one side and policy-makers on the other (cf. Weiss 1984, 1998; Sofsky and Paris 1994). It can be formulated as follows:

> A acts for B in an arena with C on interests X, trying to persuade with justifications Y.

Representatives (A) link those who are affected by decisions (B) with those who are capable of making them (C). Representatives connect and separate at least two potentially interested audiences. Often they have to generate acceptance and recognition at more sites, for example in the media, where they lobby for certain issues (X). Because CSOs usually lack sufficient material resources, they depend on the force of the better argument. They have to sustain their representative claims with good justifications (Y) that persuade and convince their audiences.

These triadic figurations are dynamic networks of interdependencies, but they are not unstructured. Structures emerge as the consequence of the flow of representative claims: A can be accepted or rejected by B or by C. Dependencies can be stronger to this or that side and thus shift the power balances with triadic figurations (cf. Jentges 2010). Since we ask how CSOs become accepted as representatives by their constituencies and by policy-makers in Berlin and Brussels, the question is also, how do CSOs position themselves as political intermediaries in the middle.

Representatives between Berlin and Brussels

Research about European civil society does not always have to be done in Brussels. In fact, a more 'representative' patch of Europe might actually be found beyond the immediate vicinity of Berlaymont. One activist even referred to Brussels as an orbiting 'space-ship' to describe the enclosed and somewhat bizarre culture in the European Quarter (interview Greenpeace). Many activists who are working on European issues are not employed by European CSOs but by national organizations. They can often be found in the government quarters of the capitals of the Member States.

How CSOs try to become representatives in the EU's multi-level system could be researched in all Member States, but zooming in on Germany delivered some advantages. Most peak associations of the organized civil society in Germany moved to Berlin when it became the capital in 1999. They have professional staff and in-house experts for EU policies and government affairs. In comparison to CSOs from smaller or newer Member States, they have relatively more resources and a relatively larger workforce specialized in lobbying. One is often not aware that national CSO offices can have more resources at their disposal than the relatively few and relatively small EU umbrella organizations which attract so much academic attention.

CSO representatives that work on European issues have to be able to navigate the intersphere between national and European institutions. As representatives of the citizen's voice, one of their tasks is to strengthen their position in the europolitical field. The political field refers to 'the place, where those actors who are present and in competition with each other generate the political products (problems, programmes, analyses, comments, concepts, events) which shall be selected by common citizens who are reduced to the status of "consumers", and where the risk of misunderstanding becomes bigger, the further they are away from the place of production' (Bourdieu 2001: 13, trans. Erik Jentges). While Bourdieu thought of the political field as a national realm, it is not limited to the state. Europeanization of the Member States requires re-drawing the political field to include supranational political arenas. The fundamental transformations of policy-making processes can be accentuated by referring to the political field as europolitical field.

In general, citizens know little about European 'political products' and are rather disconnected to the places of their production. They may not even feel as 'consumers' of Europe. But they increasingly sense that their lives are affected by EU decisions. Among other actors like the elected Members of the European Parliament, unelected representatives of CSOs also claim to speak on behalf of European citizens. They also belong to the group of those who are 'present and in competition' on the field and market their 'political products'. In this sense, CSO activists who deal with EU affairs are a nexus between national constituencies and relevant policy arenas in the europolitical field. Many frequently travel to Brussels for board meetings in EU umbrella organizations. Some regularly attend consultation groups with officials from the Commission. In these arenas they are performing as intermediaries, channelling constituency interests upwards and communicating EU decisions back down to supporters on national and local levels.

In face-to-face interviews these CSO representatives were confronted with the question 'Whom do you represent?' (see annex).[3] They were asked to make representative claims. The assumption was that when activists refer to themselves as the voice of consumers or as advocates of the environment, they would (re)create their CSO's public image and political profile for the interviewer and thus deliver a performance as representatives. Answers showed that these activists perceived themselves to act for and to stand for civil society. At the same time, they were flexible about the scope of civil society claim. They saw themselves as European civil society activists and as activists of a Europeanizing national civil society.

Case studies in the europolitical field

Religious organizations

Interest-group scholars have noted that 'the two big Christian churches and the various organizations in their environment belong without doubt to the circle of influential and successful actors in German politics' (Willems 2007: 316, trans. Erik Jentges). Only the Churches have the organizational infrastructure and the resources for strategic political interest representation in the capitals of the *Länder*, in Berlin, and in Brussels. In comparison with CSOs from other Member States, the German churches are the most influential CSOs in Europe on matters concerning religion. They have been politically active in European matters long before the EU was born and look back on a long history of interactions with state institutions. Due to the historicity of this figuration, they benefit from special legal arrangements with policy-makers on all political levels. With their economic resources, their manpower, and their expertise, they are certainly not the most influential of all interest groups, but probably the most influential CSOs involved in lobbying the EU.

In order to coordinate the representation of their political interests in Brussels, the Commission and the Churches set-up regular consultations in the early 1990s (Jansen 2000). The Churches are an example of inclusion of unelected actors as representatives. They are established insiders to the policy community on religion in the europolitical field.

The Churches are by far the biggest and most complex organizations in the civil sphere. In Germany they have about 24 million registered members each. Other religious organizations, such as the Jewish Council or the Muslim Council, or secular humanist associations, are dwarfed in relation to the political clout of the Churches. The larger and more complex network of religious organizations can be described as having at the centre the tandem of the Catholic Church and the Protestant Churches. We find the Jewish Council in a protected niche between these two insider groups. Secular CSOs and Muslim organizations are marginalized outsider groups. Smaller independent Christian associations and CSOs from other religions hardly leave their marks on the political field.

The Churches cooperate closely for the representation of their political interests. It is helpful to outline the organizational infrastructure they can rely on for addressing policy-makers. The lobby office of the Evangelical Church in Germany (EKD) had a staff of 22 and a budget of €1.2 million in 2007 (interview EKD1). In Brussels, EKD has its own lobby office since 1990, which is staffed with three persons and financed with €440,000 per year (Holzhauer 2006: 266). Additional organizational infrastructure exists in Geneva with the Conference of European Churches (CEC) and the World Council of Churches (WCC). CEC also has an office in Strasbourg and a secretariat in Brussels, located in the same building as the office of the EKD. The Berlin office of the German Bishops' Conference of the Catholic Church (DBK) had a staff of 16 and a yearly budget of a little less than €1 million (interview DBK). Embeddedness in the europolitical field is based on the membership in the Commission of the Bishops' Conferences of the European Commission (COMECE). Eleven people work in the office that is financed with €964,700 per year by yet another Catholic umbrella organization (CCEE) which is based in Switzerland.

How do the Churches ensure that the chains of delegation in these triadic figurations are actually becoming transmission belts? Their lobby efforts are coordinated at both the national and the European level. Their government affairs divisions are almost equally well equipped with resources. They publish joint statements and often team up in consultations with policy-makers. The success of their lobby activities is reflected in the Lisbon Treaty. The inclusion of a 'Church article' was a priority as representatives of DBK pointed out:

> On the European level, this exceptional standing of the Church is basically recognized and one can see this now with the Reform

> Treaty. In the Constitutional Treaty there was the article 47 about the structured dialogue with civil society. And we had – and this is where one can see that we are not classified under this label [as civil society; EJ] – we had our own article 52 about the structured dialogue with the churches. And both are now included in the Reform Treaty. (interview DBK, July 2007, Berlin [art. 52 is identical with art. 17 of the Lisbon Treaty; EJ])[4]

The claim-maker accentuated that the Churches are recognized as representatives of society, but that they are different from other CSOs. The representative claim is used to draw a line between the actors in the field. The 'Church article' is also a legal manifestation of a 'rite of institution' (Bourdieu 2000). In some sense it ennobles the Churches and secures a relatively privileged access to European policy-makers. The spokespersons of the churches meet regularly with Commission officials and representatives of the rotating Presidency of the Council of the European Union to discuss some points on the agenda that are of relevance for the Churches (interview EKD2). Their exceptionally strong standing is not unjustified. The historicity of these relations can be traced back to the beginning of state-building processes in Europe. Based on the historicity of the figuration, the Churches have strong linkages to policy-makers 'above'. But how do they integrate their members from 'below'?

The constituencies of DBK and EKD that were claimed to be represented were referred to as parishioners in Germany and beyond, marginalized groups in general, and also the core values of the faith were mentioned as the object of representative claims. In interviews and in secondary publications, church representatives referred to themselves as 'advocates for those who do not have a voice' (interview EKD2). A senior staff member of the organization of the Catholic lays, the Central Committee of German Catholics (ZdK), who looked back on almost three decades of personal involvement in political advocacy for the Catholic Church at different European institutions, answered the question 'whom do you represent?' with the following most interesting words:

> We cannot say that we represent the Catholics or the lays in a legal or political sense, that claim we should not make. Our structures and our mechanisms that create representation are neither defined nor clear.... In our statutes it says, and this is terribly unspecific, 'the ZdK represents the concerns of Catholics in the public.' Well, there one

> has to ask 'what are the concerns?' I have to admit of course that in some sense, it's us defining these concerns, under the presumption of a common consensus, for example a pro-European stance and also a Europe based on values and respect for diversity. (Interview ZdK, June 2007, Bonn)

The maker of the representative claim uses the personal pronoun 'us' to identify the organization's leadership and staff. Those who speak with authority, derived from seniority, higher status, or strong convictions, and who literally 'embody' the organization, need to define who and what is being represented. In this sense, ZdK is an example of the common pattern of an active organization with rather passive supporters. The statement also highlights the difficulties of how to aggregate concerns on a higher level. The representative later concluded that 'we organize societal communication', thereby shifting the object of the claim away from 'the concerns of Catholics' towards delivering a service to society. The claim gives the organizational image a peculiar twist, because it allows changing roles.

ZdK sees itself also as a moderator in state – society relations – and a fair moderator does not have an agenda except facilitating understanding between the parties involved. 'Proof' to substantiate the claim is delivered in various forms. Meetings are held with members and numerous press statements are published in the media. With ancillary associations like the ZdK, the Churches can anchor their representative claims and illustrate their linkages to the referents of their claims. They are in contact with people of most social milieus in all parts of Germany and Europe (for example, via priests in the parishes and church-related community activities). As political intermediaries on the europolitical field, they can offer social impact assessments to national and European policy-makers. The claims are, of course, not uncontested.[5]

If one tries to evaluate the quality of the representative claims that are made in these triadic figurations, then the Churches and their ancillary associations make relatively strong claims. Persons working in the Churches' government affairs divisions have relatively more access to policy-makers than representatives of other CSOs. Their claims show connectedness, meaning that the transmission-belt function is recognizable. Policy-makers value the contribution of the Churches because they know that they are able to create responsive channels to citizens on the local level through their well-developed and complex infrastructures. And the claims can be confirmed, meaning that linkages are evident and can be tested. The chains of delegation in the triadic figurations are unbroken. The representatives of the Churches can 'do the talk' with policy-makers and they can reach their parishioners in Germany, across Europe, and beyond with relative ease. Even though representative claims are always contested, the Churches are seen as largely legitimate representatives by policy-makers in Berlin and in Brussels.

Consumer associations

The emergence of a common market and the development of EU legislation on consumer protection are closely related processes. Today, the European Commission even sees options to repair the broken link between the EU and its citizens: 'In the period 2007–2013, consumer policy is uniquely well placed to help the EU rise to the challenges of growth and jobs and re-connecting with its citizens.' (European Commission 2007a: 3). Such statements indicate that the political opportunity structures for CSOs to participate in policy-making processes on consumer issues are rather open. How do consumer associations from Germany access these European and Europeanized policy-making arenas?

In Germany, consumer protection emerged as a policy area after the Second World War. It has traditionally been an affair of the state. The first regional consumer associations were set-up by government agencies in the 1950s and have retained close links to state institutions. These regional consumer associations have almost no individual members and rely on public funding. In 2001, the government redesigned ministerial competencies and created the Federal Ministry for Consumer Affairs, Food and Agriculture, putting consumer issues permanently on the political agenda. The most important insider group to the core of the policy community on consumer issues is the national peak association, Federation of German Consumer Organisations (VZBV). In the larger issue network around the core, we find 'independent' CSOs like Foodwatch and Greenpeace. A logic of influence determines the strategies of VZBV and a logic of reputation becomes discernible with the group of confident outsiders.

In the more complex figuration on consumer issues, VZBV occupies the central position. It was created in 2001 as a merger of several associations and unites 42 CSOs under its roof. Of these member associations, 16 are government-financed regional consumer centres. In the main office building in Berlin, up to one hundred persons are working on consumer affairs (interview VZBV). Taking all regional consumer centres and staffed CSOs together, around 1,000 experts across Germany are professionally active in political interest representation for consumers.

The actual work of aggregating, articulating, and representing interests towards policy-makers is done in Berlin.

The relative centrality compared to other CSOs in the policy field becomes apparent when looking at the access to decision-making arenas, financial resources, and the inclusion in organizational networks. A close reading of the annual report of 2009/2010 is revealing: The budget of VZBV in the year 2009 had an overall volume of €23 million including €13.8 million of project-related money that comes from various governmental bodies. The regular income of €9.3 million is also largely government-funded: 92.5 per cent comes from the Federal Ministry for Consumer Affairs, Food and Agriculture. Fees from CSO members amount to €23,750, a share of only 0.3 per cent of the regular budget (VZBV 2010). The budget numbers indicate the limits of the strategic influence of member organizations on the national umbrella. VZBV is in a strong intermediary position and relatively autonomous from its members.

The centrality of VZBV in this more complex figuration becomes even more visible when the integration into the policy community on consumer issues is highlighted. VZBV representatives are involved in regular consultations with various committees of almost all federal ministries. They have institutionalized contacts with numerous federal agencies on the national level and they have a seat on more than 20 advisory boards of consumer-related organizations, companies, and foundations on the national level (VZBV 2010).

Also at the European and international level, numerous formal and informal networks secure the exchange of information on developments in consumer policy. Institutionalized contacts exist with Consumers International (CI), European Council for Energy Efficient Economy (eceee), and Health Action International Europe (HAI Europe). VZBV representatives sit on the executive board and participate in several expert groups of the European umbrella BEUC (Bureau Européen des Unions de Consommateurs). In comparison with other national associations, VZBV provides the largest share of BEUC's membership fees. The relative significance and political weight in relation to other national consumer CSOs is indicated by the fact that VZBV is the only national consumer association in the EU that has a seat on the European Economic and Social Committee (EESC). VZBV is a very well-networked actor on the europolitical field, with many institutionalized access routes to relevant arenas.

For many years, the link towards the 'above' was realized through a government affairs department for 'EU and international relations'. It was staffed with of two full-time positions and one half-time position and was adjoined to the general secretariat. From the Berlin office, common German positions on consumer policy issues were drafted. The staff negotiated these positions at the EU level and also worked on developing transnational partnerships with consumer associations in Eastern Europe. The expert who was head of department and who retired in 2009 after three decades of political advocacy on consumer issues played a key role in networking the VZBV in the europolitical field. After her retirement, the set-up of departments within the national umbrella was fundamentally restructured. The example not only illustrates that figurations change when people change, it also reminds us that individuals and their biographies are important to understand the dynamics and effects of interest representation of CSOs.

What are the representative claims of the VZBV that link the organization with the 'below'? As can be expected, the size of membership is mentioned as an important argument. The organization claims to be 'the voice of consumers' and to speak for '20 million individual members' (VZBV 2010). The '20-million-member' claim is, however, more or less a rough estimate. It refers to individual members that are integrated by second- or third-degree affiliation. Some of the member organizations are national umbrellas themselves. For example, the German Tenants Union represents three million individual members. Other CSOs are political sections within larger organizational formations. The Association of Catholic Families can be seen as part of the Catholic Church and the German Country Women's Association has close ties with the German Farmers Federation, the key actor of the agricultural lobby. VZBV is an 'organization of organizations' and does not represent the volunteer-based stereotype of a CSO.

VZBV is located at the peak of a federally organized network of associations and can reach the local level via information desks in the 16 *Länder* and via a sophisticated communication system. Infrastructures of member organizations also establish responsive communication routes to citizens on the local level. These linkages guarantee that urgent concerns, neglected issues, and policy deficiencies are channelled upwards from citizens to the experts in Berlin – and then beyond.[6] The participation in numerous committees and working groups with government officials on the national and the European level ensure that the representative claims are based on effective chains of delegation. The acceptance of VZBV is based on being recognized by decision-makers from European and national arenas. VZBV provides expertise to policy-makers and can sustain the representative claims by unbroken hierarchical chains of delegation.

The confident outsiders on the political field, Foodwatch and Greenpeace, are CSOs that are active in the protest business (cf. Jordan and Maloney 2007: 147). They claim to be 'independent' from business and state contributions and are reluctant to join consultations and establish formally institutionalized relations with policy-makers. Their prime concern is to influence public opinion. Since campaigning groups have to finance their activities with donations, they need to be visible in the public to fundraise successfully. The claims to be 'independent' are part of a strategy to bolster their political reputation as being untainted, pure, and unbiased pursuers of public interests. Since the concept of figuration makes us sensitive towards interdependencies, we have to see that these campaigning groups are depending on journalists and other gatekeepers of the media to gain public attention and secure the means for the organization's survival.

Foodwatch has become for consumer questions in Germany what Greenpeace is for environmental concerns. It is the one CSO that is asked by the media to comment on food scandals. The media presence is enormous, taking into account that the office is staffed with just a dozen persons and runs on a budget of €920,000 (interview Foodwatch). Similarities between Foodwatch and Greenpeace in organizational structures, strategies, and tactical repertoires are not a coincidence. Also in this case, the representative's biography explains a lot. Foodwatch was founded by Thilo Bode in 2002; he had been the secretary general of Greenpeace Germany (1989–1995) and of Greenpeace International (1995–2001).

In most campaigning groups (and Foodwatch is an example of this type), the leaders decide the issues and themes that are scandalized (cf. Jordan and Maloney 2007: 10). With regard to membership and institutionalized linkages to the 'below', these organizations opt for a different strategy. They prefer supporters, because members with voting rights would be a 'nonlucrative distraction' (Skocpol 2003: 134). The statutes of Foodwatch restrict the number of members with voting rights to less than 100. Not members, but supporters, are a key resource for the organization's survival, and the numbers of supporters are rising. In January 2007, Foodwatch claimed to have more than 10,000 supporters; in July 2010 the numbers had reached 17,000. According to the website, more than 60,000 users receive the organization's newsletter. The problem with supporters and website users is that they are not full members. While credit-card activism implies recognition of the organization's aims and objectives, it does not necessarily strengthen the internal democracy within CSOs.

Campaigning CSOs do not fulfil the same kind of transmission-belt function as volunteer-based CSOs. Linkages to the 'above' and the 'below' are of a different quality in these triadic figurations. They are not responsive two-way, but one-way, channels of communication. Foodwatch's strategy towards policy-makers is usually based on confrontation. They are addressed with criticism. Negotiations in the arenas of policy-makers are not really necessary. And while national umbrella organizations are located at the peak of a 'pyramid of delegation', campaigning CSOs rather 'float on public opinion'. Their constituencies are not easily identifiable and may not even exist as a clearly distinguishable social group of people.

Consequently, the objects of the representative claims of these campaigning CSOs are broad public interests and as such rather general and diffuse. A respondent from Greenpeace said the organization represents 'the environment and consumers' (interview Greenpeace). Everyone is a consumer. Foodwatch claims to represent 'those who want to get democracy on their plate' (interview Foodwatch). Everyone likes democracy. The referents of these claims are fluid crowds. Those who can be attracted to publicly support a campaign can get disinterested quickly. Those who assemble for a rally disassemble thereafter and do not leave traces. Donors cannot always be identified. Many CSOs are dealing with volatile constituencies and they can at best make educated guesses that their supporters share post-materialist values and come from a green-liberal political milieu (interview Foodwatch).

Regarding the Europeanization of consumer issues, Foodwatch encounters the problem of national media publics. It depends on citizen-donors who have to be addressed through national media infrastructures. It makes little sense to fight a battle in Brussels where there is no broad public audience. The preferred media framing for a successful campaign requires an audience that can be convinced to support 'David against Goliath', as Foodwatch's leader described the ideal setting. The authenticity and authority of Foodwatch and Greenpeace as representatives are based on their ability to politicize and to attract attention. Because they position themselves as critical opposition to governments and claim to be 'watchdogs' of some sort, they are often cheered by media and citizens but scorned by policy-makers.

Confrontation is the preferred choice for Greenpeace and Foodwatch. Responsive relations exist only with a relatively small constituency that is addressed with newsletters and through their websites that feature options to participate in campaigns, for example, signing online petitions, downloading protest letters and information packages for product boycotts. Not surprisingly, these CSOs also use Facebook and Twitter to connect with their audiences. To sustain their argument to be representatives, campaigning CSOs are at pains to show that they are supported by public opinion. Consequently, representative claims are backed up with references to adequate polling results. Media resonance in itself is often seen as evidence of the salience of the issues.

In this sense, Foodwatch and Greenpeace can be described as dogmatic democrats with tendencies for critical populism, for example when crooked companies are called to account for health hazards that were identified by investigative research. Representatives of 'independent' CSOs frequently point out that they can say and do what national peak associations that depend on government funds cannot do. Their representative claims are based on being disconnected from the state, something that Saward calls untaintedness (2009: 19–20). At the same time, even though confident outsiders keep their distance from insider groups like VZBV, all consumer CSOs work towards the same direction. They form a dynamic issue alliance working on empowering consumer-citizens.

Conclusion

What can be taken from the case studies to understand political representation by CSOs? Once CSO experts gain access to decision-making circles, they pass modern rites of institution which authorize their inclusion in these circles (Bourdieu 2000: 242–45). They gain the capacity to actually negotiate in the name of their constituencies only after being recognized by political institutions. Recognition is a prerequisite and must come from those in power. Admittance to consultations, being called upon as experts, or being referenced in the media with a campaign, all add to the inclusion of the representatives or their concerns into policy processes. Sometimes also public protests do the job.

To make representative claims convincing, the size of membership is often referenced. Size indicates the possibility of mobilizing supporters and the capacity to frame public opinion. Membership signifies a broad societal base and responsive communication channels are associated with a 'pyramid of delegation'. Together, they are usually convincing evidence for policy-makers that a CSO can responsibly negotiate political interests for its constituencies. Campaigning CSOs deviate from this pattern and try to instrumentalize their outsider status as being independent and untainted from the interests of governments and business actors.

Beyond these contextual settings of CSOs within more complex figurations, representatives from unelected actors repeatedly stressed that on the micro-level, the most important elements of political interest representation are expert knowledge, personal contacts, and mutual trust. Organizational backgrounds are of course not unimportant. Especially the Churches, but also CSOs that rely on public funds for their regular budget, can provide relatively safe working conditions. They stabilize the dynamics of the figurations and allow building up expertise within the CSOs. In some instances, staff had been active in political interest representation for more than 30 years. Without the continuous effort of these persons, the CSO would not be linked to the relevant policy arenas and would not have established their position in the europolitical field as they did. Backed by institutional infrastructures, organizational resources, and political reputation of a CSO, individual personalities and their biographies are important sources that determine who gains acceptance as a representative.

To gain acceptance, activists who embody their organization need to create felicitous performances in front of the relevant audiences. The staging and *mise-en-scène* matters. Embedded in triadic figurations between supporters and policy-makers, they need to convince policy-makers that they speak for their constituencies, and supporters need to be convinced that the representatives can actually influence the policy process. Even though mediatized representative claims should not be neglected, at the end of the day, political advocacy work requires face-to-face interactions. It is in those settings that authority and authenticity are established and CSOs can gain or lose acceptance as unelected representatives.

Notes

1. CSOs that become active in political advocacy share three central characteristics with interest groups: political orientation, organization and informality (Eising 2008). Political orientation refers to the focus on monitoring and influencing policy processes. Organization means that they have institutionalized infrastructures, often with paid staff. Informality indicates that they refrain from claiming public offices and retain informal ways of working in the political field. Their self-image as a CSO is based on largely uncontested claims to 'be' civil society. To realize these claims the activists have to perform according to a civil society script. It includes that they narrate the founding of their organization to be rooted in social movements and that the CSO emerged from self-organizing society. They claim to promote public interests and seek to strengthen democracy. The dominant modes of behaviour are civil (peaceful protests, debates, dialogues and other non-vio-

lent modes of solving conflicts). They make use of a normative democratic rhetoric and thus imagine, practice and stage their identity as civil society (Eder 2011).

2. Figurations are characterized by fluctuating and unstable power balances, meaning that they are dynamic and that they have a political dimension. And they have a certain history as they usually evolve and transform in longer processes that stretch over generations (Schlichte and Jentges 2009).
3. Interviews were semi-structured, lasted on average 90 minutes and covered organizational structures, aims and objectives, participation in European policy-making and perceptions of the debates on the EU's legitimacy and the future of European integration. They were conducted in 2007. Secondary data sources such as press articles, publications for members (newsletters, magazines, annual reports, etc.), and the websites of CSOs were used to supplement and contextualize narrative accounts.
4. Article 17 of the consolidated version of the Treaty on the Functioning of the European Union: '1. The Union respects and does not prejudice the status under national law of churches and religious associations or communities in the Member States. 2. The Union equally respects the status under national law of philosophical and non-confessional organisations. 3. Recognising their identity and their specific contribution, the Union shall maintain an open, transparent and regular dialogue with these churches and organisations.'
5. An anecdote may help to illustrate the contentiousness of representative claims. ZdK has a facebook site where the claim is part of the self-portrait in the 'about us' section (http://www.facebook.com/ZdK.Bonn). As can happen, a facebook site 'The ZdK does not represent me!' was opened earlier in 2010 by critics (http://www.facebook.com/pages/Mich-vertritt-nicht-das-ZdK/117935994909427). Currently, followers of the critical site outnumber the ZdK by 441 to 196 (January 25, 2011). However, joining virtual groups and clicking the 'I like' button on Facebook indicate identity issues of users rather than politically motivated activism.
6. A similar infrastructure for the generation of information is provided by ECC-Net, a recently installed EU-wide network that is financed by the Commission. It monitors and reports on consumer policies across Europe and thus assists policymakers to evaluate the effectiveness and status of implementation of European legislation (interview EVZ).

Annex 1 Sample of organizations

Consumer protection	Verbraucherzentrale Bundesverband – Stabsstelle Europa	VZBV
	Stiftung Warentest – Internationales und Europaabteilung	StWt
	Europäisches Verbraucherzentrum Kiel	EVZ
	Deutscher Mieterbund – Europaabteilung	DMB
	Verbraucherzentrale Hamburg	VZHH
	Greenpeace Deutschland	Greenpeace
	Foodwatch	Foodwatch
Religion	Evangelische Kirche in Deutschland – Bevollmächtigter des Rates der evangelischen Kirche in Deutschland bei der BRD und der EU	EKD1
	Evangelische Kirche in Deutschland – Europaabteilung	EKD2
	Katholisches Büro der Deutschen Bischofskonferenz	DBK
	Zentralkomitee der Katholiken	ZdK
	Zentralrat der Juden	ZdJ
	Humanistischer Verband Deutschlands	HVD
	ProChrist	ProChrist
	Zentralrat der Muslime/ Koordinationsrat der Muslime	ZdM
	Zentralrat der Ex-Muslime	ZdExM
	Internationaler Bund der Konfessionslosen und Atheisten	IBKA
	Islamrat	IR

Part III

Repercussions of the EU on Political Representation

10

From the Margins of European Integration to the Guardians of the Treaties? The Role of National Parliaments in the EU

Tapio Raunio

Introduction

The role of national legislatures in the political system of the European Union (EU) first received serious political and academic attention in the mid-1990s in connection with debates on how to cure the EU's democratic deficit (Norton 1995; Raunio 1999). Since then, the role of national parliaments has featured quite prominently on the research agenda of both parliamentary and EU scholars, with several comparative research projects on national parliamentary scrutiny of EU policies completed during the first decade of the new millennium (Bergman and Damgaard eds 2000; Maurer and Wessels eds 2001; Auel and Benz eds 2005; Szalay 2005; Gates 2006; Kiiver 2006; Kiiver ed. 2006; Holzhacker and Albæk eds 2007; O´Brennan and Raunio eds 2007; Tans et al. eds 2007; Barrett ed. 2008). Thanks to this lively academic debate, we are now in a much better position to evaluate how national legislatures are affected by European integration.

European integration has presented a major challenge to national parliaments. According to the so-called 'deparliamentarization' thesis, the development of European integration has led to the erosion of parliamentary control over the executive branch. This argument is based both on constitutional rules and on the political dynamics of the EU policy process (Raunio and Hix 2000; O'Brennan and Raunio 2007). The EU Member States have transferred policy-making powers to the European level in a broad and significant range of questions and, as a result, parliaments have directly lost influence. The increased use of qualified majority voting and the bargaining in the Council and the European Council, in turn, make it difficult for national parliaments to force governments to make detailed *ex ante* commitments before decision-taking at the European level. But the main point is that national governments represent their countries in EU negotiations and hence this results in informational asymmetries between the executive branch and the legislature. Considering the dominance of this deparliamentarization thesis in both scholarly work and political debate, it is not surprising that national parliaments are often labelled as the main 'losers' or 'victims' of European integration (Goetz and Meyer-Sahling 2008; Raunio 2009b).[1]

Utilizing parliamentary functions as its theoretical framework, this chapter examines how national parliaments understand their role in EU governance. The next section discusses the various functions of parliaments and explains how these relate to European integration. The third section is divided into two parts, with the first part introducing the data and the method and the second part consisting of an empirical analysis of the documents produced by the European Convention and the Conference of Community and European Affairs Committees of Parliaments of the European Union (COSAC). While there is no longitudinal data that would enable us to analyse how national members of parliament (MP) perceive their role in European integration, both the Convention and COSAC are unique in the sense that they have brought together parliamentarians across Europe to reflect on the past and future role of national parliaments in EU affairs. The analysis shows that, when debating the role of national parliaments in the EU political system, domestic MPs emphasize functions related to government and policy-making, with functions relating to citizens receiving little attention. As summarized in the concluding section, this focus is more pronounced in Member States where the role of the parliament is more emphasized domestically and where the parties and the electorates are more Euro-sceptical. National parliaments are also increasingly seen as gatekeepers between national and EU politics, with the early warning system included in the Lisbon Treaty reinforcing this perception of domestic MPs acting as 'guardians of Treaties'.

The functions of parliaments

Establishing a complete list of the functions carried out by parliaments is difficult, if not almost impossible (Copeland and Patterson 1994:

153–54). Students of parliament have in fact paid surprisingly little attention to such typologies of functions. William Bagehot (1867) compiled a list of five functions: the elective function (choosing the cabinet); expressing the mind of the people; teaching the nation; informing the people; and the legislative function. But the 'classic' text is Robert Packenham (1970), who identified 11 functions that parliaments perform. Packenham divided his functions into three categories: 1) legitimation: latent (meeting regularly), manifest (formally approving public policy), safety valve or tension release (outlet for tensions); 2) recruitment, socialization, and training; and 3) decisional or influence functions: law-making, 'exit' (resolving an impasse on the system), interest articulation, conflict resolution, and administrative oversight and patronage (including 'errand running' for constituents). As Packenham based his study mainly on the Brazilian congress, he emphasized the potential role that a parliament can perform in the political system and in society at large. Packenham also rank-ordered the functions, with the legitimation function having the most consequence for the political system and the decisional functions having least significance.

In his book on the UK parliament, Philip Norton (1993) reworked Packenham's list by adding the function of educating the people and mobilizing support for particular policies. Norton also dropped the exit function, employed the category of seeking a redress of grievance, and broke the law-making function down to two phases – initiation and formulation, and legislation. Norton then divided the functions into two groups: those that relate to the government and those that focus on parliament's links with the citizens. This chapter follows Norton's approach by dividing the functions under the same two headings: government and citizen. Obviously one can argue that such a division into governmental and citizen functions is arbitrary or too simplistic as MPs are always representing citizens when performing various parliamentary activities. For example, MPs can be considered to be representing their constituents when scrutinizing EU legislation behind the closed doors in the European Affairs Committees (EAC). Alternatively one can argue that plenary debates should be seen primarily as a form of scrutiny as opposed to serving the function of articulating and representing interests. However, the main difference is that in governmental functions the parliament and the MPs interact primarily with the executive, whereas in citizen-related functions the emphasis is on representing or informing the electorate. Secondly, it is essential that the electorate can, either directly or indirectly via the media, access or follow parliamentary work. Hence, citizen-related functions need to be accessible

Table 10.1 The functions of national parliaments in domestic and EU politics

Function	National politics	EU politics
Citizen		
Acting as a safety valve and achieving a redress of grievance	Releasing tensions about national politics and taking care of demands from constituents	Releasing tensions about EU policy and taking care of EU-related demands from constituents
Mobilizing and educating citizens	Informing the citizens about national policies and mobilizing support for them	Informing the citizens about EU / national EU policy and mobilizing support for them
Interest articulation	Reflecting the views of organized interests and the electorate in domestic politics	Reflecting the views of organized interests and the electorate in European policy
Government		
Recruitment, socializing and training ministers	Recruiting and electing the members of the government	
Government oversight	Holding the government accountable	Holding the government accountable in EU affairs
Law making	Approving and amending national laws	Indirect; scrutiny of EU laws that are decided by the Council (increasingly together with the EP and by QMV)
Latent legitimation	Meets regularly and uninterruptedly (provides legitimacy to the political system)	Meets regularly and uninterruptedly (provides legitimacy to national EU policy)
Manifest legitimation	Formally approving public policy	Formally approving EU laws
International networking		Bilateral and multi-lateral interparliamentary cooperation

to the public – either in the form of live or televised coverage (like plenary debates) or of having access to the documents (like parliamentary questions). As the functions of parliaments were initially compiled in the context of national systems, it is also essential to examine whether all of these functions are applicable in the case of how national parliaments get involved in European affairs (Table 10.1).

Let us first examine the functions that relate to the linkage between citizens and parliaments. I have combined the functions of acting as a safety valve and achieving a redress of grievance into one category. However, I have retained interest articulation as a separate category. Acting as a safety valve and achieving a redress of grievance relate to parliaments', and specifically to MPs', contacts with constituents – releasing tensions and taking care of demands from the constituents. Interest articulation, instead, refers to the parliament reflecting the views of the whole electorate in societal affairs. Hence I use this function more broadly than Packenham and Norton, who primarily referred to parliaments articulating the views of organized interests, political parties, and interest groups. Mobilizing and educating citizens refers to the ability of the parliament to 'teach the nation' about issues and to increase support for specific policies. In the case of the EU, this function can refer to teaching the citizens about integration or mobilizing support for EU or national EU policy (which may be at odds with one another). I have excluded the function of conflict resolution as it is already incorporated into the functions of interest articulation and acting as a safety valve and achieving a redress of grievance.

The second set of functions deals with parliament–executive relations. The function of recruiting, socializing, and training ministers only applies to national politics, as domestic legislatures do not recruit or elect members of the Commission or the persons for any positions in the EU institutions. Government oversight refers to the parliament holding the cabinet accountable, both in national and EU politics. As for law-making, with the partial exception of Treaty amendments and other issues decided by unanimity, in EU affairs the influence of national parliaments is mainly limited to scrutinizing the Commission's initiatives and to influencing the government that represents the country (and can find itself in the losing minority in matters decided by qualified majority) at the European level. In terms of latent legitimation, through meeting regularly and practically uninterruptedly, the parliament provides legitimacy to national governance. In European affairs, this aspect of legitimation applies directly only to national EU policy (and, perhaps, by extension to the whole process of European integration). The function of manifest legitimation operates partly in the same way in both national and EU politics: the parliament legitimates public policy through formally approving domestic laws and those European laws (such as Treaty amendments) that require the approval of national parliaments.[2]

I have also added to the list the function of international networking, as national parliaments engage in the EU in both bilateral – between individual parliaments or between a national parliament and the European Parliament (EP) – and multi-lateral interparliamentary cooperation, with the latter exercised mainly through COSAC (Larhant 2005; Neunreither 2005).[3] Obviously national parliaments have also other kinds of international contacts, but it is plausible to argue that such interparliamentary cooperation has become (really) much more extensive and regular through the EU (see the chapter by Fasone in this volume).

Turning to legal regulations, national constitutions typically give domestic legislatures certain rights (such as to receive information from the government on EU affairs) and set them specific responsibilities (such as transposing directives or approving Treaty amendments), with the constitutions often also containing rules about how EU matters are processed by parliaments. Beyond such rules, parliaments are free to decide how and whether to become involved in EU politics. Treaties of the EU give national parliaments certain rights (such as to receive EU documents) and allocate them certain specific duties that mainly deal with the division of competencies between the EU and its Member States.

The Lisbon Treaty is the first time that national parliaments are mentioned in the actual main text of the EU's 'constitution' – as opposed to Protocols and Declarations attached to previous Treaties. According to Article 10 (2) 'Citizens are directly represented at Union level in the European Parliament. Member States are represented in the European Council by their Heads of State or Government and in the Council by their governments, themselves democratically accountable either to their national Parliaments, or to their citizens.'[4] Indeed, the main Treaty-derived function of national parliaments is to control their governments that represent Member States in the Council and the European Council. Article 12, in turn, lists the basic functions of national parliaments and refers to the two Protocols attached to the Lisbon Treaty that focus on domestic legislatures: the Protocol on the role of national parliaments in the European Union and the Protocol on the application of the principles of subsidiarity and proportionality. The former is designed to make national MPs better informed about the European decision-making process and essentially strengthens and consolidates similar provisions attached to the Maastricht and Amsterdam Treaties. But the main novelty of the Lisbon Treaty is the 'early warning system', with the national legislatures assigned the right to monitor whether initiatives for EU laws comply with the principle of subsidiarity. In addition, national parliaments have some specific rights referred to in

Article 12, such as having a stronger role in Treaty revision (COSAC 2008: 20–6). It is worth emphasizing that practically all of the rights and responsibilities assigned by the Treaties deal with government-related functions of parliaments – mainly with the functions of government oversight, law making, and manifest legitimation.

The next section examines which of these parliamentary functions have received attention in the European Convention and COSAC. More specifically, the empirical analysis illustrates how domestic MPs are primarily concerned about government accountability and that these concerns are more prominent in Member States where the parliament has traditionally occupied a stronger role in public policy-making.

Empirical analysis of convention and COSAC documents

Data and method

The empirical data consists of European Convention and COSAC documents. As explained in the introductory section, this data was chosen because both forums are exceptional in the sense that they have brought together MPs from across the EU to debate the role of national parliaments in European integration. Hence these discussions and documents enable us to examine how domestic parliamentarians understand their role in EU governance. Subsequently, these two forums are briefly introduced; the analysis of the data then follows in the second part of this section.

The role of national parliaments featured quite prominently on the agenda of the Convention on the future of Europe (2002–2003). This was perhaps not that surprising given that national MPs comprised 56 out of 105 Convention members. The Convention established a Working Group (WG IV) entitled 'The role of national parliaments', while their role in monitoring the subsidiarity principle was primarily discussed in WG I on 'The principle of subsidiarity'. The proceedings of the Convention illustrated both the desire to improve national scrutiny of governments in EU matters and the lack of enthusiasm for the establishment of a collective organ of national MPs or for changing the functions of COSAC (Brown 2003; Raunio 2007). But the Convention did result in a novel institutional innovation by introducing the 'early warning system', with the national legislatures assigned the right to monitor whether initiatives for EU decisions comply with the principle of subsidiarity (CONV 286/02; CONV 353/02).[5] The data consists of the 48 working documents (WD) and a final report produced by WGIV.[6] The selection of categories found in Table 10.2 was driven primarily by the mandate of WGIV, whereas the categorization was based on simply reading the documents and then assigning them into one category depending on the main emphasis of the WD.

COSAC is the main forum for interparliamentary cooperation (Bengtson 2007; Knudsen and Carl 2008). The biannual COSAC meetings bring together delegations from the EACs of the national parliaments and the EP. COSAC decides normally by consensus, but following a rule change adopted in May 2003, its non-binding decisions (called 'contributions') can be passed with three-quarters of votes cast (which must constitute at last half of all votes). COSAC also has a secretariat in Brussels. According to the Protocol on the Role of the National Parliaments in the European Union attached to the Amsterdam Treaty, COSAC 'may make any contribution it deems appropriate' for the attention of EU institutions. The areas of freedom, security and justice, fundamental rights, and subsidiarity were mentioned as areas where COSAC could be particularly active. However, 'contributions made by COSAC shall in no way bind national parliaments or prejudge their position'.[7] According to COSAC's rules of procedure, it 'enables a regular exchange of views, without prejudicing the competences of the parliamentary bodies of the European Union'.[8]

Agendas of COSAC meetings are drawn up by the body's leadership (the Presidency and the Presidential Troika assisted by the COSAC secretariat) paying account to the provisions of the Amsterdam Treaty's Protocol and to the working programmes of the EU institutions. The Presidential Troika consists of the Presidency, the preceding Presidency, the next Presidency, and the EP. The Presidency is held by the parliament of the country holding the Presidency of the Council. But 'the principal business on every draft Agenda shall be derived from COSAC's role as a body for exchanging information, in particular on the practical aspects of parliamentary scrutiny'.[9] Within these limits, COSAC is free to choose its own role and agenda items.

For COSAC, the primary data consists of its biannual reports published between 2004 and 2009. The first such report was published in May 2004 and by the end of 2009 COSAC had produced 12 reports. These reports have in turn been divided into 58 chapters, which also form the basis of the categorization found in Table 10.3.[10] The selection of categories was driven primarily by the 'mandate' of COSAC (as stated in the Treaty of Amsterdam and in COSAC's rules of procedure). COSAC produces three kinds of documents: brief contributions, conclusions, and longer biannual reports. Contributions and conclusions are short notes adopted at the end of the meetings, with the conclusions summarizing the sessions and the contributions, in the spirit of the Amsterdam Treaty, adopting positions on various items that should be addressed by the EU institutions (such as emphasizing the importance of the Lisbon strategy or calling on the Commission and the Council to adopt procedures that facilitate national parliamentary scrutiny). Biannual reports are more detailed analyses or comparisons of the involvement of national parliaments in the EU's policy process, often based on questionnaires circulated among national parliaments. COSAC secretariat shall 'compile a factual report on developments in EU procedures and practices relevant to parliamentary scrutiny every six months in order to provide the basis for debate in COSAC'.[11] COSAC is free to decide the content of these reports and, hence, they provide a good indicator of what are the main interests of COSAC.[12]

Analysis

WG IV of the European Convention convened on 26 June 2002 and submitted its final report on 22 October 2002 (CONV 353/02). The Praesidium issued a discussion paper on 29 May which was 'intended to serve as a basis for the discussions on that subject in the plenary session of the Convention on 6 and 7 June'. That paper discussed three sets of functions or proposals related to national parliaments: enhanced scrutiny of national governments in EU affairs; Treaty amendments providing for compulsory consultation of domestic legislatures; and potential changes to interparliamentary cooperation and the EU's institutional architecture (CONV 67/02). In a subsequent Praesidium note, published two days later (CONV 68/02), Convention members were encouraged to use that plenary debate to give 'preliminary guidance' to WG IV, and the Praesidium listed five questions that were meant to guide the plenary debate. The first question put forward was 'how could one assist the national Parliaments to play their crucial role in ensuring the democratic legitimacy of Union action?'

The mandate of WG IV had meanwhile been outlined by the chair, Gisela Stuart, in a paper circulated on 30 May (CONV 74/02) that set the terms of reference for the WG as follows: How is the role of national parliaments exercised in the current architecture of the European Union? What national arrangements function best? Is there a need to consider new mechanisms/procedures at national level or at European level? It went on to state that the WG

> will therefore concentrate its attention on the following matters: consideration of existing scrutiny and consultation mechanisms of

> national parliaments at national level, with a view to drawing attention to those systems which work best; examination of those aspects of legislative procedures and working practices at European level which may create difficulties for national parliaments attempting to carry out effective scrutiny of their governments' activities; reflection on the role we believe national parliaments could/should play; identification and evaluation of the different means by which we enable parliaments to fulfil this role in the future by examining the proposals made by Convention members and others for formal and/or informal involvement of national parliaments at European level.

Considering these guidelines and instructions for subsequent debates, it is hardly surprising that the plenary debate, held before WG IV commenced its work (CONV 97/02), and the agenda of WG IV focused almost exclusively on these same topics. The thematic focus was confirmed by the final report of the WG, according to which the 'work of the Group can be brought under three distinct headings: the role of national parliaments in scrutinizing governments (national scrutiny systems); the role of national parliaments in monitoring the application of the principle of subsidiarity; the role and function of multilateral networks or mechanisms involving national parliaments at the European level' (CONV 353/02). Also the plenary debates on national parliaments, held after the WG had concluded its work, focused on the same themes (CONV 378/02; CONV 630/03).

Categorization of the documents produced by WG IV shows how the work and the discussion in the WG were structured around the themes specified in its mandate (Table 10.2). Seventeen documents were comments on the draft final report of the WG, with the delegates providing quite detailed and minor comments on the wording of specific points. Ten documents were general papers on the role of national parliaments in EU governance. However, these papers focused almost exclusively on the themes specified in the Praesidium discussion paper and in the mandate of WG IV (CONV 67/02; CONV 74/02) – mainly scrutiny of government in EU matters, various forms of interparliamentary cooperation, and the monitoring of the subsidiarity principle. Nine documents were descriptions of how scrutiny of EU affairs works in individual parliaments. Monitoring the subsidiarity principle was the main focus of four documents. Also four documents highlighted challenges or problems related to scrutiny performed by individual parliaments, such as the delays in receiving information about legislative proposals or the closed nature of Council meetings. None of the documents focused mainly

Table 10.2 Categorization of the working documents of WGIV in the convention

Category	Focus of document	Total (n = 48)
Final report	Comments on the proposed final report	17
General contributions	Papers that discuss the role of national parliaments in EU governance (on the basis of the WG's mandate)	10
Models of national scrutiny	Descriptions of how scrutiny of EU affairs operates in the country	9
Scrutiny	Papers on problems related to scrutiny by individual parliaments	4
Subsidiarity	Monitoring of the subsidiarity principle	4
Interparliamentary cooperation	Forms of cooperation between national parliaments or between EP and domestic legislatures	
Citizens	The parliament as a forum for debate or information about EU	
Other	Documents that do not fit any of the above categories	4

on interparliamentary cooperation. Finally, four documents were not assigned to any of the categories.[13]

Examining the distribution of WDs between nationalities, most active members came from Member States that normally both emphasize the value of national parliaments and also have more stringent control mechanisms in EU matters. Finland and Sweden provided five WDs, Denmark and the Netherlands four, Cyprus (and the Commission) three, France, Ireland, Italy, Luxembourg, Malta, Portugal, and the United Kingdom two each, with delegates from Austria, Belgium, Hungary, and Poland providing one WD. When considering also that the WG was chaired by a British delegate, it is clear that the more 'northern' member countries largely dominated the proceedings and showed more interest in the topic. In fact, many of the contributions from Central and Southern European delegates were more cautious about strengthening the role of national legislatures, preferring instead to emphasize the role of the EP.

None of the documents focused on how national legislatures could 'link' with citizens in EU affairs (for example, through plenary debates or providing information about EU to the electorate). Some WDs mentioned the need for debating EU matters in national parliaments, arguing that this could bring Europe closer to citizens.[14] Interestingly, while several WDs argued that the Council should become a more open and transparent institution (particularly when acting in legislative capacity), only one delegate explicitly argued for increased domestic parliamentary transparency.[15] Arguments on citizen-related functions were thus clearly exceptional in both the WDs and in actual discussions of the WG. The WG nonetheless ended up recommending in its final report a specific 'European week' for holding simultaneous debates on the EU's policy agenda:

> As a part of the process to bring the EU closer to the debate within Member States the Working Group further recommends that once every year an EU-wide European week be organised to coincide with the presentation of the Commission's annual policy strategy. This would create a common window for debates in the national parliaments, involving Members of the European Parliament, and possibly also Members of the European Commission as well as representatives of national governments, thus raising national awareness of the activities of the European Union. These European weeks would require a certain coordination of scheduling of the European Parliament and national parliaments, to ensure that MEPs [members of the European Parliament] have the possibility to take active part in the national debate. (CONV 353/02)

Despite receiving wide support in the WG and in the plenary, the 'European Week' was not included in the Draft Treaty establishing a constitution for Europe published on 18 July 2003, but a week later the Convention President, Valéry Giscard d'Estaing, received a declaration from two Convention delegates (and co-signed by 50 Convention members and alternates), requesting that the idea of 'European week' be transmitted to the forthcoming Intergovernmental Conference (CONV 834/03).

COSAC picked up on this idea the following year[16] and re-stated its position in late 2004, calling 'on the European Conference of Speakers to provide for its prompt implementation by putting forward a proposal, in consultation with the European Parliament, on the specific week in which all the national parliaments will hold a debate on the annual legislative and work programme of the European Commission'.[17] COSAC (2005: 38–41) reviewed the situation in the summer and fall of 2005, noting that at least the parliaments of Austria, Belgium, the Czech Republic, the Netherlands, Slovenia, and Sweden had either held such debates or were planning to organize them. However, many parliaments showed little interest in such debates. It appears that since

Table 10.3 Categorization of COSAC reports

Category	**Focus of document**	**Chapters of biannual reports (n = 58)**
Scrutiny of policies	Comparisons or reports on national scrutiny of specific EU policies	18
National scrutiny	Comparisons or reports on national EU scrutiny procedures	12
EU institutions	Comments on the roles or working procedures of EU institutions	9
Constitutional process	Comments or reports on the 'constitutional process' resulting in the Lisbon Treaty	8
Subsidiarity	Monitoring of the subsidiarity principle	6
Interparliamentary cooperation	Forms of cooperation between national parliaments or between EP and domestic legislatures	2
Citizens	The parliament as a forum for debate or information about EU	2
Other functions	Documents that do not fit any of the above categories	1

then the initiative has quietly withered away, with few such 'European weeks' organized in domestic parliaments.

Categorization of COSAC's biannual reports produces a rather similar picture (Table 10.3). Half of the items in the reports focused on national scrutiny, with 18 of the chapters comparing parliamentary involvement in various EU policies (Schengen area, the Mediterranean Dimension, Common Foreign and Security Policy, etc.) and 12 comparing national scrutiny procedures. Nine chapters dealt with EU institutions, for example transparency in the Council or the functioning of legislative procedures. Eight chapters looked at the state of the 'constitutional process'; six focused on monitoring subsidiarity; and two on interparliamentary cooperation.

Only two of the chapters focused on citizen-related functions of national parliaments: the comparison of 'European weeks' discussed above and a comparison of the transparency of the national scrutiny procedures contained in the twelfth report.[18] The remaining chapter was an evaluation of the COSAC reports found in the eleventh report. Interestingly, when asked as part of that evaluation to suggest topics for future reports, none of the national parliaments felt that the reports should cover themes that focus on the link between citizens and the EU – such as the parliament providing a forum for debate about Europe or informing the public about the EU (COSAC 2009: 44–5). Examination of the conclusions and contributions also confirms this bias in favour of government-related functions.[19]

Concluding discussion

European integration may not have transformed the basic functions or 'ways of doing things' of national parliaments, but domestic MPs have certainly become increasingly aware of how European integration impacts on their work and on legislature–executive relations at the national level. In addition to concerns about deparliamentarization, there is evidence that EU matters have increased the workload of national legislatures (Raunio and Wiberg 2010). Hence it is perhaps not that surprising to find that the debates at the European level have largely focused on how to recover that ground lost to the executive branch. This chapter has clearly shown how the debates in the Convention and COSAC have been dominated by government-related functions. This was more understandable in the Convention where the WG on national parliaments had a rather specific mandate and was expected to make concrete proposals about whether and how national parliaments should be recognized in the EU's constitution. COSAC in turn has a basically unconstrained agenda and can discuss any issue it wants. It is also worth emphasizing that practically all of the rights and responsibilities of the national parliaments assigned by the EU Treaties deal with government-related functions of parliaments – mainly with the functions of government oversight and law-making.

These concerns about losing ground to the executive have also domestically been more pronounced in countries where the role or sovereignty of the parliament has traditionally been more emphasized and where the parties and the electorates are more Euro-sceptical (see, for example, Maurer and Wessels eds 2001; O´Brennan and Raunio eds 2007; Tans et al. eds 2007; Barrett ed. 2008). It appears that there is a rough 'north-south' divide, with the role of domestic parliaments and national sovereignty in general receiving more attention in the Northern Member States (particularly the three Nordic EU countries, the United Kingdom, and many of the countries that joined the Union in 2004). On average, these are also the countries where citizens are, according to public opinion surveys, more satisfied with how national democracy works.

MPs from these countries were also more active in the WG on national parliaments in the Convention. However, interestingly, the parliamentarians from the more 'Northern' Member States have also been more cautious about EU-level rules on domestic parliamentary EU scrutiny. This attitude appears to be mainly explained by the fact that legislatures with a stronger role both domestically and in EU affairs are worried that too extensive European regulations about national parliaments might undermine or interfere with their established scrutiny practices.

The new role accorded to national parliaments in monitoring subsidiarity can also be seen as belonging to the sphere of legislature–executive relations, with national MPs called upon to check that EU laws respect the division of competencies between the national and European level. There is broad scholarly consensus that the 'early warning system' was mainly introduced in response to legitimacy concerns, and it is probable that its impact will remain modest (for example, Rittberger 2005: 189–92; Kiiver 2006: 153–68; Raunio 2007, 2010). Also the constitutionalization of the Convention procedure and the strong role of national parliaments in the simplified revision procedures – which both, in fact, reduce the likelihood of the subsidiarity control mechanism being used – mean that domestic MPs are now more effectively the 'guardians of the Treaties'.[20] But whatever the impact of the subsidiarity control mechanism, it does reinforce the perception of domestic MPs acting as 'gatekeepers' of European integration.

To conclude, national parliaments, often identified in both academic literature and political discourse as the main losers of European integration, have invested resources into recovering ground lost to the executive branch. In the context of their national political systems, parliaments have reformed their EU scrutiny systems, primarily through upgrading the powers of EACs and gaining better access to information in EU affairs. European level cooperation has largely also focused on facilitating better national scrutiny, with interparliamentary networking in COSAC contributing to the sharing of best practices and Treaty amendments giving national legislatures stronger rights in EU governance. This is of course not bad news, as stronger domestic scrutiny improves the democratic accountability of decision-making in the Council and the European Council through forcing Brussels-bound ministers to explain their positions and negotiating strategies to the parliamentarians.

But perhaps the main message of this chapter is that the electoral dimension of representation has clearly received less attention than government accountability – both at the European level (COSAC, Convention, Treaty amendments) and in domestic debates on the role of national parliaments. It must of course be simultaneously acknowledged that such emphasis on government accountability does not necessarily tell us anything about whether and how national parliaments and MPs actually perform citizen-related functions in EU affairs. This is clearly a question that should be addressed by future research as existing studies have focused almost exclusively on parliament–executive relations (Auel 2007; Goetz and Meyer-Sahling 2008; Raunio 2009b). Among questions deserving scholarly attention are how MPs defend constituency interests in European affairs, what types of European debates are organized in national parliaments, or to what extent media covers the handling of EU matters in domestic legislatures (see the chapter by de Wilde in this volume).

Notes

1. It must also be understood that the debate about deparliamentarization or 'executive drift' has not been restricted to factors related to European integration (Raunio and Hix 2000; O'Brennan and Raunio 2007). Party discipline and centralization of power within parties to the leadership (who often are cabinet ministers), together with the more complicated and detailed nature of the issues on the political agenda, are often identified as key variables in explaining the drift of power from the parliament to the government. National parliaments are also facing many more external constraints than before (in addition to the EU), with particularly global rules and the stronger role of courts impacting on the sovereignty of parliaments. Parliaments have fought back and have in many ways become better at controlling governments – they have reformed their rules of procedure and committee systems to facilitate oversight of the government, with MPs also making more active use of various control mechanisms. But even though there is by no means unanimous agreement among legislative scholars that parliaments have indeed declined, much less on the degree of that alleged decline, only a selected few studies have argued that parliaments have become stronger or have not lost power to the executive branch. (Strøm et al. eds 2003; Bergman and Strøm eds 2011)
2. Both Packenham and Norton placed the functions of latent and manifest legitimation under the category of 'legitimation' functions. As I use no such category, both are placed among the government-related functions as they emphasize the ability of the parliament to provide legitimacy to the process of governance.
3. See the Guidelines for Interparliamentary Cooperation in the European Union, adopted by the Conference of Speakers of the European Union Parliaments in Lisbon on 21 June 2008, which lists the objectives and frameworks for interparliamentary cooperation (www.cosac.eu/en/documents/basic/guidelines.pdf).
4. Consolidated version of the Treaty on European Union, *Official Journal of the European Union* C 83/13, 30 March 2010.

5. For reasons of space, the Convention documents are referred to by their number instead of full title.
6. The WDs are available at http://european-convention.eu.int/dynadoc.asp?lang=EN&Content=WGIV.
7. Protocol on the Role of the National Parliaments in the European Union, Treaty of Amsterdam, *Official Journal* C 340, 10 November 1997.
8. Rules of Procedure of the Conference of Community and European Affairs Committees of Parliaments of the European Union, *Official Journal of the European Union* C 27/6, 31 January 2008. The rules were adopted in 2003.
9. Rules of Procedure of the Conference of Community and European Affairs Committees of Parliaments of the European Union, *Official Journal of the European Union* C 27/6, 31 January 2008.
10. The biannual reports are available at www.cosac.eu/en/documents/biannual/.
11. Establishment of A Secretariat of the COSAC Troika Presidency and Presidential Troika, Document adopted by XXX COSAC, 7 October 2003.
12. According to COSAC (2009: 43), 'topicality is the main criterion for determining the subjects of the Reports. Indeed, in most cases, the choice was made on the basis of: the issues at the centre of the debates in the EU at the time of the Presidency; the priorities defined by the government in charge of the Presidency of the EU Council; the decisions taken during the previous COSAC meetings.'
13. These documents were an introductory note from Gisela Stuart (WD 1), a list of relevant Convention documents for the working group (WD 2), an academic paper by Andreas Maurer on comparing the national scrutiny mechanisms (WD 8), and a paper providing the numbers of national MPs and MEPs per country (WD 15).
14. WD 4 by MEP Andrew Duff, WD 29 by MEP Johanna Maij-Weggen, WD 18 by Swedish MP Sören Lekberg (WD 18), and WD 25 by Portuguese MP Eduarda Azevedo.
15. Commenting the draft final report, Renée Wagener from Luxembourg (WD 37) argued in favour of 'widest possible transparency: The handling of the EU matters should be public. Publicity is guaranteed thorough complete access to documents and public registers.'
16. Contribution, XXX COSAC, 7 October 2003.
17. Conclusions, XXXII COSAC, 23 November 2004.
18. In addition, some sub-chapters have dealt with citizen-related concerns. Examples are sub-chapter 1.2. (Providing citizens with information about the new Treaty) in the ninth report and sub-chapters 1.3. (Engaging a debate with citizens on European affairs) and 1.4. (Additional parliamentary communication efforts) in the tenth report.
19. See http://www.cosac.eu/en/documents/contributions/.
20. There is also the possibility or danger of parliaments not becoming more strongly involved in day-to-day EU affairs because they can ultimately veto any Treaty amendments or the move to qualified majority voting or co-decision procedure in specific policy areas.

11
The Europeanization of Regional Assemblies: A Comparison between Different Ways of Approaching the Representative Challenge in EU Affairs

Elena Griglio[1]

Introduction

In the last decades, parliamentary representation at domestic level has been challenged in multiple ways by so-called 'passive' Europeanization (Auel 2007: 427). On the one hand, the EU integration process has clearly favoured the predominance of the executive branch (Weiler, Haltern and Mayer 1995: 7; Schmidt 1999: 25) in so-called 'ascending' subsidiarity – the stage of participation in the production of EU norms (Garofalo 2006: 28) – and often also in 'descending' subsidiarity, the phase dedicated to the transposition and implementation of EU legislation. On the other hand, the national parliaments have been coming to terms with the idea that they are not isolated, but are, instead, involved in a complex network of representation in which collective decisions are taken at multiple levels (Crum and Fossum 2009: 267). National parliaments have lost their role as single representatives of popular sovereignty as a consequence of the dissolution of nation-state sovereignty in a supranational and transnational governance model (Cohen 2004). The EU impact on regional assemblies has been even stronger, overwhelmed by the enlargement of the executive branch both at the national and regional level (Pérez Tremps 1991: 93).

The impact of these trends on the 'democratic deficit' of the European order has contributed to the consolidation of the idea that a major change is needed in the role played by parliaments in the EU decision-making process. This belief, rooted not only in the scientific debate, was perceived by many legislatures as an institutional priority. It is upon such a basis that a 'representative challenge' was diffused among parliaments (and often by parliaments), as a form of competition for the establishment of the representative assemblies' role in the political and institutional arena where collective decisions concerning EU affairs are taken.

The representative challenge has also involved regional assemblies which, after the rediscovery – at EU level – of the role of the regions as the authentic interpreters of the popular will, have started implementing their role of representatives in EU affairs, often by re-thinking their internal organization and functioning. With regard to these tendencies, the literature has focused on the powers directly assigned to regional assemblies by the European Union (Vos 2005; Jeffery 2005; O'Brennan and Raunio 2007) or on their role in legitimizing the constitutional set-up of both the Member States and the Union (Maurer 2002; Weatherill 2005). However, much less attention has been paid to the adaptations *autonomously* promoted by regional assemblies in order to interpret the needs and interests of their own constituencies in EU matters better.

It is specifically this field that the present chapter focuses on. Its aim is to deepen our understanding of the issue regarding regional assemblies' 'active' Europeanization, questioning if, and, if so, how, they have interpreted the representative challenge issued by the EU. In what ways have they fulfilled this task by focusing on the ascending or descending forms of subsidiarity? What are the most promising practices of regional assemblies in the EU arena and what factors condition them?

The EU impact on the domestic balance of powers differs according to the unitary, regional, and federal nature of the nation-state (Schmidt 2006: 54). Here, we will focus on the 'regional' experiences of Italy and Spain, both of which are characterized by the presence of regional authorities endowed with a large amount of legislative and administrative powers, but both of which lack a form of permanent representation of regional interests at state level. The absence of an authentic 'federal' senate, in fact, weakens the role of regional assemblies even in the representation of EU-related territorial interests (Thym 2009: 65).

In particular, Section 2 focuses on the capacity and willingness of regional assemblies to interpret and carry out their role of representatives in EU affairs. Section 3 provides a general outline of Italian and

Spanish law provisions concerning the representative function of regional assemblies in EU affairs. In Section 4, we will see what the main parliamentary tools used by regional councils to implement such a representative function are. Section 5 draws some conclusions on the aptitude of regional assemblies to assess the representative challenge.

The role of regional assemblies in the EU context: a dynamic approach to the issue of representation

In the last decades, the role of regions has become increasingly important within the EU political system. The cooperation between regions and the European Commission on regional policy (started in 1975), the participation of regional ministers in the Council allowed by the Treaty of Maastricht in 1992, and the establishment of the Committee of the Regions (CoR) in 1994 are all signals of the ongoing 'opening' of the EU to the active participation of regional representatives in EU decision-making (Cole 2005). The process was continued by the Treaty of Lisbon, which extended the principle of subsidiarity to the local and regional level (Article 5), which envisages the participation of regional parliaments with legislative powers through the 'early warning system' (Article 6 of Protocol n. 2 annexed to the Treaty of Lisbon).

Given this general legal background, the section focuses on the role of regional assemblies in EU affairs based upon a conception of representation that does not only capture individual representatives but also legislatures as a whole in their relationships with their constituencies. In competitive arenas, representation is a function which not only falls upon individual representatives, but also upon assemblies. As developed by Scharpf for Member State governments (2006), on issues of institutional reform legislatures represent 'not only the interests of their constituents but also their own institutional self-interest which, in the present context, can be interpreted as a concern for autonomy and influence' (ibid.: 846). This means returning to the original idea of political representation as a function which is first attributed to the whole legislature before being assumed by individuals (Castiglione and Warren 2008: 8).

For regional assemblies, EU affairs constitute an ideal testing-ground for endorsing the representative challenge. This is not so much due to electoral reasons (sensitivity to EU integration does not represent a generally shared political message), but to the attempt of regional legislatures to affirm their role of representatives in a more comprehensive mode, participating in decisions taken outside their remit (often in competition with national parliaments). This change seems to have interested regional assemblies, above all. National parliaments, in fact, are overloaded with ordinary domestic work and thus often find it difficult to get more involved in EU affairs (Norton 1996: 32; Sejersted 1996: 156).

The problematical side of this transformation is that, for a long time, Europeanization has enabled regional parliaments to expand their areas of intervention, for instance by participating in the EU regional development policies, but not to identify new patterns for the accomplishment of such responsibilities. Parliaments were for a long time constrained in the exercise of traditional functions (control of the executive, social representation and participation), without the opportunity to affirm new methods of involvement (Liebert 2002: 12). Most recently, though, the upturn of the ascending subsidiarity dimension seems to have re-invigorated regional assemblies' attempts to be active in the representative arena on EU issues. In these latter cases, the legitimization of regional parliaments is based, above all, upon their capability to give space to the opposition as well as to the majority rights in EU affairs (Strøm 1998; Holzhacker 2005) and to coordinate and compose different forms of territorial, political, and corporative representation (Manzella 2002: 36).

Regional assemblies' strategies of enhancing their representative role in EU affairs can be empirically assessed by investigating the possible changes in parliamentary functions and in the tools applied to fulfil these functions Consequently, the empirical comparison of the Italian and Spanish cases is based upon the following set of indicators:

i) the main **functions** that identify the role of regional assemblies in EU affairs (Álvarez Conde 2006: 26; Fasone 2009: 420):

- legislative function: according to the CoR, roughly 70 per cent of EU legislation is implemented by regions and local authorities; moreover, regional parliaments with legislative powers often transpose EU directives themselves;[2]
- control of the executive: parliaments' aptitude for controlling executive performances is ranked among the 'classic' forms of accomplishment of the representative function;
- subsidiarity monitoring procedures: after the Treaty of Lisbon, regional parliaments are being asked to re-think their traditional function, investing effort in the so-called 'early warning

mechanism', the subsidiarity control procedure based upon the cooperation among national and regional parliaments;

- cooperation with other regional assemblies: the development of cooperative interparliamentary networks can help regional assemblies to strengthen their participation in the EU decision-making process (Smets 1998);
- information to citizens: input democracy should be considered to be one of the main duties of regional assemblies (Peterson and Shackleton 2002: 356); for input legitimacy, transparency is a central precondition since it promotes the information and participation of citizens in EU affairs (Culpepper and Fung 2007: 734).

ii) the **tools** that favour the exercise of the representative function in EU-related issues (Wessels and Katz 1999: 11):

- organizational tools, with specific regard to the presence of an EU affairs committee. Standing committees devoted to EU affairs do not clash with the idea that European issues must be integrated in the ordinary activities of parliaments (Sejersted 1996: 156), but instead represent an instrument for strengthening the exercise of parliamentary functions (Dann 2003: 556) – with specific regard to the control of the executive (Bilbao Ubillos 2003) – and interact in a more proactive way with electors. In the relationship with the EU, in fact, parliaments with strong committees are ranked among the most powerful in Europe (O'Brennan and Raunio 2007: 7);
- procedural tools, which regard, in particular, the procedures for the EU law transposition;
- statutory tools, consisting of the principles and rules on the participation in the EU introduced by regional statutes;
- cooperative tools, which enable multilateral interaction among regional assemblies in EU-related issues;
- informative tools, provided by the institutional websites of the regional assemblies on EU affairs and related activities.

This layout is based upon the idea that the assessment of parliamentary strengths and capacities in EU affairs cannot be based upon *formal* parliamentary participation rights alone, but also have to acknowledge the assemblies' aptitude to translate formal capabilities into parliamentary behaviour (Auel 2007: 503).

Table 11.1 Functions played by regional assemblies in EU affairs and parliamentary tools for the endorsement of those functions

	Legislative functions	Control of the executive in the ascending subsidiarity	Subsidiarity monitoring procedure	Cooperation with other regional assemblies	Information to citizens
Organizational tools	Presence of an EU affairs committee	Presence of an EU affairs committee	Presence of an EU affairs committee		Presence of an EU affairs committee
Procedural tools	Procedures for the adjustment of domestic regulation to EU law	Procedures for the parliamentary control of the executive in the ascending subsidiarity	Procedures for the implementation of the early warning mechanism		
Statutory tools		Principles on regional assemblies' participation in the EU decision-making	Identification of the role of the assembly in the subsidiarity control		
Cooperative tools			Cooperation with national parliament in the early warning procedure	Participation to the CoR Subsidiarity Monitoring Network	
Informative tools					Information on EU affairs/EU related parliamentary activity

Regional assemblies and the legal arrangement of representation in EU- related issues

The case of Italy

Article 117 of the Italian Constitution – as modified in 2001 – attributes to the national legislator the discipline of EU – state relations; at the same time, concurring regional legislation applies to the EU relations of regions. According to this norm, Italian regions are able to regulate their participation at the EU, providing they respect the principles introduced by Member State law.

Italian legislative assemblies have traditionally focused on descending subsidiarity in their participation in EU matters. This has been favoured by the fact that, since 1989, the national legislator (law n. 86/1989) has given regions the power to adjust their norms to the EU law directly. EU legislation, therefore, does not change the internal distribution of competences.

Italian regions have adopted different solutions in order to fulfil this task. Sixteen out of the twenty regions provide (in their statutes, standing orders, or, most often, with regional laws of procedure) a specific procedure for the adjustment to EU law, consisting of the transposition/implementation of expiring EU legislation with a single law, to be approved every year by the council (the so-called regional *legge comunitaria*, moulded on the EU norm adjustment model established at the national level since 1990).

Moreover, 12 out of the 21 regional councils[3] introduced the so-called *sessione comunitaria*, an assembly session dedicated to the examination of EU-related issues and acts. The nature and role of this *sessione* varies from region to region. Apart from the approval of the *legge comunitaria*, in some regions (Calabria, Marche, and Molise), it focuses on the control of executive performances in EU-related issues, in one case (Campania) extended to the national government. The *sessione* can also be used for monitoring the enforcement status of regional programmes co-financed by the EU (Basilicata) or for promoting the proactive role of the assembly in this area; in this latter case, the *sessione* is usually concluded with the adoption of guiding acts addressed to the regional government (Emilia-Romagna, Marche, Molise, Sardinia, and Sicily). Sometimes (Emilia-Romagna) it is used to favour the broad circulation of EU-related documents and reports among citizens.

The energy invested by Italian regional councils in the descending subsidiarity phase have not been accompanied by a significant involvement in the EU decision-making process (ascending subsidiarity phase where the role of the national and regional executives remains predominant. The absence in the two national chambers' standing orders of specific rules enabling the involvement of regional councils in EU-related decisions (Lupo 2008: 98) seems to have hindered stable cooperation among assemblies at both national and regional levels on EU affairs. The Treaty of Lisbon has not changed the situation, since neither the *Camera* nor the *Senato* has taken formal decisions on the participation of regional councils in the subsidiarity monitoring.[4]

A possible solution to the problem of the participation of regional parliaments in the ascending (and also descending) phase could be provided by strengthening the Conference of the Chairmen of the Regional Councils, a voluntary interregional organism which supports regional assemblies in the gathering and analysis of information and documents concerning the EU. This activity, formally recognized by Article 5 of the law n. 11/2005, has recently been implemented by the Conference through the promotion of the 'RIPEX' project, a mechanism for the regional interparliamentary EU information exchange.[5]

The case of Spain

The Spanish Constitution of 1978 does not formally discipline the participation of the *Comunidades autonomas* in EU matters. Neither the state nor the regions have a specific competence with regard to the internal transposition of EU norms and it is only through the intervention of the Constitutional Tribunal that the regions have obtained the right to adjust to EU law in their own areas of intervention directly.[6] The general principle of non-distortion of the internal distribution of competence – as affirmed by the constitutional court – has found a much weaker implementation in Spain than that of Italy. The possibility for regional parliaments to adopt laws in order to adjust to EU legislation is very limited, given the fact that this task is usually assured by the *Cortes Generales* or by the national government through the exercise of the so-called 'horizontal' competences (such as economic competition and the protection of fundamental citizenship rights).[7] Even in those regional areas of intervention most affected by EU law (finance, agriculture, environmental protection, and the single market), regional parliaments tend to delegate the transposition of EU directives to the government.[8] Some regional statutes explicitly limit the role of the region in the adjustment to EU law to the exercise of administrative powers. Only seven *Comunidades autonomas* (Pais Vasco, Andalusia, Canarias, Madrid, Castilla La Mancha, Cataluña, and Comunidad Valenciana) are endowed with a wide range of normative powers in the transposition of EU law, while others (Murcia, Asturia, Baleares, Extremadura, Castilla-Leon, and Galicia) cannot adopt rules of implementation before a specific national law of execution has been approved.

The praxis developed in this field seems to confirm the aptitude of regional parliaments to dismiss their potential role as legislators in the descending subsidiarity phase. Since the entry into force of the Treaty of Lisbon, the intervention of regional parliaments has been focused on the ascending subsidiarity stage, thus taking advantage of the early warning mechanism. The procedure has found advanced implementation both at the national and regional level: the Mixed Committee on EU affairs – composed of representatives of the two chambers and managed by the *Cortes Generales* – has first established, with the agreement of 24 March 2009, temporary criteria for the introduction of experimental subsidiarity monitoring. Afterwards, with the approval of l. 24/2009, the national parliament conclusively disciplined the procedure, assigning four weeks to the regional assemblies for the approval of a motivated report on subsidiarity.

Moreover, Spanish regional assemblies participate in the COPREPA, the Conference of the Chairmen of the Regional Parliaments, which mainly functions as a forum of debate and for the drafting of proposals focused on the promotion of the involvement of the regional parliaments in the ascending subsidiarity and on the arrangement of accessible information on EU-related activity. In the annual interregional meetings, held since 1983, the COPREPA has carried out 11 debates on EU-related issues.

A comparison of the use of the representative tools in Italy and Spain

Bearing in mind the different role of Italian and Spanish regional assemblies with regard to the EU decision-making process, it is now time to examine how the different representative tools – as listed in Table 11.1 – are implemented in the two cases.

The empirical data which will now be analysed refer to the experience of the 21 Italian regional councils and the 17 Spanish regional parliaments, and they have been collected mainly by using the official websites of the regional assemblies. In particular, the following sources of information have been considered as being relevant: the provisions on the participation at the EU by regional statutes: the national/regional legislation on the subject; the EU-related rules of the regional assemblies' standing orders; the agenda/activities of regional assemblies' standing committees/plenum; the acts concerning EU affairs approved by standing committees/plenum; the parliamentary debates on EU matters; the institutional reports on the subject; the institutional news and press releases on EU-related parliamentary activities; and the institutional website of the CoR.

Organizational tools: the creation of EU affairs committees

The analysis of the Italian and Spanish experiences and sources reveals that many regional assemblies provided for the creation of a standing committee or sub-committee specialized in EU affairs (9 out of the 21 regional councils in Italy; and 11 out of the 17 regional parliaments in Spain); the nature and role of such committees, though, appears rather different in the two countries.

In Italy, EU affairs committees (endowed with a wide range of competences, from the legislative and control powers to the exercise of advisory and administrative functions) clearly operate as an incentive for the proactive implementation of EU assignments, including the analysis of non-legislative acts, which, in contrast, are rarely taken into consideration by regional assemblies that attribute the competence on EU affairs to multi-disciplinary committees.

In Spain, however, the creation of EU standing committees or specialized sub-committees (the so-called *ponencias*) has been favoured by the implementation of the subsidiarity-control procedure. Such bodies do not share a wide range of competences (they are never involved in the legislative procedures), but their presence has clearly enabled the regional parliaments to begin/initiate intense activity in the ascending subsidiarity phase (which, in most cases, represents their core area of intervention).

Procedural tools for the transposition and implementation of EU legislation

As evidenced in Section 3, the role of regional parliaments as legislators in the adjustment to EU law has been fully exploited only by Italian regional councils. This trend has deeply conditioned the procedures for the transposition and implementation of EU law.

In Italy, the regional *legge comunitaria* seems to offer a number of advantages from the perspective of representation: it enables a joint debate on all EU-related issues, thus favouring public control and participation; it promotes an active role of the regional council in the implementation of EU acts delegated to the executive; and it favours an accountable and efficient exercise of regional legislative functions in EU-related issues, thereby avoiding infraction procedures. These advantages are partially counterbalanced by the dissemination of the procedure; only a minority of regions has effectively approved one or more EU laws,[9] while the others have continued with the old praxis of adjustment to EU law with sector-oriented legislative disciplines or other regulatory and administrative acts.

In contrast, Spanish regional parliaments have not developed specific legislative procedures for the transposition of EU law. The first remarkable parliamentary experiences in the direct adjustment to EU law have been put into practice in the transposition of the so-called 'Bolkenstein Directive' on Services in the Internal Market, achieved by many regions (8 out of the 17) with the adoption of a parliamentary law.

The 'procedural' approach confirms that there is a parallelism between the need to develop original procedures for the adjustment to EU law and the representative role played by regional assemblies in the descending subsidiarity phase.

Statutory tools: the parliamentary control of the executive

Different parliamentary forms of control of the executive in EU affairs can be found in the Italian case, where some regions experienced real cooperation between the legislative and executive powers; in contrast, in Spain, the relationship between the two branches is either related to the independent participation of the respective bodies to the production of EU law, or to the prevalence of the regional executive over the parliament.

The cooperative bent is favoured in Italy by the fact that here the regional councils (unlike Spanish regional parliaments) usually regulated the subject through the adoption of EU laws of procedure. Generally speaking, the more the regional law is vague in regulating the ascending subsidiarity procedures, the more the arena will be covered by the regional executives (Rivosecchi 2009: 389). This explains why dedicated rules in this field often constitute the necessary premise for an active intervention of legislatures.

Italian regions usually base cooperation between the two branches on different patterns: the exchange of mutual information on the activity developed or to be started in the ascending phase (Emilia-Romagna; Sardinia); the definition of common positions, often through the approval of parliamentary guidelines destined for the executive (Friuli-Venezia Giulia; Tuscany; Umbria). Even some regions formally characterized by the prevalence of the regional executive over the parliament (Lombardy and also partially in Sicily) introduced forms of weak cooperation between the branches, based on the advisory role of standing parliamentary committees.

In Spain, in contrast, those regions with recently reformed statutes either restrict themselves to generally recognizing the participation of the *Comunidad autonoma* (as a whole) to the ascending phase (Aragon, Baleares, Comunidad Valenciana) or tend formally to legitimize the overriding role of the government in the EU (Andalucia). Other regions (Castilla y Leon, Cataluña) explicitly state the right of the two branches to submit their remarks to national institutions independently during the ascending phase.

Cooperative tools: the implementation of the subsidiarity monitoring

As mentioned before, an emerging opportunity for regional assemblies is represented by the subsidiarity-monitoring mechanism shaped by the Treaty of Lisbon. Tools introduced by parliaments in order to adapt to this new procedure can be seen as forms of cooperation among different institutions (regional assemblies, national parliaments, and EU institutions).

Italian regional councils in many cases (9 out of the 21 regional councils) have regulated the subject in their standing orders or in EU laws of procedure, specifying which parliamentary body (standing committee, floor, other specialized organism) is entrusted with the task of monitoring EU draft proposals sent by the national government or by the EU Commission, and formulating specific comments in cases of presumed violation of the subsidiarity principle. Unfortunately, these provisions have been implemented in very few cases. Only Sicily has started the subsidiarity monitoring.

Instead of participating to the ascending phase, up to now Italian councils have been more interested in the consultation procedures on EU non-legislative documents (which do not usually generate much interest among Spanish regional assemblies), promoted by the EU Commission or by the CoR. Paradoxically enough, most of the Italian regional councils declare themselves to be interested in a reform which would strengthen their role in the ascending subsidiarity phase, eventually adopting (as in the case of Marche, Sardegna, and A.P. Trento) binding resolutions directed at the national parliament.

The subsidiarity monitoring enforcement status in Spain is quite different: under the impulse of the national parliament, regional assemblies provide well-timed implementation of this mechanism. All the reformed statutes (Comunidad Valenciana excluded) envisage new principles on the subject. Some regional parliaments (Asturias, Cataluña, Comunidad Valenciana, and Extremadura) disciplined the mechanism, anticipating the intervention of the national parliament. Only five regions (Aragon, Baleares, Galicia, La Rioja, and Región de Murcia) have not formally disciplined the procedure, but in three of these five regions (Aragon, Galicia, and Región de Murcia) the subsidiarity control is implemented by standard procedure.

The subject in charge of the control is generally the EU affairs committee or *ponencia*, but, in most cases, the proposal can be submitted also to the plenum (Canarias, Cantabria, Cataluña, Com. Valenciana, and Extremadura). Many regional regulations (Andalucia, Canarias, Cantabria, Cataluna, Com. Valenciana, Extremadura, and Pais Vasco) provide for an effective involvement of all parliamentary groups; sometimes the participation is extended to regional governments (Andalucia, Aragon, Cantabria, Madrid, and Pais Vasco) and, in the case of the Pais Vasco, also to the 'historic territories'. Only in a few cases has the procedure explicitly included participative patterns aimed at acquiring qualified opinions on the proposal (Castilla La Mancha, Castilla y Leon, and Navarra).

Another cooperative tool related to the early warning mechanism is represented by the adhesion to the Subsidiarity Monitoring Network, created in 2005 by the CoR in order to involve local and regional authorities in the development, implementation, and evaluation of EU policies.[10] The network operates as a voluntary association which now has more than 120 partners. In Italy and Spain, only a minority of regional assemblies has adhered to the network (five Italian regional councils; six Spanish regional parliaments; and three executives both in Italy and in Spain). The number of assemblies actively participating to the subsidiarity test is even more limited: only six regional parliaments (Emilia-Romagna, Marche, and Tuscany; Asturias, Cataluña, and Extremadura) sent their reports and only two keep ongoing participation in such tests (Emilia-Romagna and Extremadura).

These data confirm that participation in cross-border projects pursuing the development of new methods of participation in the EU decision-making process is still low, but, at least in Spain, a shift towards the strengthening of the ascending subsidiarity cooperative procedures was initiated in 2010.

Information on EU affairs/EU-related parliamentary activity

In order to verify how the regional assemblies fare with regard to informing the public of their activities, we have submitted their institutional websites to a transparency test, based upon the following steps:

a) How do regional assemblies provide general information on the EU? Italian councils (10 out of the 21) tend to focus on the most relevant EU norms and decisions of the EU institutions. In contrast,

Spanish regional assemblies seem to be more interested in providing information about their participation in the meetings of interregional organisms, such as the COPREPA on EU affairs (Cantabria, Castilla y Leon, La Rioja, Madrid, and Murcia). In some cases (Calabria, Campania, Valle d'Aosta; Asturias, Castilla La Mancha, Extremadura, and Navarra) the duty is carried out simply through the publication of links to the main European institutional websites. Not many assemblies include general information on the role of the region in EU decision-making processes (Emilia-Romagna, Piedmont, Tuscany, A.P. Trento, and the Veneto; Aragon and Cantabria);

b) Do the websites of regional assemblies give citizens the opportunity of a specific survey of the parliamentary debates, proposals, acts, deliberations, and news relating to the regional participation at the EU? Most regional councils (with the exception of Abruzzo, the Baleares, La Rioja, Madrid, and Murcia) include search engines for this purpose, but the access to thematic data is not always immediate and easy (on average, it seems to be favoured by the presence of an EU committee, which can positively filter such data);
c) Do legislative reports published by the assembly provide information on EU-related activity of the committees and the plenum? Results achieved are not very satisfactory. Usually such reports do not include a specific chapter on EU-related activities and rarely do they offer some (often unsystematic) information on EU affairs (Abruzzo, Emilia-Romagna, Lazio, and Lombardy) or on the participation of the region in the meetings of the competent interregional associations on EU affairs (Castilla y Leon);
d) Do the parliamentary websites include thematic pages dedicated to the information about the relevant EU parliamentary activities? This only happens for a minority of regions (Emilia-Romagna, Friuli Venezia Giulia, Sicily, and the Veneto; Aragon, Comunidad Valenciana, and Galicia). In comparing these 'best' practices, we should mention in particular the cases of Comunidad Valenciana and Galicia, which provide citizens with a personalized information service on EU-related parliamentary activities. However, none of these websites includes participative patterns which could allow citizens the possibility of interacting with their representatives on EU-relevant topics.

Curiously, it is difficult to find a direct relation between the degree of transparency of the institution and its capacity to interpret the representative challenge in EU-related issues. As for the Italian regional councils, only one of the four 'best' regions is endowed with a standing committee dedicated to EU affairs, and only two of these adhere to the Subsidiarity Monitoring Network (but one does grant ongoing participation to the subsidiarity tests). One of these four regions has structurally started to implement the subsidiarity control procedure, and two have introduced a cooperative relational model between the legislative and executive branches. Similar conclusions can be drawn by examining the Spanish experience: the three regional assemblies providing most information to citizens on EU-related activities have all started to implement the subsidiarity-control procedure, but they do not coincide with the two regions (Cataluña and Extremadura) most active in the Subsidiarity Monitoring Network.

Conclusion: are regional assemblies self-sufficient in the arrangement of representation in EU affairs?

The analysis of the tools implemented by regional assemblies in EU-related activities has evidenced that not all the parliaments tend to interpret the representative challenge in the same way. Italian regional councils seem to have invested, above all, in the exercise of the normative function, thus focusing on the descending subsidiarity phase. In contrast, Spanish parliaments have tried to imitate the so-called 'Danish model', characterized by the attempt to strengthen the role of regional assemblies, especially in the ascending subsidiarity phase (Fitzmaurice 1976: 291).

Generally speaking, the results suggest that the most proactive assemblies in assuring the task of fulfilling the representative function in EU affairs are those more willing to affirm their autonomy and their role of territorial representatives at the national level. In both Italy and Spain, the capacity of regional assemblies to interpret the representative challenge in the EU arena seems to be influenced by the so-called 'autonomist' factor rather than by other socio-economic elements (such as the availability of financial resources and the geographical location or dimension). Such an 'autonomist' factor could be defined as the institutional propensity of the region to see its political role recognized as being distinct from that of the central state, thereby extending its decisional powers to new areas of intervention; it is influenced not so much by the amount of powers/competences attributed to the region, but rather by the search for further autonomy, which, in its turn, can be considered to be the result of historic, social, cultural, and political elements (as, for example, with the presence of strong autonomist parties).

Given this general tendency, though, there is no assembly which performs equally well in all the areas of intervention. Some assemblies, thanks to their EU-dedicated committees and sessions, are particularly active in the examination of EU non-legislative documents; others focus on the implementation of the subsidiarity procedure instead. Some assemblies have started an intense control of the executive in EU affairs, while others maintain their ongoing participation in the CoR Network tests. Some assemblies provide citizens with detailed information on the activities of EU institutions, while others prefer to talk of the activities developed by the region in EU-related issues.

A justification of these different choices can be found in the fact that, paradoxically, the representative role of regional assemblies in EU-related issues seems to work only when it is supported by the national legislation (Rivosecchi 2009: 402). For instance, the introduction of a regional EU procedure by most of the Italian regional councils has been encouraged by the approval, at national level, of law n. 11/2005; also in the implementation of the early warning mechanism by Spanish parliaments, the intervention of the national parliament favoured the well-timed implementation of the subsidiarity monitoring by the majority of regions (while the lack of such a 'national' initiative seems to have slowed down the adoption of similar reforms by Italian regional councils). These experiences seem to reveal that adaptations to the EU challenges by regional assemblies are favoured by the proneness of the national parliaments to consent and/or to promote such arrangements.

Moreover, some elements confirm that the attempt to strengthen the position of regional assemblies in EU-related issues (at least in countries where they are devoid of a permanent representation within the national parliament) requires the promotion of interregional initiatives or cooperative actions. Regional assemblies, in fact, receive an enormous amount of information from EU institutions, but are often incapable of coping with such documents; it is in this area that interregional cooperation can serve as a valid instrument for the selection of most relevant acts and the exchange of best practices.

The problem is that, by adopting such an interpretation, we would have to recognize that the representative role of regional assemblies in EU affairs depends on some variables (the cooperative attitude of the national parliaments; the effectiveness of interregional cooperation) which are often beyond their control. This remark does not exclude that proactive regional assemblies are autonomously able to meet the representative challenge in EU affairs. But the interpretation clearly challenges – at least for regional councils whose competences are devoid of a strong constitutional warranty – the traditional image of representative assemblies as self-sufficient in the arrangement of representation, given their autonomy in moulding the political tactics (Bentham 1843).

Notes

1. Ph.D. in Public Law at the University of Turin (Italy). Holder of a research grant in Public Comparative Law at the Faculty of Political Science – Luiss University, Rome.
2. CoR, 'A new treaty: a new role for regions and local authorities', http://www.cor.europa.eu, date accessed 20 August 2010.
3. Italy is composed of twenty Regions, but Region Trentino Alto Adige is divided into two Autonomous Provinces (Trento and Bolzano), represented by two separate assemblies endowed with legislative powers. Later on, we will therefore refer to the '21' Italian regional councils.
4. Only the Chamber of Deputies debated, during the first official subsidiarity test (Meeting of the 17 February 2010, in www.camera.it), on the opportunity of involving regional councils.
5. http://www.parlamentiregionali.it/dbdata/documenti/%5B4a9f983446967%5DPROTOCOLLO_DI_INTESA_luglio_2009.pdf, date accessed 18 January 2011.
6. See, in particular, the sentences of the *Tribunal Constitutional* n. 252/1988, 76/1991, 79/1992, 80/1983.
7. See, in particular, Articles 149.1.1. and 149.1.13 of the Spanish Constitution. The literature has deeply criticized such a legislative trend (Montilla Martos 2004: 211). Some examples of direct adjustment are instead represented by the r.l. of the Pais Vasco n. 2/1986 and the r.l. of Cataluña n. 4/1986.
8. See, for instance, the r.l. of Baleares n. 1/1997 for the transposition of the Dir. CEE 409/1988 or the r.l. 6/1997 of Murcia on the adjustment of the commercial fairs legislation to EU law.
9. Friuli-Venezia Giulia: r.l. n. 11/2005, r.l. n. 9/2006, r.l. n. 14/2007, r.l. n. 7/2008 and r.l. n. 13/2009; Valle D'Aosta: r.l. n. 8/2007, r.l. n. 6/2008, r.l. n. 12/2009, r.l. n. 16/2010; Marche: r.l. n. 36/2008; Emilia-Romagna: r.l. n. 4/2010; Umbria: r.l. n. 15/2010.
10. http://portal.cor.europa.eu/subsidiarity/pages/welcome.aspx, date accessed 18 January 2011.

12
Interest *Representation* in the EU – Is There Any? A Top-Down Perspective

Stijn Smismans

Introduction

Interest groups have played a role in European policy-making ever since the European Economic Community was created. Their influence, functioning, and regulation have been extensively analysed in the academic literature. Interestingly enough, the concept of 'interest representation' is hardly used in this literature and the question of 'representation' in relation to interest groups remains absent as a topic of systematic inquiry, as is well illustrated by two recent literature reviews on 'interest groups' (Eising 2008) and 'civil society' (Finke 2007) in the EU.[1]

The EU Institutions themselves have referred to the role of interest groups with different concepts over time, but the concept of 'interest *representation*' has hardly ever (and only very recently) featured in the EU's official discourse. The focus has been on 'lobbying' or encouraging 'participation' and 'involvement' of 'interest groups', 'special interest groups', NGOs, 'civil society organizations', and 'interested parties'. However, the absence of the concept of 'interest representation' does not imply that the EU Institutions have not been concerned with the representative nature of interest-group participation. This concern emerged particularly from the 1990s onwards, when the EU attempted to develop measures and discourses that would improve its perceived lack of legitimacy (Smismans 2003). The structuring of interest representation has been occasionally an issue of concern and debate among European political actors from the start of the EEC (see Rittberger 2009), but it was only during the 1990s that the EU adopted horizontal, cross-sectoral initiatives and an official discourse on it.

This chapter analyses to what extent and how the EU Institutions attempt to regulate or set conditions on the representative character of interest-group participation in European policy-making. The EU's concern with the representative character of interest-group participation takes two forms. On the one hand, the EU takes initiatives to structure the overall system of interest-group participation in order to make it more 'representative', which I will refer to as 'system representativeness'. On the other hand, the EU sometimes also sets conditions of representativeness on the organizational features of the interest groups themselves in order to be involved in policy-making, which I will refer to as 'organizational representativeness'.

The aim of this contribution is not to provide an exhaustive overview of all measures through which the EU structures interest-group participation, but to analyse to what extent and how 'representation' is an *explicit* concern of the EU Institutions in their dealing with interest groups. It analyses how the EU Institutions set conditions on their interaction with interest groups in terms of representation and representativeness.[2] This chapter does not intend to provide a normative model for interest representation in the EU, but has the more modest objective of analysing how representation is voiced as a concern and taken into consideration by the EU Institutions in their relations with interest groups.

In section 2, I will first analyse how 'representation' has not figured at all as an explicit concern of the EU Institutions when dealing with interest groups. The focus has been on 'participation' rather than 'representation'. However, in the context of an increasing concern about the legitimacy of European policy-making – particularly addressed by the White Paper on European Governance – and of the emergence of a discourse on the role of 'civil society organizations', the European Commission has more explicitly dealt with the representative dimension of interest-group participation. While not using the concept of 'interest representation', it addressed questions both of organizational representativeness and system representativeness. This will be analysed in section 3. The fourth and final section focuses on the more recent European Transparency Initiative (ETI). Transparency, rather than the representative character of interest-group participation, is the central concern of the ETI. Surprisingly enough, it is in the context of the ETI that the concept of interest representation first emerges in the European institutional discourse.

Participation rather than representation

Interest-group participation in the EU has developed largely informally. Only in the 1990s did the Commission attempt to develop some cross-sectoral initiatives and a more formalized approach, first by two Communications adopted together in 1992 – one on 'An open and structured dialogue between the Commission and special interest groups' (Commission 1993a) and one on 'Increased transparency in the work of the Commission' (Commission 1993b). The two Communications are referred to as 'twin' documents and should be read together. The focus is on transparency in the Commission's relation with interest groups, and not on the representative nature of interest representation. The Communications function as an 'exchange'. On the one hand, the Commission promises to increase transparency of its own functioning in a way that would facilitate the participation by interest groups which is understood to improve more effective policy-making. On the other, it is noted that 'some problems with aggressive styles of lobbying have occurred' (Commission 1993a), and the Commission therefore expects that, in exchange for its 'open dialogue', interest groups will respect some minimum rules of fair lobbying practice and are therefore invited to adopt their own code of conduct. The Commission's approach is thus one of encouraging participation, without setting any requirements on the representative character of interest groups, as long as they do not engage in aggressive or illegal lobbying.

Participation rather than representation is also the keyword when EU Institutions, and in particular the European Commission and the European Economic and Social Committee (EESC) develop a normative discourse on the role of civil society organizations (CSOs) in European governance at the end of the 1990s (Smismans 2003). Whereas 'encouraging participation' in the 1992 Communications was mainly a question of increasing effectiveness of policy-making, the discourse of the Commission and the EESC at the turn of the century defines encouraging participation of interest groups or CSOs both as an issue of effectiveness and of enhancing democratic decision-making. The White Paper on European Governance (2001) identified 'participation' (and not representation) as one of the five principles of good governance, which would ensure 'the quality, relevance and *effectiveness* of EU policies' and 'more *confidence* in the end result'. Civil society plays a particular role in this participatory process. Civil society is said to 'play an important role in giving voice to the concern of citizens and delivering services that meet people's needs', and to 'act as an early warning system for the direction of political debate'.

However, it has been the EESC which most explicitly stressed the democratic added value of encouraging the participation of CSOs, with reference to the concept of participatory democracy. In its Opinion of 1999 on 'The role and contribution of CSOs in the building of Europe' (EESC 1999), the EESC defined its own role as guaranteeing 'the implementation of the *participatory model* of civil society; [enabling] civil society to participate in the decision-making process; and [helping] reduce a certain "democratic deficit" and so [underpinning] the legitimacy of democratic decision-making processes'. The Committee argued that 'the democratic process at European level – even more so than at the national level – must provide a range of participatory structures in which all citizens, with their different identities and in accordance with their different identity criteria, can be represented, and which reflect the heterogeneous nature of the European identity'. The EESC concluded that, being itself composed of representatives of intermediary organizations, it could act as a representation of the people's way of identifying with CSOs, and that it could complement the legitimacy offered by the EP as the representative of citizens' national (territorial) identity. The Committee – in its contribution to the White Paper – did not claim a monopoly of this role, and argued that 'the "European democratic model" will contain many...elements of *participatory democracy*', but it also stressed that 'a basic precondition and legitimising basis for participation is adequate representativeness of those speaking for organised civil society' (EESC 1999).

The debate on participatory democracy as a complement to representative democracy in European policy-making intensified during the European Convention and the adoption of both a principle of representative democracy and participatory democracy under the title of 'the democratic life of the Union' in the Constitutional Treaty (for details, Smismans 2004a). This dichotomy between representative and participatory democracy suggests that 'representation' is a concern for the former but not for the latter. Political theory has mostly linked the concept of 'participatory democracy' to ideas of 'direct democracy', although the two are not synonymous. 'Direct democracy' has mainly referred to the referendum model and the classical city-state democracy of ancient Greece. 'Participatory democracy' emerged as a concept to revive the idea of direct participation in the complex society of the second half of the twentieth century (Pateman 1970; Barber 1984). It extended the idea of direct participation from the political world to other sectors of social life, such as the workplace, education and local public administration, and gave particular attention to 'self-realization' and to deliberation in face-to-face relations, so stressing mostly a 'small-group' model of democracy (Sartori 1987: 112). Both direct and participatory democracy share the focus on democratic mechanisms in which individuals participate personally in the deliberations which concern them, in which there is no representation by intermediary bodies between those who make the decisions and those affected by them. However, the conceptual use of 'participatory democracy' in the EU official discourses is less coherent. The Commission and the EESC have used the concept also, and in particular to refer to the intermediary role of CSOs in policy-making. By using the concept of participatory democracy they have thus obfuscated the question of representation in what is substantially a representative and not a direct participatory mechanism.

However, this blurred use of the concept became an issue of debate in the European Convention (Smismans 2004a: 133; Kohler-Koch 2011: 59), with some arguing that participatory democracy is (also) about direct citizen participation and others arguing it is about the participation of interest groups. The article on participatory democracy in the Constitutional Treaty (article I-46) included references to both, although the initial comments accompanying the article had focused on the civil society dimension.[3] The citizen is directly addressed by the citizen's initiative (paragraph 4) (Dougan 2008) and the requirement that 'the institutions shall, by appropriate means, give citizens and representative associations the opportunity to make known and publicly exchange their views on all areas of Union action' (para. 1). Intermediary organizations are further addressed by the requirement for the institutions to 'maintain an open, transparent and regular dialogue with representative associations and civil society' (para.2), and the obligation for the Commission to 'carry out broad consultations with parties concerned in order to ensure that the Union's actions are coherent and transparent' (para.3). This entire article has been taken over by the Lisbon Treaty (article 11 TEU) but with the remarkable difference that the article has no longer a title and the concept of 'participatory democracy' has thus entirely disappeared from the text.

Two remarks regarding the question of representation need to be made in relation to the new Treaty text. First, while the concept of participatory democracy has disappeared, the article on representative democracy (art. 10 TEU) still makes a clear statement that 'the functioning of the Union shall be founded on representative democracy'. That a similar statement on participatory democracy is lacking suggests that the mechanisms of direct citizen involvement and of interest-group participation provided in article 11 TEU are clearly subordinated to the main principle of 'representative democracy', which in article 10 TEU is defined with reference to the role of the European Parliament, the Council, the European Council, the national parliaments, and the political parties at the European level.

Secondly, the question of 'representation' is not entirely absent from article 11 TEU. Reference is made twice to '*representative* associations'. The Convention debate on the article indeed did not only raise questions on whether participatory democracy was about interest-group or direct citizen participation, but also on whether groups had to be 'representative' in order to be involved in policy-making (Smismans 2004a: 133). The final phrasing in article 11 TEU is far from clear on the EU's requirements in relation to the representative nature of intermediary groups. Paragraph 2, for instance, requires the institutions to 'maintain an open, transparent and regular dialogue with representative associations *and* civil society', thus opposing the two concepts. According to the explanatory note that accompanied the first draft of the Constitutional Treaty, 'associations are mentioned in addition to civil society since there are associations which do not come under the civil society heading (employers' and employees' trade unions, associations representing the interests of the regional and local authorities etc).' It is also remarkable that representative associations are mentioned in the first and second paragraph of article 11 TEU, which set out requirements for all EU Institutions, whereas they are not mentioned in the specific requirement of the third paragraph for the Commission to 'carry out broad consultations with *parties concerned*.' Read together, the three paragraphs seem to suggest that 'representative associations' play a particular role in ensuring wider public debate, but that they have no privileged role in the specific consultation mechanisms of the Commission. As we will see in the next section, this is in contrast with the approach the Commission proposed in the White Paper on European Governance.

Concerns about the representative character of civil society *participation*

That participation rather than representation has been the core concept in relation to the role of interest groups in European policy-making does not exclude that the EU Institutions did express concern about the representative nature of such participation. The concern about the representative character of interest-group participation only first emerged in relation to the social partners. The concept of 'representativity'[4] was introduced in the early 1990s as a tool to structure their role in European policy-making. By setting criteria of representativeness, the EU makes an explicit statement on the conditions under which representative claims by social partners will be accepted as valid.

The Social Agreement attached to the Maastricht Treaty introduced the European social dialogue, which provides that the Commission has to consult the European social partners on all legislative initiatives in the social field, and allows them to sign collective agreements which can either be implemented with the means of industrial relations or by Council decision. Providing the social partners with regulatory competence, the question of their representativeness came prominently to the fore. In its 1993 Communication on the Social Agreement, the Commission set out for the first time formal criteria of organizational representativeness.

In order to be *consulted* under the European social dialogue procedure, a social partners organization has to be organized at the European level and be representative of all Member States (MS) 'as far as possible'. The required territorial organizational representativeness is thus not absolute, namely the social partner organization does not have to be representative of all MS. The rationale behind this may be that shortcomings in the territorial scope of one organization may be compensated by other consulted organizations. So system representativeness rather than organization representativeness is the ultimate objective. The European social partners should also be associations of national social partner organizations 'which are themselves an integral and recognised part of Member States' social partners structures and with the capacity to negotiate agreements' (Commission 1993c). This means that an organization based in Brussels with only individual members or no members at all cannot be consulted under the social dialogue. A European association must be a confederal organization of national social partners. This also implies that the EU has to rely indirectly on the criteria the MS use to consider their social partners representative.

Overall the criteria of organizational representativeness defined by the Commission are not particularly 'interventionist', relying mainly on the criteria set out by the MS. The Commission abstains from setting any conditions on how a European association should relate to its member organizations or individual members by way of mandated authority, accountability, or internal democratic procedures. Equally remarkable is the absence of a requirement for a minimum amount of individual members. This has been criticized by labour lawyers since membership numbers have been the predominant criterion to decide on the representativeness of social partners at the national level (Bercusson and Van Dijk 1995). This does not mean that membership numbers are entirely irrelevant in the European social dialogue, but the extent to which it is required is delegated to the national level.

Surprisingly enough the Commission is less explicit in setting requirements for the *negotiation* stage of the European social dialogue than for the consultation stage, despite the social partners' regulatory powers. Respecting the principle of 'mutual recognition' of collective bargaining, the Commission leaves it up to the social partners to decide who is sitting at the negotiation table (Commission 1993c, para.31). Yet, if the Commission and Council are asked to implement the collective agreement by Council decision, the Commission will check (again)[5] the representativeness of the social partners, adjusting pragmatically the criteria established for the consultation stage. The requirement to have 'adequate structures to ensure their effective participation in the *consultation* process' is re-phrased as 'adequate structures to ensure effective participation in the *negotiation* process',[6] but no further indications are given on what such adequate structures for negotiation would be, and to what extent they would differ from those for consultation. The Commission's concern appears also very 'functional', it seems mainly concerned with the *effectiveness* of the social partners' internal structures, rather than with an idea of representativeness and accountability in democratic terms. There is one exception to that. Sometimes the Commission also checks whether the signing social partners have been mandated by their national member organizations to negotiate on that particular topic. However, this requirement has never been set out as an official policy and the Commission has been inconsistent in implementing this criterion; it thus failed to apply such a check to agreements by sectoral social partners, which in fact often lack clear internal procedures to mandate European negotiations (Franssen 2002: 199).

The European Court of Justice has been more explicit in setting out further criteria of representativeness for the social partners when negotiating agreements to be implemented by Council decision. In the *UEAPME* case,[7] the General Court of the EU emphasized that representativeness of the social partners should be assessed 'in relation to the content of the agreement' (*UEAPME*, para.90). An organization representative in relation to the content of one agreement may not be representative for another agreement. Second, the Court talks about 'sufficient representativeness'. The requisite degree of representativeness is not absolute. If the signatory parties are 'sufficiently representative' it does not matter whether there are other organizations which might be representative too.[8] Third, the Court introduced the concept of 'sufficient collective representativeness', that is, the required representativeness is the representativeness of the signatory parties 'taken together' (*UEAPME*, para.90). The final objective is thus system representativeness rather than organizational representativeness. Taken together the social partners ensure that the system of interest representation, namely the social dialogue procedure, is representative. Fourth, the Court did not provide clear criteria on how such 'sufficient collective representativeness in relation to the content of the agreement' would be realized, but it gave some additional indications. The criterion of numbers represented 'may be taken into consideration...it cannot be regarded as decisive' (*UEAPME*, para.102). The Court pays particular attention to the relation between the content of the agreement and what it calls the 'mandate' of the organizations. Yet, unlike the Commission in relation to the cross-industry social partners, the Court does not focus on whether the organizations have been internally mandated. With 'mandate' the Court refers to the overall objectives of an organization[9] rather than the internal procedures. It assesses whether these overall objectives correspond with the content of the agreement, in which case the organization is considered representative for the agreement.

While the EU started to set conditions on the representativeness of the social partners during the early 1990s, its main approach regarding interest groups remained focused on encouraging participation rather than being worried about representation. This changes by the end of the 1990s, when the EU, and in particular the European Commission and the EESC, starts to develop a normative discourse on 'civil society' and 'CSOs' in European policy-making as part of a broader attempt to legitimate European decision-making and their own institutional position in particular (Smismans 2003).

However, while the concept of civil society evokes certain normative expectations in relation to democratic decision-making, the relationship between civil society and the question of representation is under-theorized.[10] Depending on the definition, civil society has been attributed different roles in a democratic society (for an overview see Foley and Edwards 1997; Rossteutscher 2000). Yet much of the popularity of the concept results particularly from a dissatisfaction with representative democracy. Civil society theories often refer to civil society as a societal sphere independent from the state, which is essential for democracy but stands to a great extent separate from state institutions, while representation seems an issue that only relates to the latter. Communitarians, for instance, stress the role of traditional family, functioning neighbourhoods, and volunteer associations to revive feelings of community and shared values (Etzioni 1998) while theorists of 'social capital' (for example, Putnam 1993, 1995; Fukuyama 1995) focus on voluntary organizations, such as neighbourhood associations, choral societies, bird-watching clubs, sport clubs, or bowling leagues, which are supposed to generate social capital by supporting norms of reciprocity and civic engagement, building social trust and providing networks of social relations that can be mobilized for civic action. In Central and Eastern Europe the concept of civil society re-entered the political debate stressing the role of the democratic societal forces in opposition to the state-led communist society (Carter 1998; Hirst 1997: 156), whereas in South American and African countries it has been used to draw attention to traditional forms of social organization in confrontation with Western European – imposed state structures.

The EU's reliance on the concept of civil society therefore functions as a double-edged sword. On the one hand, it allows reference to interest groups without a need to address the issue in terms of 'interest *representation*' while nevertheless providing some democratic and legitimating flair to their role beyond the mere argument of increasing effectiveness of policy-making as put forward at the start of the 1990s. On the other hand, by justifying their role in decision-making increasingly in normative terms of democratic added value rather than simply effectiveness, questions about the exact democratic features and representative character of the CSOs themselves would unavoidably emerge after some time.

It is in the 2001 White Paper on European Governance (WPEG) that the discourse on civil society becomes most explicitly mixed up with concerns about the representative character of such participation. The White Paper commits to ensuring better involvement of CSOs in European governance due to their 'important role in giving voice to the concern of citizens and delivering services that meet people's needs' and to 'act as an early warning system for the direction of political debate'. However, 'with better involvement comes greater responsibility' (Commission 2001: 15). The WPEG promises 'additional consultation in return for more guarantees of the openness and representativity of the organizations consulted' (Commission 2001: 4). If CSOs enjoy privileged access to the institutions due to their particular democratic or representative added value, they should be able to give evidence of their representativeness. To this end, the WPEG proposes three follow-up initiatives, namely a database of CSOs, CONECSS, 'which should act as a catalyst to improve their internal organization' (Commission 2001: 15); standards of consultation that 'should improve the representativity of CSOs and structure their debate with the institutions' (Commission 2001: 17); and the development of 'extensive partnership arrangements' which 'in return, will prompt CSOs to tighten their internal structures, furnish guarantees of openness and representativity' (Commission 2001: 17).

The White Paper's concern with the representative character of interest-group participation is characterized by several aspects. First, it proposes organizational representativeness as a central tool to strengthen the representative nature of the overall system of interest participation. Yet organizational representativeness is not applied to all interest groups as a criterion for participation, but only to CSOs. Representative CSOs would profit from 'extensive partnership arrangements', but the Commission does not limit its consultations to them. The White Paper also refers to the consultation of 'interested parties', through Green and White Papers, advisory committees, business test panels, and online consultations. It thus proposes a dual approach, distinguishing between CSOs for which the test of representativeness could imply privileged partnerships, and other 'interested parties' for which such a test does not apply but which could not profit from such privileged partnerships. This creates not only a problem of identifying what the criteria of representativeness are but also of which interest groups and participatory actors would be considered CSOs and which not.

Second, the White Paper and follow-up initiatives remain unclear on the exact scope of application of the concept of representativeness. Not only is there a problem in identifying to which type of interest groups the concept would be applied (CSOs or not), but also for which types of consultative mechanisms. The White Paper links representativeness to 'extensive partnership arrangements' but these have never been developed. The CONECCS database set some criteria of organizational representativeness in order to be included in the list of European CSOs, but it did not identify what the advantage would be for these included organizations in relation to different consultation mechanisms. The standards of consultation, on the other hand, focus on different mechanisms for interest-group participation, but seem to give up on organizational representativeness as a structuring tool (see below).

Thirdly, neither the White Paper nor its follow-up initiatives define clear criteria of organizational representativeness. The White Paper does not define criteria at all. The CONECCS database set out criteria to be included in its list of European CSOs.To be included a CSO needed to be organized at the European level and have member organizations in at least two MS or candidate countries. As for the social partners, full territorial organizational representativeness is not required, assumingly because the plurality of consulted actors could ensure system representativeness. CONECCS also required the CSOs to be non-profit and to have expertise in one or more of the Commission's policy areas. This reads more as answering a functional need of the Commission for expertise, rather than a concern on how representative an organization is in relation to societal demands. The same can be said of the requirement to need 'some degree of formal or institutional existence' and 'be prepared to provide any reasonable information about itself required by the Commission, either for insertion on the database or in support of its request of inclusion'. Only the requirement that a CSO needed 'the authority to speak for its members' suggests a concern about the internal representativeness of the organizations, but the Commission did not outline how this would be verified. A CSO 'should [also] operate in an open and accountable manner' but this reads more as accountability towards the outside world (formulated together with the requirement to provide information to the Commission) rather than a strong concern about internal representativeness. It is thus hard to see how CONECCS could function as a catalyst to 'improve the internal organization' of CSOs as the White Paper had promised.

Finally the standards of consultation do not define criteria of organizational representativeness. The standards of consultation are more concerned with the representativeness of the overall system of interest participation rather than with organizational representativeness, and the latter is not considered a central tool to realize the former. 'For consultation to be equitable' the Commission promises to ensure adequate representation of 'those affected by the policy; those who will be involved in its implementation; and bodies that have stated objectives giving them a direct interest in the policy'. It will take into account the wider impact of the policy, specific experience and expertise, the need to involve non-organized interests 'where appropriate', and participants' track record in previous consultations, and will consider the need for a 'proper balance' between social and economic bodies, large and small organizations or companies, wider constituencies, and organizations in non-member countries (Commission 2002c). All these statements express concern about system representativeness, but organizational representativeness is never proposed as a central tool in that. The representativity of the overall system of interest-group participation is mainly aimed at by pluralizing mechanisms for consultation, in particular by increased use of online consultations, rather than by setting criteria of organizational representativeness for more selective consultative forums. The standards thus fall short from the White Paper's promise that they 'should improve the representativity of CSOs'.

One can conclude that, although the relationship between civil society and the question of representation in a democratic society is not straightforward, the EU's turn to the civil society discourse led to some concern on the representative character of interest-group participation. However, the Commission's attempt to introduce organizational representativeness as a tool to structure interest intermediation, in particular in relation to CSOs (and beyond the particular category of the social partners), faced strong implementation problems both in defining the criteria of representativeness and defining the scope of application of the concept. The more recent European Transparency Initiative (ETI) seems therefore to give up on the idea of representativeness and focuses on transparency rather than representation.

Interest representation and the ETI: transparency rather than representation

In 2006, the European Commission adopted a Green Paper on the European Transparency Initiative (ETI) (Commission 2006) in order to launch a debate on a structured framework for the activities of lobbyists, on the principles and standards of consultation, and on the idea to disclose information on beneficiaries of EU funds. Following the Green Paper's consultation process, the Commission adopted two Communications (Commission 2007b, 2008) providing in particular for a Register of Interest Representatives linked to a Code of Conduct. The Register aims at gathering information on *all types* of interest groups interacting with the European Commission,[11] unlike CONECCS which it replaces and which focused only on European CSOs. Although the Register remains voluntary, the Commission takes a more proactive approach by requiring its staff in their interactions with interest groups to advise them to register. It also provides more information on each interest-group than CONECCS, in particular by requiring financial disclosure of the interest groups' means.

The objective of the ETI is to guarantee a 'high level of transparency' to ensure that the Union is 'open to public scrutiny and accountable for its work'. Unlike the White Paper, the ETI is not focused on structuring interest-group participation, and the concept of 'representativeness' or 'representativity' is completely absent. This goes together with a more general return to the concepts of interest groups and lobbyists rather than talking about CSOs. While the latter are still occasionally mentioned in the ETI, they are not given any differential treatment compared to other interest groups.

The focus is on transparency rather than representation and the idea of organizational representativeness as a structuring device for interest-group participation seems entirely abandoned. Yet the ETI does present some concern about the representative character of interest-group participation. Thus it states that 'it must ... be clear who they [interest groups] represent, what their mission is and how they are funded' (Commission 2007b). Yet this follows the statement that 'when lobby groups seek to contribute to EU policy development, it must be clear *to the general public* which input they provide to the European institutions'. The requirement to be clear on who they represent is more a question of overall accountability than a tool to structure interest-group participation. In a similar way, 'the main objective of revealing how interest representatives are funded is to ensure that decision-makers and the general public can identify and assess the strength of the most important driving forces behind a given lobbying activity'(Commission 2007b: 4). Although this would also allow for the EU Institutions to give more consideration to interest groups that appear 'more representative', the ETI does not provide any guidance on what would be considered representative nor on how exactly this would affect particular consultation mechanisms. While one of the main critiques formulated during the ETI Green Paper consultation related to the fact that there is no mechanism to ensure that targeted consultations are sufficiently balanced, the ETI does not provide a solution for this.

Two remarks need to be made. First, given the predominant focus of the ETI on transparency rather than representation, it may come as a surprise that it is the ETI that introduces for the first time the concept of 'interest representation' in the Commission's official discourse. The use of the concept, however, does not go hand in hand with a particular intention to structure system representativeness or organizational representatives. 'Interest representation' is used as a synonym for 'lobbying' and defined as 'all activities carried out with the objective of influencing the policy formulation and decision-making processes of the European institutions' (Commission 2006: 5, and 2007b: 30), which clearly does not include any reference to the representative nature of such activities. The Commission's recourse to the concept of 'interest representation' seems to stem from a fear that the concept of 'lobbying' will be perceived in a negative way. The Commission stresses that when referring to 'lobbying' it does not include any negative value judgement (Commission 2007b: 3) Yet by using 'lobbying' and 'interest representation' as synonyms, the ETI seems to fight the negative perception other actors might have. The Commission admits that for that reason the new register is called 'Register of Interest Representatives' (Commission 2007b: 3), rather than, for example, 'lobbying register'. This conceptual choice may not be the most accurate as 'representatives' invokes particularly the persons who represent, whereas the Register includes organizations and not persons.

Secondly, while the ETI abandons the concept of representativeness, it may actually contribute to the re-emergence of the concept in the future. The Register provides more systematic information on interest groups than ever before, and structures them in five different categories: professional consultants and law firms; 'in-house' lobbyists and trade associations; NGOs; think tanks; and 'other organizations' (including academic and religious organizations and associations of public authorities). This would facilitate the structuring of interest intermediation by way of organizational representativeness for certain categories as opposed to others. Given the latent struggle of the Commission with organizing its targeted consultations the return to the tool of organizational representativeness is not excluded.

Conclusion

While the EU Institutions have mainly referred to the role of interest groups in European policy-making in terms of *participation*, rather than *representation*, the representative concern has not been entirely absent in the EU's approach and discourse. This concern first emerged in relation to the social partners as the social dialogue provides them with regulatory powers, and takes the form of defining criteria of organizational representativeness. However, the Commission has not been particularly 'interventionist' in setting criteria that would make the organizations more representative in democratic terms. First of all, overall system representativeness of the social dialogue procedure is more important than organizational representativeness of each participating social partner organization. Moreover, the Commission's concern about the internal organization of the social partners seems primarily inspired by functional effectiveness rather than by democratic accountability. It has not been particularly demanding in terms of internal representative structures or in terms of membership numbers. These criteria may play a role in as far as the European social partners have to be confederations. Besides setting a criterion of territorial representatives in relation to the number of Member States represented, the EU thus mainly relies on a decentralized definition of representativeness leaving it up to the Member States to define them and not adding much as European level requirements.

The use of organizational representativeness as a tool to structure interest intermediation was subsequently extended to the larger category of CSOs, in the context of the EU's legitimating move to talk about CSOs rather than interest groups. While organizational representativeness was proposed as a tool to contribute to overall system representativeness of interest intermediation, the definition of criteria and of the scope of application of representativeness proved particularly difficult. As a consequence, the idea to set clear criteria of organizational representativeness seems to be abandoned in the ETI. Yet, while the ETI focuses on transparency rather than representation, the information provided by the Register of Interest Representatives might facilitate the application of representativeness requirements in the future.

Notes

1. For a rare exception see Beate Kohler-Koch (2008) and (2010) on the relation between civil society and representation within the EU as well as the contributions by Jentges, Kröger, Pleines and Rodekamp in this volume.
2. My approach is the flipside of Michael Saward's focus on representative claim-making (Saward 2010). His focus is bottom-up on how actors in a polity make representative claims. Although Saward pays attention to the 'audience' of representative claims, i.e., the group that is spoken to (Saward 2010: 49), his focus is on the democratic legitimacy of representative claims which depends on the 'acceptance by appropriate constituents' (Saward 2010: 144), i.e., the group the claimant claims to speak for (Saward 2010: 49). I look instead top-down at the criteria under which representative claims by interest groups are recognized by the EU institutions.
3. 'The purpose of this Article is to provide a framework and content for the dialogue which is largely already in place between the institutions and civil society', Note from Praesidium to Convention, CONV 650/03: 8 (2 April 2003) as quoted by Bignami 2004: 81.
4. Representativity and representativeness appear to be used as synonyms in EU official discourse, although in particular in relation to the social partners representativity is used more systematically.
5. Negotiation can follow initial consultation by the Commission (at which stage representativeness will already have been checked a first time), but can also emerge at the autonomous initiative of the social partners.
6. This requirement is not set out in the 1993 Communication, but has always been mentioned in the explanatory memorandum sent to the Council when the Commission proposes the implementation of a collective agreement by Council decision.

7. Case T-135/96, Union Européenne de l'Artisanat et des Petites et Moyennes Enterprises (UEAPME) *v.* Council (1998) ECR II-2335.
8. UEAPME was considered representative of small- and medium-sized undertakings but failed to obtain annulment of the collective agreement to which it was not part because the signing social partners were considered by the Court as 'sufficiently representative' of this category. *UEAPME*, para. 110.
9. Thus it refers to the 'general mandate' of Business Europe to represent all types of employers, while UEAPME has a more specific mandate to represent only small- and medium-sized undertakings.
10. For a recent exception, see Kohler-Koch (2008) who distinguishes two main ways in which 'civil society' relates to the question of representation in the European context. The first one focuses on an abstract representation that equates civil society with an active European citizenship. The EU's social constituency is foremost a formation of discourse made up of claims for representation and legitimacy that operates through the imaginary of European (civil) society (Kohler-Koch 2008: 8, with reference to Trenz 2007: 16). The second image of European civil society focuses on 'organised civil society' and its role in a system of political representation.AU: CHANGE OK? For another model of representation of CSOs in EU policy-making, see Kröger in this volume.
11. Negotiations are in place to extend the use of the Register also to the European Parliament and the Council.

13
Democracy Promoter or Interest Defender? How the European Commission Influences Non-Electoral Representation by Civil Society Organizations

Sandra Kröger

Introduction

In the context of the perceived democratic deficit of the EU, and its possible solution with an increase in citizen involvement and participation, much attention has been given to Civil Society Organizations (CSOs), and to whether their inclusion in policy-making can be a means for the democratization of EU politics (Kohler-Koch and Finke 2007; Ruzza 2005). It is often believed that CSOs could serve as a remedy to the legitimacy crisis of the EU by bringing the political system closer to the citizens and vice versa (Kohler-Koch and Edler-Wollstein 2008). In particular, the European Commission has actively engaged in a systematic attempt to promote and develop 'societal representation' at EU level (Bellamy and Castiglione 2010), something reflected in the much debated White Paper on Governance (2001), where the Commission argued that 'its legitimacy today depends on involvement and participation' (Commission 2001: 11).

Ever since the White Paper, the involvement of CSOs in EU policy-making has been on the research agenda. The main focus has been on what CSO involvement contributes to deliberation, participation, and the emergence of a public sphere (Della Sala and Ruzza 2007; Hüller 2010; Steffek and Nanz 2008). We now have a fairly good understanding of the involvement of CSOs in EU policy-making as well as of the

Commission's consultation regime (Kröger 2008). What we lack is theoretical reflection and empirical research into the influence of the institutional environment of the EU on CSOs and their capacities and strategies to represent a constituency or a cause democratically. This is where the present contribution steps in. The specific context conditions that we will consider are the funding and consultation regime of the Commission and the multi-levelness of the EU. The Commission has a vested interest in defending and possibly expanding its competences, not least through the legitimacy that broad CSO consultation seemingly lends it (cf. Greenwood 2010). As a result, CSOs may find themselves co-opted by the Commission (cf. Eder 2011; Kohler-Koch 2010b). The multi-levelness may be an aggravating factor with regard to accountability. CSOs must satisfy multiple 'forums' with, possibly, different preferences: the 'principals' at domestic level and the peers and the Commission at EU level (Papadopoulos 2010: 1038).

The remainder of this contribution is as follows. Section 2 is interested in the ways in which the Commission – CSO relationship has been conceptualized and actually been implemented by the Commission. In order to know whether participating in EU policy-making promotes or hinders non-electoral representation, we need to develop an understanding of democratic representation by CSOs, and this is what section 3 will provide. The next section (4) discusses the ways in which the Commission influences the activities and capacities of CSOs to represent a constituency or a cause, before the final section (5) concludes and discusses to what extent participating in EU policy-making promotes or hinders democratic non-electoral representation.

Three rationales of the European Commission for consultation

Before we address how the Commission can influence the capacity of CSOs to represent democratically, we need to shed some light on the rationale of the Commission to consult CSOs at all. This is important as different rationales should imply different behaviour on the part of the Commission: if it is purely interested in expertise, it must not pay attention to the internal organization of a CSO, whereas, if, for example, the promotion of democracy is the rationale, then the internal structure of CSOs as well as the choice of the CSOs that are consulted are important elements for the Commission to consider. Three such rationales can be identified, and they correspond to three streams in the literature (Kohler-Koch 2009). From a first perspective, the focus is on CSOs and their role in the system of European Governance. The point of departure is the crisis of the welfare state and the apparent weakening of the state and its political authority, which the involvement of civil society is called upon to compensate. It should be mobilized so as to supplement activities formerly performed by the state, allowing the state to focus on the organizational reproduction of society and other, more external, tasks. In this approach, civil society (and representation) is an underdeveloped concept. Instead, the focus is on effective problem-solving, to which CSOs can contribute their knowledge, expertise, and resources, not least in the hope of increasing the loyalty to the decisions taken.

Empirically, with the White Paper on European Governance, civil society participation became associated with 'good governance'. Behind this term, we can identify two expectations, namely, that the inclusion of civil society would contribute to more effective problem-solving, through involving the relevant partners early on, through pooling experiences and ideas, collectively searching for the best solution, and to securing loyalty to decisions through the involvement of the actors in the process, all of which would help to overcome problems of implementation. The Commission obtains expertise at low cost, which CSOs, in the hope of obtaining political influence, are generally happy to provide. In order to obtain the desired expertise, the Commission is keen on interacting with the representatives of European umbrella organizations, such as the Social Platform. Dialoguing with the Social Platform gives the Commission the opportunity to argue that it has consulted with 'the social CSOs' in the EU. However, the Social Platform is an umbrella organization of European umbrella organizations such the European Anti-Poverty Network (EAPN). This means that, if the Commission consults the Social Platform at short notice, it is impossible to reach down to all the local members of the regional members of the national members of the European umbrella organizations of the Social Platform. It is much more likely that the Social Platform will consult its European members (umbrella organizations) in Brussels, which will prepare a reaction, which, at times, could include some brief input by a national EU officer. Here participation is functionally defined according to the value and resources that actors can bring to the policy process (Schmitter 2002: 62–3), and thus belongs to the first rationale of civil society in the EU identified above.

From a second perspective, scholars ask whether CSOs can be a source of democratic legitimacy for the EU, assuming that the EU is a political system in need of democratic legitimation. They are interested in assessing the ways in which CSOs are included in policy-making processes at

EU level, and the impact of this inclusion. CSOs function as transmission belts that bring the interests and values of citizens to the EU (Steffek and Nanz). From this perspective, the role attributed to civil society is to 'mediate between the national and the supranational, thereby connecting national society to transnational governance' (Rumford 2003: 32). Little attention has been given, in this context, to the organizational structure of participating CSOs, and to whether they are internally democratically organized (however, see Altides and Kohler-Koch 2009; Steffek et al. 2010b).

After periods characterized by consultation (1960s and 1970s) and partnership (1980s–1990s), the consultation regime dubbed 'participatory democracy' (Kohler-Koch and Finke 2007) also began with the process around the White Paper on European Governance, published by the Commission in July 2001 (Commission 2001). The White Paper, in contrast to previous Commission Communications, no longer focuses on interest groups and lobbyists, but, instead, refers 20 times to civil society (Smismans 2009). The preliminary peak of these developments was Article 47 of the Draft Constitutional Treaty, which specified that 'the Union's institutions shall maintain an open, transparent and regular dialogue with representative associations and civil society' (European Convention 2003) and a legal duty is now established in the Treaty of Lisbon to consult CSOs. Most recent developments, in contrast, indicate that, under the Barroso leadership of the Commission, CSOs have almost disappeared from the discourse, whereas interest groups and lobbyists are back in the game (see the contribution by Smismans in this volume).

From a third perspective, the EU is seen as an emergent polity. Here scholars focus on the link between a social constituency and active citizenship (Fossum and Trenz 2005; Trenz 2009a) and on the creation of a demos-equivalent outside the framework of the nation-state (Eriksen and Fossum 2000). As an emergent polity, the EU is in need of direct legitimacy, a necessary condition of which is an (emergent) political community and a European public sphere, to which CSOs could possibly contribute. Approaches belonging to this realm are interested in the social space(s) of the EU, distinct from state and market, in their active constructions, and in the norms that are constructed within them. These spaces and the claims expressed in them, so the assumption goes, are a necessary precondition both for further polity-building as well as for further democratization.

Empirically, this rationale corresponds to a more hidden agenda in civil society consultation by European institutions, which is that of system integration. If the Commission can argue that its position is based upon broad consultation with CSOs, its bargaining power vis-à-vis the Council will be increased (Greenwood 2007a). By consulting diverse actors, the Commission can claim more legitimacy for its own proposals, be they of a legislative character or not. The Commission, like other actors in the institutional triangle of the EU, is in a never-ending quest to defend, and, if possible, to expand, its competences. In order to do so, particularly in policy areas where it enjoys restricted competences, it is of the utmost importance to show that it is acting in line with the so-called 'European interest'. According to the Commission, nothing could show this better than an apparently broad consultation (with pro-European) CSOs. Thus, the consultations of CSOs also serve the objective of legitimizing non-elected institutions such as the Commission itself (Bauer 2002; Saurugger 2008: 1284; Smismans 2004b). In principle, we can thus identify in practice all three rationales for including civil society: effective policy-making, the function of a transmission belt, in order to enhance the democratic legitimacy, and system integration.

While the second of these rationales is generally concerned with the issue of democratic legitimacy, it has not paid sufficient attention to the issue of democratic representation by CSOs, and this is what the next section sets out to do.

Non-electoral representation of constituencies

Representation traditionally relates to a complex relationship between a principal (the represented) and an agent (the representative), concerning an object (a claim), taking place before an audience. The relationship has traditionally been seen as consisting of authorization and accountability (Castiglione and Warren 2008). The typical institutional translation of representation has been for the constituents periodically to elect representatives who are, in some way, accountable to the constituency. More recently, it has been argued that representation is much more diverse than elected legislatures, that it is realized by a great variety of actors, that it is more dynamic than the principal–agent model assumes, and that it takes place in more spaces and instances than through elections, in parliament and in the nation-state (Lord and Pollak 2010; Rehfeld 2006; Saward 2006; Taylor 2010; Trenz 2009a; Warren and Castiglione 2004). Michael Saward, in particular, understands representation as claims-making, a constantly changing and dynamic social dialogue in which different actors make claims to audiences who discuss, reject, or amend them (Saward 2006). Conceiving of political representation as a dynamic relationship opens the door to reflect the political field in which it takes place as well as the power relationships that operate within it.

So, how can we think of representation in non-electoral modes, and in the multi-level context of the EU? And which sort of non-electoral representation could be called democratic representation? Indeed, there are forms of ('surrogate') representation that transcend the limitations created by territoriality (Mansbridge 2003), and CSOs can have an important role in making up for the deficiencies of territorial representation in that they are not necessarily linked to a territory, but, often enough, linked to a cause. In order for representation to be called democratic, certain criteria have to be met. Such representation either requires a reliable link to a constituency that is actively involved in the will-formation process and is its ultimate author. From such a perspective, a rather minimalistic, procedural definition of democracy will suffice (Dahl 1989; Schumpeter 1950). Political representation here is democratic if certain procedural minima are respected (one person, one vote; fair and free elections; etc.). Alternatively, representation can be called democratic if it represents interests that are otherwise not represented. From such a perspective, a minimalistic definition of democracy will not do. Instead, the quality of democracy is taken into consideration, so that the more the members of a political system are included in decision-making, the more the political system is democratic (Young 2002). Given these considerations, two kinds of ideal types of representation by CSOs, which can be called democratic, come to mind, dubbed 'member representation', and 'solidarity' (cf. Halpin 2006).

'Member representation' is available to constituencies that are human, and are capable of presence and voice. Members of such organizations are identical with the constituency whose interests are being advocated (Binderkrantz 2009; Halpin 2006; McLaverty 2002: 309–10). Here, delegation chains from the local/regional level to the EU level typically exist so that members can authorize their representatives and can hold them to account. Representation, therefore, can be expected to function according to a delegate model of representation. Mechanisms are typically in place which, theoretically, assure that what the European umbrella organization does is linked to what national policy-officers asked it to do, while the latter's preferences are linked to will-formation processes by national and regional members. This has been the dominant way of looking at the issue of a legitimate role for functional representation in EU policy-making, as it (theoretically) provides citizens with a regular opportunity to voice their preferences and to take part in EU policy-making. Accordingly, empirical research has asked what are the ways in which members can participate in the agenda-setting, will-formation, and decision-making of the CSO of which they are a member. Whether or not representation can actually be called democratic depends on whether CSOs are including their constituencies in will-formation processes and the extent to which, and by which mechanisms, this inclusion is procedurally institutionalized (see the contribution by Meike Rodekamp to this volume).

Who or what is being represented is typically accompanied by different capacities to organize and mobilize. Member-based CSOs typically organize and mobilize (sectoral) professional interests, often with (re-)distribution effects that directly concern their members, leading to strong competition among the actors involved. Such CSOs are typically well-resourced, not least due to membership fees. Against this background we can expect that the members themselves have a strong personal incentive to influence will-formation within the CSO, as the success of its activities will – (more or less) directly – influence the (economic) well-being of the members.

Accountability is the other side of the representative relationship and a key feature of democratic checks and balances, which demands that those who exercise power can be controlled in their function (Stewart 1992), in this case by the members. It assures that exercising power is conditional, that representatives must be responsive to feedback, and, in the event of dubious or erroneous behaviour, that they must take the blame and suffer the consequences of their actions (Arnull and Wincott 2002; Papadopoulos 2007). How can we think of accountability in the context of member-based, non-electoral representation in the EU? The preconditions of accountability would, here, consist of internal transparency and access to the relevant information throughout the policy process, informed debates among members and their representatives about policy options, and the institutionally foreseen possibility of holding representatives to account and of choosing other representatives in the event of discontent.

Transparency mechanisms enable the free flow of information between organizations and their members in decision-making, performance, and reporting. Reporting and disclosure systems, and processes that enable information-sharing among parties, are central to an effective accountability relationship. Examples include audited accounts and annual reports made available to members, organizational or project evaluations, strategic plans based upon external assessments, and regular communications (newsletters, updates, briefs). They all provide channels for access to information about the organization's work, financial status, governance structure, and operational impact. Informed debate among members is crucial, as it is here that all the relevant reasons, their benefits and shortcomings, as well as political alternatives, can be exchanged and discussed. Transparency and informed debate allow for responsiveness. Evaluation mechanisms such as monitoring and impact assessments or the simple exit of members are examples of ways to support responsiveness. Responsiveness, in turn, can, theoretically, lead to sanctions. Violations of constituent mandates can lead to the replacement of the elected leadership if the respective transparency and sanctioning mechanisms are in place (Kohler-Koch 2010).

Not all CSOs function according to a logic of 'member representation'. There are also organizations that function according to a logic of 'solidarity' (Halpin 2006), that is, they represent a cause that does not relate to a living human constituency, such as the environment, animals, or future generations. In the literature, these CSOs are often called public interest groups (White 2010). Here, the people affiliated to the organization are not those for whom the organization advocates. Accordingly, identifying affiliates (as supporters or members) is more difficult than for the previously discussed organizations, with the consequence that such organizations are typically not grounded on members who will authorize representatives and hold them to account (although this does not preclude such organizations from offering membership to supporters). The people who affiliate with such organizations will, in turn, commonly be less interested in influencing will-formation in the organization; for them, it is sufficient to support the abstract cause by being affiliated with the organization in some, more or less direct way, for example, by financial support (Binderkrantz 2009; Maloney 2009). Such CSOs seek to gain their legitimacy from the force of the better argument, ideally supported by scientific expertise (Halpin 2006), from pursuing the 'public good', and from bringing in perspectives which are frequently overseen by conventional political institutions (Mansbridge 2003: 524). Broad, public communication strategies are developed in order to attract support for abstract causes (Binderkrantz 2008).

Contrary to what is commonly assumed – public interest organizations are particularly democratic in the sense that they involve broad member involvement – these organizations can be expected to correspond less to traditional democratic standards than sectoral organizations. The central difference between organizations that work according to a logic of 'representation' and those following a logic of 'solidarity' (or public interest) is that the former work to advance their own benefit, whereas the latter defend a broader cause. Again, this corresponds to organization and mobilization capacities. When diffuse interests are mobilized, affiliates are not *immediately* concerned about the results of the organizations' activities, not least as no (re-)distributional issues that directly involve the affiliates are at stake. In such cases, there is commonly a rather broad consensus about the issue at stake (the protection of the environment, of animals, future generations, etc.) rather than a competitive logic, as occurs in sectoral cases. Finally, these types of organizations are, generally, weakly equipped in terms of financial and human resources.

In this type of non-electoral representation, where there are no regularized means of authorization through members, authorization can grow from the ability of groups to attract supporters. Such support can take different forms: petitions, demonstrations, donations, or broad media support, but also members. Identifying the accountability processes of such CSOs is, due to the lack of one clearly identifiable constituency, inherently difficult. Are they exclusively accountable to universal ideas or should their activities also be subject to internal control mechanisms? These CSOs tend to have several constituencies at a time: activists, beneficiaries, members, donors, and parts of the public, and these different addressees may have different accountability standards which may, at times, be incompatible with one another. However, we may find in-built accountability mechanisms even here. The first is the potential distance between the values which CSOs defend and their actual practices. If this distance becomes too obvious, they will lose support (and funding) due to a credibility gap. The second is competition between CSOs with similar goals, which tends to work in favour of mutual oversight and peer review, including that of the media (horizontal accountability). The third is related to the effectiveness of CSOs. If they fail to accomplish what they were set up for, vanishing support is also likely to happen. Thus, even in the case of informal accountability mechanisms, CSOs can be held to account.

Let us now turn to how the Commission's consultations can potentially have an impact on the capacities and strategies of CSOs to represent constituencies or causes in the multi-level system of the EU.

The potential influence of the commission practices on CSOs

The Commission carries out consultations in almost all policy areas today. The consultation of CSOs takes place in the context of preparing

Green and White Papers, consultation reports, and communications. There are several forums for consultation, such as advisory committees, expert groups, and ad hoc consultation structures, and there are also more informal consultations. Consultation through the Internet is also increasingly frequent, as reflected, for instance, in the 'Interactive Policy-Making Initiative' and websites that organize public consultations. How can the capacity of CSOs to represent a constituency or a cause be affected by the practices of the Commission? It is to this question that we now turn. We can picture two main ways in which the Commission influences CSOs and their capacities and strategies, namely, through its consultation regime, and through funding, as we will see in more detail below.

One way of potentially having an impact on CSOs lies in their inclusion in consultation processes at EU level. The Commission has developed very different ways of involving CSOs in EU policy-making (Mahoney 2004). After very diverse consultation traditions in the different Directorates General (DGs) throughout the period from the 1970s to the 1990s, the Commission's legitimacy crisis in 1999 led to a massive change towards more institutionalized dialogue with CSOs in all DGs, even though differences remain between them, with some of the DGs consulting more than others (Kröger 2008).

Does the Commission consider the principle of representation when choosing with whom it will consult? When looking at the broad definition of 'civil society' by the Commission, it does not seem so: 'Civil society includes the following: trade unions and employers' organizations ("social partners"); non-governmental organizations; professional associations; charities; grass-roots organizations; organizations that involve citizens in local and municipal life with a particular contribution from churches and religious communities' (Commission 2001: 14). Nevertheless, the Commission has started to consider that CSOs should be representative: 'With better involvement comes greater responsibility. Civil society must itself follow the principles of good governance, which include accountability and openness' (Commission 2001: 15). The Commission thus asks for organizational representativeness (see the contribution by Stijn Smismans to this volume), in particular with regard to the so-called partnership arrangements that institutionalize a privileged dialogue with the actors chosen:

> In some policy sectors, where consultative practices are already well established, the Commission could develop more extensive partnership arrangements. On the Commission's part, this will entail a

> commitment for additional consultations compared to the minimum standards. In return, the arrangements will prompt civil society organisations to tighten up their internal structures, furnish guarantees of openness and representativity, and prove their capacity to relay information or lead debates in the Member States. (ibid. 17)

Indeed, we do find an evolving body of documents by the Commission and by CSOs on reciprocal expectations and the modalities of consultations.[1] Notwithstanding this, the representativity of CSOs continues to be provided upon a voluntary basis and the Commission does not exclude non-representative organizations and actors from its consultation process, either: 'Representativity, though an important criterion, should not be the only determining factor for membership of an advisory committee, or to take part in dialogue with the Commission. Other factors, such as their track record and ability to contribute substantial policy inputs to the discussion are equally important' (Commission 2000: 9; see also Commission 2002a: 11–12). In other words, good policy ideas are not necessarily representative ones. This policy clearly upsets organizations which are, or which consider themselves to be, representative, because they fear that their (potential) influence will decrease in favour of non-representative organizations. By way of example, the European Social Platform has found common cause with Business Europe, the principal EU business group, in advocating an accreditation scheme with criteria which very closely reflect its own status as a designated principal social partner organization. These are based upon a high threshold of 'representativity', centred upon geographic coverage and the ability of members to speak for their constituencies.

If CSOs want to be capable of influencing the Commission, then they need to be able to react quickly, 'on demand', and they need to be capable of providing specific expertise. In particular, if representation corresponds to a mandate by members and relies on structures of internal democracy, then the normally allocated period of eight weeks for consultation is clearly insufficient (Ruzza 2005: 22). These requirements will structure the work organization of the liaison offices in Brussels, which will become ever more specialized and professionalized in the context of their lobbying activities (Maloney 2009) while increasingly losing contact with the grass-roots level of their organizations with which there is seldom any direct exchange. Officials of the CSOs themselves do not seem to be too troubled by this development: 'While ideally it would be good to get people involved... my role is not to encourage the most participatory governance, but to ensure the best results for the environment' (Senior officer, European Environmental Bureau, quoted in Sudbery 2003: 91–2). In order to be heard, most of the time CSOs will, furthermore, adopt consensus-seeking strategies and positions, and seek to avoid conflict (Beyers and Kerremans 2007), thereby possibly deviating from what their members at the grass-roots level would opt for.

Another central way of influencing the activities of CSOs is through funding (Greenwood 2007a). Indeed, European funding schemes and the expenditure for NGO activities have constantly risen since the 1970s (Commission 2000): 'It spends approximately 1 percent (1bn) [euro] on funding groups and almost the entire (300) citizen interest group universe (excluding Greenpeace) mobilized at the EU level receives some EU funding' (Maloney 2007: 77), with some umbrella organizations receiving up to 90 per cent of their total funding from the Commission (see the contribution by Johansson in this volume). Funds to support EU level civil society are available from various sources. They come from specific budget lines,[2] especially with a view to promoting the so-called European interest. By now, the different budget lines have been transformed into a programme called the Community Action Programme to promote active European Citizenship. Its goal is to promote the European idea and to bring citizens closer to the European institutions through conferences, seminars, workshops, networking, exchanges, and education and training events (European Council 2004).[3] Important budget lines are, of course, also found in the context of the European Structural Funds in which CSOs participate.

How does giving money to CSOs influence them in ways that distort their capacity to represent democratically? The money, to put it in a nutshell, is not provided unconditionally. Rather, the money is given to CSOs in order to strengthen the bargaining position of the Commission (Bauer 2002; Maloney 2007): 'One of the most visible methods governments employ to guide activity is government contracts. By deciding what projects are to be funded and who will be responsible for bringing the projects to fruition, institutions guide policy debates and wield considerable control over interest activity' (Mahoney 2004: 444). Many of the supported actions consist of seminars, workshops, information diffusion and/or awareness-raising activities, to name the most current ones. These activities clearly do not prioritize the original activity of each and every CSO; instead, they prioritize the setting-up of transnational networks, and through them, 'European ways' of doing things. Accordingly, the bulk of the money provided to each CSO is linked to these activities, so that people can come together, meet, exchange, learn from each other, and so forth, all of which are respectable aims, but they do also redirect the human resources of CSOs away from their original purpose.

Another requirement in order to attract EU money, intended to work in favour of network-building, is that CSOs increasingly have to be part of a transnational Co-operation Partnership (Commission 2003). While the Commission was at first somewhat vague about what was meant by these partnerships, it now clearly sets out their format and their specific characteristics. This implies, first, that CSOs must become active and find potential partners both within and outside the EU, which takes time away from their other activities while leaving the added value of the emerging transnational partnership completely open. Second, it implies that those CSOs which cannot identify such potential partners, for whatever reasons, are excluded from European funding, as are those CSOs which cannot assure the demanded amount of co-financing. Thus, the funding schemes privilege the larger CSOs over the smaller ones, with the implication that CSOs will seek to assemble under umbrella organizations, which, by definition, assemble a broad variety of organizations. They also privilege those CSOs which are ready to use the dominant EU-speak as well as the dominant approaches to specific policy areas over more critical ones.[4] Call for proposals lay out in detail which sort of activities are open to funding, thereby excluding other activities which do not appear in the proposals, but which CSOs may wish to pursue. Overall, this means that the Commission sets the tone for who will obtain funding and who will not, and that it privileges certain CSOs over others.

Conclusion and discussion

The Commission influences the activities of CSOs through its consultation regime and through direct subsidies and other financial incentives. It determines which issues are granted attention in formal debates and who participates in these debates. In so doing, the Commission pursues two major aims. First, it gets expertise at low cost by relying on the willingness of the CSOs to provide such expertise in the hope of exercising some political influence. Second, by consulting diverse actors, the Commission can claim more legitimacy for its own proposals in the name of the so-called 'European interest'. Like other actors in the EU institutional triangle, the Commission has a vested interest in defending, and, if possible, expanding, its competences. These two goals are in support of effective governance and of system integration, but not of enhancing the democratic quality of policy-making.

As a result of the influence of the institutional environment, CSOs 'may be trapped by the need to adapt to the "logic of influence" prevailing in Brussels' (Kohler-Koch, Quittkat and Buth 2008: 6). The price of participating in EU policy-making, and of access to it, may be that CSOs will have to act like any other interest group and transform themselves from 'an instance of defence against state power to a partner of political power' (Eder 2009: 25). The representation of a human constituency or of a public cause, which may stand in contrast to the Commission's standpoint or agenda, may take second place to the more functional objectives of being part of the policy-making process.

What are the consequences in terms of democratic representation? Connecting EU policy processes to real people in the Member States, who could be democratically represented by CSOs, might, in the context of the multi-level structure and the pressure towards professionalization and adaptation, in effect, be impossible to realize. The institutional environment of the Commission may imply, occasionally, that members, or strong public support by larger publics, are no longer necessary if CSOs are broadly funded by the Commission, that is, that a constituency is increasingly rendered obsolete. Or as Maloney puts it: 'Why spend a great deal of organizational resources seeking and servicing members, when patronage permits fully focussed professional lobbying?' (Maloney 2007: 80). If there are (involved) members, then the professionalization implies that they are not necessarily the ones who decide upon the topics with which they wish to deal, and the activities which they wish to pursue (at least, not if they are interested in EU funding, which has become a major funding source for many CSOs, to the point of their being dependent on it), but that the Commission does.

To put it in a nutshell: the way in which the Commission chooses its civil dialogue partners, the way it organizes consultation, and the influence that the latter has on CSOs does not support the democratic representation both of and by CSOs. The Commission uses a wide and ambiguous 'definition' of civil society: the representativeness of the CSOs that participate in the consultations is not assured, and the funding and consultation regimes of the Commission leave traces on CSOs that distance them from their grass-roots organizations, thereby decreasing their democracy-enhancing potential. Democratic representation either requires strong ties between CSOs and their members, or requires CSOs to be in a position to represent weak interests, both of which are not given. We are thus left with the effectiveness and system integration rationales, both of which are centred around the interests of the Commission. Here, however, CSOs lose their theoretical capacity of independently promoting interests, as they increasingly become interwoven with both state and market structures, and their respective funding, and therewith also become increasingly dependent on these (Kohler-Koch and Edler-Wollstein 2008).

Should we be surprised? Not really. The Commission is the guardian of the Treaties and, as such, is partial. It will support initiatives which, in its view, are in line with the Treaties, and it will not support initiatives that it sees as being in conflict with the Treaties. This is clearly an aim other than the promotion of democracy, with which it is meant to conflict. The promotion of democracy would call for a Commission that is open to criticism of those self-same Treaties. These structural barriers are difficult, if not impossible, to overcome. We are therefore likely to continue to see a Commission that is primarily acting according to its own (particularistic) interests, rather than being interested in realizing the democratic representation of all EU citizens.

Notes

1. http://europa.eu.int/comm/civil_society/apgen_en.htm
   http://europa.eu.int/yourvoice/consultations/index_en.htm
   http://europa.eu.int/comm/civil_society/coneccs/index.htm
   Commission (2002a), *Communication from the Commission: Towards a reinforced culture of consultation and dialogue – General principles and minimum standards for consultation of interested parties by the Commission*, COM (2002) 704 final.
2. See, for instance, Commission 2005.
3. For the programme period 2007–2013, 232 million euro are available for these purposes (Commission 2005).
4. This evidently also holds true for research funded by programmes that the Commission administers.

14
Representing Workers or Presenting EU Prescriptions? Trade Unions from Post-Socialist Member States in EU Multi-Level Governance

Heiko Pleines

Introduction

From both the historical and legal perspectives, trade unions belong to the non-state actors with the highest degree of involvement in political representation in European societies. From a historical perspective, trade unions were one of the first collective actors with a mass following to emerge in the wake of industrialization and, therefore, received special attention from policy-makers. As a result, their prerogatives, over other interest groups, together with those of employers' associations, were codified in most European countries through special legislation on wage bargaining and social dialogues. Through the European Social Dialogue they also have – at least de jure – a privileged position in EU level policy-making.

At the same time, their role involves specific challenges for representation, as their constituencies (just members, all workers, or also the unemployed?), the major addressee (employers or the state?), and the major arena of representation (enterprises, national collective bargaining, or political arena?) differ both among Member States of the European Union and over time. In this context, weak trade unions offer an interesting case of interest representation in the EU, as they are more likely to reflect the impact of the EU on their role than to bend the EU to their liking. This is why this chapter will examine the impact EU membership has had on the political representation by trade unions from the new post-socialist Member States.

The following analysis is based on 70 interviews with representatives from 13 trade unions in new Member States and experts conducted in summer 2007, and on detailed case studies of trade union actions concerning specific policy issues.[1] Three of the larger new Member States, Poland, the Czech Republic, and Slovakia, were chosen for the empirical analysis. Taken together, these countries have a large number of trade unions, and their trade unions also possess different organizational structures. In each of the three countries national umbrella organizations were selected alongside the branch unions for the metal and for the mining industries. The trade union studies include the most powerful trade unions in the larger post-socialist EU Member States, which joined in 2004, as most other trade unions from the new Member States are not active at the EU level. Although there are strong differences between the trade unions selected concerning their position in the national political arena, their stance towards the EU and their performance in political representation are quite similar. Accordingly, the following analysis treats all trade unions covered as one case of political representation by relatively strong trade unions from new post-socialist Member States.

First, the representative function of trade unions is discussed with reference to Hanna Pitkin's dimensions of representation in order to illustrate the forms of representation feasible for trade unions in their respective states and at the EU level (section 2). After that, the integration of trade unions into policy-making in the system of EU governance is briefly described in order to assess the governance structures to which trade unions from the Member States had to adapt when they joined the EU (section 3). Third, the actual integration of trade unions from the new Member States at the EU level (section 4) and into decision-making processes in EU multi-level governance (section 5) will be examined in order to assess the representative functions they perform. These sections will argue that the political representation by trade unions can only be explained as a result of the interrelation between the EU and the national level. The analysis of trade unions' representative functions in EU multi-level governance also allows for an assessment of Europeanization tendencies (section 6). The final section then concludes and discusses the results.

Trade unions and representation: an analytical framework

In contrast to political parties and similar to other non-state actors, trade unions do not see political representation, that is, participation in public policy-making processes, as their main task. Instead, the major focus of trade unions is traditionally on representing workers vis-à-vis the employers. In a broader perspective, Ewing (2005) distinguishes five core functions of trade unions: service provision; representation in the workplace; rule making (through collective bargaining); governing (through direct or indirect participation in policy-making); and public administration (through participation in the implementation of legislation). Thus the core functions of trade unions related to representation are directed first at employers and second at public policy-makers and state bureaucrats. The focus of this analysis is on the governing and public administration functions, which are based on political representation as the organized representation of working people in the political arena at all governance levels.

In order to assess the different representative functions performed by trade unions in the political arena, they will be linked to the basic dimensions of representation as described by Hanna Pitkin (1967): formalistic representation; substantive representation; descriptive representation; and symbolic representation.

In Pitkin's typology, formalistic representation refers to the institutional mechanisms which legitimize or initiate representation. She differentiates between authorization and accountability. The first refers to a representative as someone who has been authorized through election. The latter focuses on the possible termination of representation, seeing a representative as someone who will be held to account for his or her performance. Substantive representation looks at what the representative does for his or her constituency. Here, Pitkin distinguishes between three types of 'acting for' the represented: the idea of substitution (i.e. acting instead of someone as a trustee); the idea of taking care (i.e. acting in the interest of someone as a caretaker); and the idea of subordination (i.e. acting on instructions as an agent). Descriptive representation refers to the resemblance between constituency and representative. This aspect of representation does not look at the action of the representative, but rather at common features shared by the constituency and the representative. Likewise, symbolic representation does not refer to anything that a representative does, but highlights a symbolic 'standing for' someone or something. Symbolic representation is thus based on the beliefs of the constituency and does not require any rational or objective connection between the constituency and the representative (Pitkin 1967).

The representation of employees in political arenas, that is, political representation by trade unions can take on different forms. As internal democracy is normally required by national legislation, the representative function of trade unions within the EU is based on formalistic representation, namely through authorization based on the election of the leadership, while accountability mechanisms are often more weakly developed. In collective bargaining, that is, in representation vis-à-vis employers, the substantive representation by trade unions often takes the form of agency as members have to approve the agreement reached. In political representation, however, trade unions are more likely to act as caretakers not bound by specific orders or the preferences of their constituency. Descriptive and symbolic representation may also play an important role in the case of trade unions, especially as a source of legitimacy, but they are not formally required or regulated.

Representation of trade unions in EU governance

At the EU level political representation by trade unions can take place through five channels: (1) direct consultations with the European Commission; (2) consultations with national representatives in the Council of Ministers; (3) direct consultations with the EU Parliament; (4) participation in the Social Dialogue; and (5) involvement in the European Economic and Social Committee (EESC).[2] An office in Brussels and membership in European umbrella organizations are also frequently cited as ways to obtain influence. However, both in and of themselves they do not guarantee involvement in decision-making processes. They can just facilitate the pursuit of the avenues listed above.

The first three options are based on access to the standard EU decision-making process, while the fourth option, the Social Dialogue, is available only to the social partners, and the fifth, the EESC, only to selected non-state actors. The Social Dialogue offers trade unions, together with employers' associations, privileged access to political representation. Within the legal framework of the European Social Dialogue the social partners have the right to initiate regulations in the area of social policy if they express interest. However, the Social Dialogue has not had a broader impact on EU policy-making, as it has resulted in a very small number of agreements on regulation and none at all since the EU's Eastern enlargement of 2004. Another institutionalized possibility for trade union participation in the EU decision-making process is via the EESC, which, however, is endowed solely with an advisory capacity to the European Commission, Council, and Parliament (Obradovic and Alonso 2006).

Moreover, at the EU level, competences in labour-market regulation and social policy are limited in scope and largely focus on establishing health and safety regulations in the workplace, regulating labour migration within the EU and equalizing the status of female employees. Collective wage bargaining, one of the major tasks of trade unions, is still done exclusively below the EU level. Nevertheless, the competences of the EU in the field of social policy have been systematically expanded since the beginning of the 1990s. And through the Open Method of Coordination (OMC), a more sweeping EU-wide harmonization of social integration, pension funds, and health care has been attempted since 2000 (for an overview see Kröger 2009). Moreover, the EU competences in the economic sphere also possess implications for labour-market regulation, as, for example, the EU Service Directive has shown (Falkner 2006; see also Edquist 2006; Falkner 2007; Schäfer and Leiber 2009).

Due to the limited competences of the EU in labour-market and social policy, and also the inertia of the EU Social Dialogue, the national level is still of major importance in these fields of social and labour policies. At the national level the regulation of political representation by trade unions shows considerable variations across EU Member States. This concerns not only the organization and competences of national social dialogues and further avenues of formal involvement in policy-making processes,[3] but also rules for establishing the status of a trade union or regulation concerning forms of engagement; for example, in Germany strikes as a form of protest are restricted to collective bargaining, but in France strikes can be highly politicized.

As a result, labour relations continue to be strongly organized along national lines. Large differences in the national regulations of the collective bargaining process also lead to large differences in the interests and policy preferences of trade unions (Busemeyer et al. 2007). All this does not prevent transnational trade union solidarity in specific cases, especially against specific EU directives (such as the Bolkestein draft on service liberalization, see Gajewska 2008) or against specific employers (for instance in the Laval, Viking, and Rüffert cases of 2008, see Zahn 2008). But, due to different national concerns, consensus on concrete policy measures is difficult to reach between the social partners. In addition, national trade unions – even as members – are often reluctant in their support for European umbrella organizations (Falkner 2000; Hyman 2005; Rojot 2004).

Trade unions from the post-socialist member states at the EU level

Weak trade unions have been chosen for this study, as they are more likely to directly reflect the impact of the EU on their role and thus allow for a clearer assessment of the impact the EU has on political interest representation. Trade unions in the post-socialist Member States, with the exception of Slovenia, are considered to be very weak (Crowley 2004; Ost 2006; Vanhuysse 2007). Due to their socialist legacy, many trade unions in the new, post-socialist EU Member States still boast relatively large numbers of members, but are organizationally limited in their ability to represent interests in the political arena. The trade unions are only associated in comparatively loose umbrella associations. Trade union representatives often shy away from political responsibility and have barely any experience in working with supranational committees. The weakness of the post-socialist trade unions is also demonstrated by the fact that none of the national level tripartite committees in the new Member States has led to successful trade union participation in political decision-making processes in the new EU Member States (Casale 2000; Mailand and Due 2004). The trade unions' influence on national politics is generally perceived as minimal (Ost 2006; Sil and Candland 2001; Avdagic 2005; Matthes and Terletzki 2005). On the basis of a comprehensive study, Stephen Crowley concludes that labour relations in the new EU Member States tend to resemble the American model, and therefore might not be compatible with the EU's system (Crowley 2004; similarly Vanhuysse 2007).

The relative weakness of trade unions in the political arenas was confirmed in our study of the EU level. Even the most influential trade unions from Poland, the Czech Republic, and Slovakia barely exert any influence on EU decision-making processes via direct consultations with EU organs. Direct consultations with the European Commission are a rare exception and were cited by only two trade unions. Consultations with the national representatives in the Council of Ministers were mentioned by three trade unions. Consultations with the European Parliament occur somewhat more frequently. Five of the trade unions polled have access to the Parliament, mostly because some trade union members are Members of the European Parliament. Only the three largest national trade union organizations from Poland and the Czech Republic have any meaningful access to direct consultations.

One reason for the limited use of direct consultations by trade unions from the new Member States is that none of them has an office in Brussels (Krech 2008: 58). The trade union members responsible tend to travel to Brussels only when they have a concrete appointment there. Their interests are instead represented by a European umbrella organization (10 of the 13 trade unions) and by the Economic and Social Committee (8). Accordingly, only 3 per cent of the interviewees felt that their trade union was capable of representing their interests at the EU level adequately. The great majority depend on a European umbrella organization to further their interests, and roughly a third relies on cooperation with other national trade unions.

The participation of the Polish, Czech, and Slovak trade unions in the decision-making processes at the EU level thus takes place almost exclusively via EU-wide umbrella organizations or through membership in EU committees, above all the EESC. The trade union representatives interviewed perceive cooperation with the European umbrella organizations, above all the European Trade Union Confederation (ETUC), as overwhelmingly positive. Only 4 per cent reported having had predominantly negative experiences. The fixation of the new trade unions on the European trade union federations is also underscored by the fact that nearly every trade union interviewed named these as the best cooperation partners at the EU level. However, Józef Niemiec, from Poland's Independent and Self-Governing Trade Union Solidarność (NSZZ Solidarność), has been the only trade union representative from the post-socialist Member States to gain a leadership position in one of the corresponding European umbrella organizations (Krech 2008).

Accordingly, it can be argued that trade unions from the new Member States are being represented by the European umbrella organizations at the EU level. Thus, the representation of workers is delegated twice, first from the original constituency to the national trade unions and then from the national trade unions to the European umbrella organizations. Hence, formalistic representation is institutionalized only between the direct representatives of the national level and the indirect representatives at the EU level. As Lis (2012) demonstrates, there is also a relation of substantive representation between national and EU level trade union leaderships. However, the 'membership-chain', conceptualized by Kohler-Koch and Buth (2009) as the number of organizational levels which have to be bridged to communicate from Brussels to the grass roots and vice versa, is quite long for trade unions, though less complex than for many NGOs, where heterarchy and organizational nestling blur or transcend direct bottom-up and top-down links (Kohler-Koch and Buth 2009: 18–20). The link across the different governance levels is rather weak in the case of trade unions, but it still follows a functional bottom-up/top-down logic.

Based on the empirical findings, it can be assumed that trade unions from the post-socialist Member States have very limited access to channels of influence at the EU level. Not even a handful of the trade unions from the new Member States are visible in the relevant forums of political decision-making. Although trade unions from the post-socialist Member States consider the EU to be highly relevant, they primarily rely on collective interest representation through the European trade union movement, if they are active at the EU level at all (Pleines 2008b; Einbock 2008; Mansfeldova 2008; Cambalikova 2008).

This means that the trade unions from the new Member States do not really engage in interest representation at the EU level; they are only present through membership in the umbrella organizations and the EESC. Accordingly, an analysis restricted to the EU level would find that trade unions from the new Member States are unable to perform any representative functions at the EU level. However, if the perspective is broadened to include the full multi-level system of EU governance, one can see that EU integration has had a distinct impact on political representation by trade unions from the new Member States.

A multi-level perspective

Although their link to the EU level is rather weak, the trade union representatives from the new Member States attribute great importance to the EU. More than half of them consider the EU and national levels to be of equal importance, while one-third thinks that the EU is even more important than national politics. At the same time, the role of the EU is viewed very positively. Nearly 90 per cent report that the EU has a positive effect on their own trade union work. Accordingly, two thirds of the trade union representatives interviewed hope that the influence of the EU on national politics will grow in the future.

All of the trade union representatives interviewed agree that the activities at the EU level influence the work of their trade union on the national level. Roughly half believe this is often true and half perceive it as sometimes true. A similar view is expressed with respect to the importance of EU standards. The EU is actively used by all trade unions as an argumentation aid at the national level. More than half of the trade union representatives interviewed claim to frequently use the EU to justify arguments at the national level or to support their position or activities.

From the trade unions' perspective, EU integration means, above all, that the EU supports their interest representation at the national level insofar as its guidelines and standards bolster the trade unions' position in negotiations with the government or employers. Furthermore, the trade unions do not have to grapple with implementing worker-friendly regulations on their own; they receive backing from European law and EU standards. The representative of a national Polish trade union explained:

> It is certainly true that membership in the EU can hinder the government from acting without consulting the social partners. EU membership also offers an additional arena for the protection of Polish workers' rights, for example through the Fundamental Rights Charter.... When the Polish government wanted to change the European directive on weekly working hours without consulting us, we found out about it – among other things – thanks to our participation in the European Trade Union Confederation and we had a chance to present our own opinion. The result was that the government's action without consulting the public could be hindered. Membership in the European Federation of Trade Unions thus represents an additional information source. It enables one to learn not only about European opportunities, but also about national ones. (Project interview, summer 2007)

Representatives of the Slovak trade unions mentioned the revision of the labour code as a current national debate in which the harmonization of EU regulations was a central issue and representatives of the Czech trade unions added a broad spectrum of topics from wage issues to job security and from telework to pension reform. In each case, they explicitly used the relationship to the EU to underpin their argumentation in the national debate.[4]

In summary, this means that the big trade unions of the new Member States use access to the EU level not to perform a representative function there, but to gather information which is then used to improve representation at the national level. At the same time it can be argued that many of the trade unions of the post-socialist Member States do not see a need for active participation at the EU level, as they are largely satisfied with EU policies.

This illustrates an important difference between new and old Member States. Trade unions in the large, old Member States have already consolidated their influence at the national level, and have already contributed to the introduction of labour standards above the EU average. In contrast, the trade unions in the new Member States (and to a certain degree also in Southern Member States) profit from EU guidelines and standards that bolster their position in negotiations with the national government. They also support the implementation of EU regulation in their policy fields, as EU standards are regularly higher than their respective national standards.

Accordingly, the most important task for trade unions in the new Member States is – in their own perception – not to participate in policy-making at the EU level, but to support reforms at the national and sub-national level. And for this task the EU Commission is on many occasions a very powerful and helpful ally. As a result, trade unions in the new Member States have partly assumed the de facto role of a watchdog for the EU Commission, monitoring the implementation of EU policies at the national and sub-national level and putting pressure on the respective domestic governments to adhere to EU regulations. This function is in most cases not based on a partnership with national or sub-national governments, but on a confrontational stance, which might alienate trade unions from the national political elite and foster their image as EU agents. In this perception, they are representing the EU, and namely the European Commission, in the national arena.

Moreover, membership of European umbrella organizations can have a similar impact on political representation by trade unions from the new Member States in their respective national political arenas, especially in the case of the large Polish trade unions. The more they support European positions in their national arena, the more they are seen as agents of EU level actors. In this respect the debate on the EU Service Directive (Bolkestein Directive) was a crystallization point for the post-socialist Member States. The planned liberalization benefited service providers from countries with low standards, such as the post-socialist Member States. The public debate in the EU was focused on the symbolic figure of the 'Polish plumber', who would benefit from the liberalization at the expense of service providers in the old Member States. The great majority of the political elites in the post-socialist EU Member States thus supported the original version of the directive. The trade unions meanwhile feared social dumping and wanted to codify the national standards for all service providers. In the conflict between national public opinion and the European trade union position, the large trade unions from the post-socialist Member States decided overwhelmingly in favour of European trade union solidarity. The Polish trade unions, for example, found themselves in opposition not only to all of the political parties represented in parliament, but also to public opinion (Gajewska 2008, 2009). However, this case is so far exceptional and on other occasions attempts by the Polish trade unions to establish an alternative to the ETUC's position have failed (Lis 2012).

Opportunistic Europeanization

As the national trade unions from the new Member States actively support the transfer of regulation and ideas from the EU level to the national arena, they can be seen as agents of Europeanization, according to Radaelli's often-quoted definition of Europeanization as the transfer of rules, values, or behaviour from the EU level to the national level (Radaelli 2004: 3–4).

However, as described above, this does not imply blind acceptance of decisions made at the EU level, but rather indicates an instrumental use of EU standards to improve one's own negotiating position at the national level. The director of NSZZ Solidarność's Department for International Affairs explains: 'When we feel it's the right thing to do, we invoke the European Union'.

This form of Europeanization is thus predicated on opportunism rather than on conviction. Accordingly, EU guidelines considered undesirable are not accepted. Europeanization in this sense serves to compensate for organizational and programmatic weaknesses in the national political arenas as well as for comparatively weak national labour-market and social standards.

This suggests that, as the harmonization of national regulations and EU standards progresses, this form of Europeanization will lose most of its relevance. When the employees' situation ceases to benefit from the adoption of EU standards and the trade unions can no longer bolster their demands with EU guidelines, the trade unions will no longer cite EU regulations and standards in their arguments.

However, their membership in European umbrella organizations is also linked to two further forms of Europeanization. First, information transfer from the European level to the national level is involved. This form of passive profiting from membership is widespread, but will probably also cease to be important in the longer term once the trade unions' EU competence grows and interest in adopting EU regulations, as described above, wanes. Second, membership in European umbrella organizations also means active engagement with the EU level, especially for the large Polish trade unions. In this case, an internalized Europeanization via networking and collaboration is more likely to occur. The key factor is the development of European solidarity in the trade union movement.

However, the development of European trade union solidarity in the post-socialist Member States should not be overestimated for a number of reasons. First, it requires an EU-wide, unified trade union position, which rarely exists (Busemeyer et al. 2007). Second, active European solidarity in the post-socialist EU Member States is limited – including in the case of the Service Directive – to the few large trade unions that have the capacity for engagement at the EU level. Whether they possess the potential to act as a Europeanizing force at the national level is questionable. Third, one must keep in mind the fact that European solidarity was made easier for the trade unions in that the Service Directive primarily pertained to small-scale service companies, and the members of the trade unions from post-socialist Member States, demonstrating their European solidarity, were for the most part not directly affected.

A true test case for trade union solidarity, not only against the national public, but also against the interests of its own constituency, is yet to come. Nevertheless, the principle tension between European solidarity, that is, representation of common transnational trade union interests, and representation of the interests of the national workforce is clearly visible.

Conclusion

The basic idea embodied in the social dialogues and the related regulations at the different governance levels is that trade unions represent the interests of employees in the political arena. In Pitkin's terminology, this would imply formalistic representation (mainly through authorization) and substantial representation with the trade unions as caretakers acting on behalf of the employees. But if we now relate the actual engagement of trade unions from the new Member States in multi-level EU governance to Pitkin's different types of representation and differentiate between various constituencies being represented by national trade unions, a more complex picture emerges. This picture demonstrates that an analysis of representation in multi-level governance has to move beyond the bilateral relationship between constituency and representative as it has been conceptualized by Pitkin. When there is a longer membership chain and when representative links can be multi-lateral, conflicts of interest and split loyalties are more likely to occur. In addition the question emerges vis-à-vis which audiences' representation takes place.

First, trade unions of the new Member States do not represent workers' interests at the EU level. Instead of representing interests they are on most occasions just present as observers – if at all. As they do not perform a representative function at the EU level, they can by definition not make any direct contribution to representative democracy at the EU level. Instead, it can be argued that trade unions from the new Member States are represented by the European umbrella organizations at the EU level in a formalistic and also partly in a substantive way. In this case, the 'membership-chain' is rather weak, but it still follows a functional bottom-up/top-down logic.

Second, trade unions from the new Member States are sometimes seen as representing the interests of EU level actors. They utilize the information and experience they gather at the EU level to improve their political representation at the national level. The constructive relationship between the EU and these trade unions in the new Member States can be attributed to common interests, as both want to strengthen specific regulations. As a result, the integration of these trade unions can be in the direct political interest of the EU Commission, as it can, at least in some countries, use them to further the implementation of EU policies at the national and regional level.

Thus, third, these trade unions provide not only, and perhaps not even primarily, a link between their constituency and the EU Commission, but also a control mechanism between the EU Commission and the national and regional governments. However, as they do not have a mandate from the EU Commission and are not accountable to it, aspects of formalistic representation do not come into play. Accordingly, although they are sometimes criticized as agents of the EU in national debates, national trade unions in the new Member States do not represent the EU Commission in the national arena, but just use it as a strategic partner where they deem this helpful.

From a functional point of view, a similar relation has occasionally emerged in the relationship between the European umbrella organizations and the national trade unions from the new Member States. Above all, in the debate on the EU Service Directive, the national trade unions acted as representatives of the ETUC's position. However, whereas the national trade unions relation to the EU Commission is instrumental and thus limited to cases of mutual benefit, in the case of the ETUC an emotional link in the form of European solidarity of workers has been evoked and has caused the national trade unions to support a position which is not in their own interest. In this case, the relationship between the ETUC and national trade unions comes closest to symbolic representation, as the national trade unions literally stand for and speak for the European trade union position in their national political arenas.

Accordingly, in relation to the EU level, the stance of the trade unions at the national level seems to be shaped more by the opportunities or demands coming from Brussels than by the interests arising from their prime constituency (i.e. the employed). This dependence on positions formulated at the EU level is increased, as Grosse (2010) argues, by the fact that the opportunities and demands coming from the EU level take the form of precise prescriptions and leave no room for negotiations, thus rendering the national Social Dialogue meaningless. A similar situation emerged in the case of the Service Directive, where the national trade unions could just represent the position of the European umbrella organization as an agent, without any chance to change it and, therefore, without any opportunity to engage in negotiations at the national level.

Although trade unions from the new Member States do not provide any significant input into political representation at the EU level, engagement at the EU level has considerably transformed the established forms and practices of representation employed by trade unions. Most notably, the national trade unions in the new Member States have partly been converted into representatives of EU prescriptions. This strengthens their position in national politics, but at the same time it limits their room for manoeuvre in the national political arena and it could potentially alienate them from the national elites and their original constituency.

The latter implies a potential weakening of substantive representation of employees in the national political arena as trade unions are no longer focused solely on the demands of their constituency. The employees do not have efficient means to change this, as formalistic representation is weak and substantive representation in the political arena is based on the caretaker principle and not on agency. Therefore, for trade unions in the new Member States, engagement at the EU level has the potential to weaken the representative link between constituency and representatives.

Notes

1. A documentation of empirical results is given in Pleines 2008a. The research project, which received financial support from the Otto Brenner Foundation, was conducted by the Research Centre for East European Studies at the University of Bremen in collaboration with the Institute of Sociology of the Czech Academy of Sciences, the Institute of Sociology of the Slovak Academy of Sciences and the Koszalin Institute of Comparative European Studies. Brigitte Krech was responsible for conducting the interviews in Brussels.

2. The Social Dialogue and trade union engagement on the EU level have already been thoroughly researched for the EU 15. For an overview see Greenwood 2007b: 94–115; see also Erne 2006, Martin/Ross 2001, Neal 2004.
3. For a systematic and concise overview for the EU-15 see Leiber 2009.
4. Respective excerpts from the guided interviews are documented in Pleines (2008a: 31–39).

Conclusion

15
Transformation As Differentiation: The Diversity of Representation in the European Union

Dawid Friedrich and Sandra Kröger

In the first decade of the twenty-first century, the theory of political representation experienced significant developments. The conventional model of democratic representation has been questioned, as various other forms of representation have been recognized by representation theory, beyond party competition and elections, and beyond national borders. There are three main theoretical developments. First, the representative relationship is not exclusively perceived as a static principal–agent relationship anymore. Second, additional actors have entered the field of political representation. Third, the representation of weak interests has increasingly attracted scholarly attention.

In this volume, we aspired to investigate the extent to which the developments in representation theory are underpinned by empirical developments in the context of the European Union, thereby adding to the emerging debate on political representation and democracy in the EU. As we argue in this conclusion, it is impossible to separate neatly the empirical developments of representation from the normative discussions about its impact on democratic representation, from conceptual discussions about the nature of representation, and from methodological considerations about how best to analyse the new diversity of representative practices.

The contributions disclose a wealth of multi-faceted practices of representation in the EU. Accordingly, one of the key messages of the book is that of differentiation. Contemporary political representation in the EU is characterized by a simultaneity of different representative practices of formal, semi-formal, and informal agents at different geographical and spatial levels. This diversity of practices and actors establishes a system of representation in the EU (Bartolini 2005; see the Introduction to this volume) whose contours are still in the making. Following from this, we wish to summarize and to discuss the key results of the foregoing chapters in order to describe this system of representation alongside the following aspects:

1. Different actors claim to represent a constituency in EU politics. But it is far from evident which constituencies are meant, whether a multitude of different constituencies are represented by these actors, or whether they target a single European constituency.
2. How do the different actors that claim to be representative actually bring representation into practice, and how is representativeness organized?
3. The European integration process has a significant influence on the way political representation is both practiced and imagined in the EU. Which roles do European institutions play for political representation?
4. If political representation shall be democratic, the repercussions of its institutionalization and conceptualization on political equality need to be addressed.
5. Finally, a representation perspective on the EU cannot be separated from reflections on the EU's alleged democratic deficit. What can we say, upon the basis of the contributions to this volume, about the democratic quality of political representation in the EU?

Each of these aspects deserves a much longer discussion than can be offered in this conclusion. Nevertheless, by stressing the key topics raised by our contributors, we will be able to show avenues that further research on representation in the EU should address.

Representation of (too) many constituencies?

The conventional model of democratic representation was established in the context of sovereign nation-states. There, democratic representation was used more or less synonymously with electoral representation (Pitkin 2004: 336), as it could be reasonably argued that the constituency is composed of all those (adult) citizens who are living within the confines of a particular nation-state. In the context of the EU, however, this link has been questioned, as the electoral route to democratic representation did not result in the establishment of truly pan-European elections of the European Parliament.

In line with this diagnosis, the chapters dealing with the key actors of electoral representation, that is, parliaments and parties, unequivocally show that the national constituencies will remain of high importance for political representation in the multi-level structure of the EU. Emmanuel Sigalas and Johannes Pollak (Chapter 2) show that, even in the election campaign of the EP, the European Party Federations are not capable of successfully encouraging their national members to establish coherent trans-European party manifestos. Instead of adopting a pan-European election program, it seems to be most important for the national parties to establish a party manifesto that talks to their respective national constituencies. Consequently, they pick and choose (or not) their topics from the European manifestos at will, so that, in the foreseeable future, European elections will remain organized nationally. At first sight, the picture seems to be more ambiguous regarding national parliaments, because national parliaments do engage actively in a multiplicity of interparliamentary cooperation, as shown by Cristina Fasone (Chapter 3) and Tapio Raunio (Chapter 10). However, Fasone argues that interparliamentary cooperation has not evolved into venues in which the representatives of national constituencies make claims to represent a transnational constituency. Furthermore, they fail to communicate their transnational activities to their respective national electorate. Moreover, in his contribution, Raunio analyses how national parliaments even weaken the links to their own electorate. This is so because the EU accentuates the general trend of parties and parliaments towards controlling the executive, rather than towards representing the constituency more actively (Mair 2006). Finally, the analysis by Simona Piattoni (Chapter 4) shows that the representatives of regions – unsurprisingly – identify with their own regions first, next with other regions, their own party, and their home country. A common European constituency finds no correlation in their self-perception.

Not only do the representatives of classical electoral representation largely stick to a national concept of constituency, the people themselves also seem to conceptualize multiple national constituencies rather than to construct a European constituency. Asimina Michailidou and Hans-Jörg Trenz (Chapter 8) analyse discussions on the Internet surrounding the EP election campaign in 2009. They illustrate that the people themselves overwhelmingly refer to their nationalities and national politics, even when they publicly discuss EU-related topics. However, in their propositions, they do not introduce the notion of a multi-level or federal EU as a legitimate reference-point for democratic politics. Rather, to the contrary, the chapter suggests that the majority of the involved citizens is of the opinion that the EU cannot legitimately represent them.

The contributions that deal with Civil Society Organizations (CSOs) also point in this direction. Not only are they more often than not representing particularistic interests, they are also organized along national lines, as is shown in the chapters by Håkan Johansson (Chapter 5), Meike Rodekamp (Chapter 6), Erik Jentges (Chapter 9), and Heiko Pleines (Chapter 14), respectively.

Deviating somewhat from the above-mentioned results, Pieter de Wilde (Chapter 7) shows that, with regard to the issue of EU budget negotiations, different constituencies are addressed by different makers of representative claims. In his in-depth analysis of representative claims-making patterns of (self-proclaimed or elected) actors, de Wilde argues that the competitiveness of representative claims-making moves – at least partially – beyond national frontiers. He observes, in these claims, a struggle to address different, often functional, constituencies, such as farmers, of which the classical demos in the nation-state is only one category among others. Overall, then, the evidence in this book suggests that representative politics in the EU is, to a large extent, structured along the lines of nationally separated constituencies and public spheres.

The organization of representativeness

In the conventional model of electoral representation, representativeness is sought through regular and free elections, following the rule of one –person, one vote. Elections serve the double purpose of authorizing new representatives, and of making the old representatives accountable for the actions of the past legislature. While this formal mechanism of establishing representativeness through elections has been criticized for insufficiently representing different societal groups (Young 2000), the organization of representativeness beyond the ballot box of the nation-state is even more precarious. A central message of many contributions is that there is not *one* mode of organizing representativeness, but that several complementary or conflicting modes exist; it often remains unclear, however, whether representativeness is actually being achieved or not.

The EU's Committee of the Regions (CoR) has found, according to Piattoni (Chapter 4), an interesting way of combining two different forms of organizing representativeness, namely, territorial and socio-economic representativeness. The selection mechanisms of CoR members, which are based upon both direct election (regional level) and more functional (national selection) criteria, serve, according to Piattoni, as devices to filter out the 'parochial interests of their particular territory' in favour of a trans-European representativeness of all similar sub-national regions. In a similar vein, Stijn Smismans (Chapter 12) shows that the European Commission seeks to combine both functional ('system') and territorial ('organizational') representativeness. As Smismans shows, the Commission has recently tended to privilege system over organizational representativeness, not least because it failed to define clear criteria for the latter.

In her contribution, Sandra Kröger (Chapter 13) develops two models of representation: dubbed 'representation' which relate to the delegate model of representation, and 'solidarity', whereby weak or abstract interests which cannot represent themselves (environment, peace, etc.), are represented. The more empirical chapters show that these are indeed the two types of functional representation that we can identify. In his analysis of the European Anti-Poverty Network (EAPN), Johansson (Chapter 5) identifies tension between the different modes of representativeness inside the network. On some occasions, the EAPN acts for poor and excluded people; on others, it claims to stand for them, or it even claims to be a network of the socially excluded itself. Thus, Johansson characterizes the EAPN's organization of representativeness as 'chameleonic' as it changes between the delegate and trustee models of representation, or even claims to be a self-help organization rather than a representative one. Which claim of representativeness prevails in a specific situation appears to depend on the specific audience that is addressed. Similarly, Jentges (Chapter 9), in his analysis of the narratives of national CSO representatives, stresses the simultaneous presence of elements of both mandate and delegate forms of representation. He also finds that, in the communication with EU institutions, the role of expertise and policy advocacy, thus of a trustee-like form of representation, prevails. Rodekamp (Chapter 6) concentrates her analysis on the internal practices of Civil Society Organizations (CSOs). She focuses on the relation between the Brussels-based organizations and their national member organizations, and attempts to identify the operation of the transmission-belt function that CSOs purportedly have (Steffek und Hahn 2010). She finds that representativeness functions largely according to the trustee model, but that equal consideration of the diversity of member organizations cannot be achieved due to insufficient formal and participatory measures.

The results discussed so far already provide indications of a specific shape of the representative system of the EU. The issues of constituency formation and of the organization of representativeness are strongly linked to each other. Representativeness can only be unambiguously organized if there is certainty about the constituency and its boundaries. Almost all the actors that have been analysed share the difficulty of clearly defining their constituency. The organization of non-electoral representativeness is meandering between trusteeship and attempts to establish delegation. Unlike the classical vision of electoral forms of organizing representativeness, the representative relationship in non-electoral forms of representation is more complex as non-electoral representatives are often couched between different, sometimes transnational, constituencies, on the one hand, and the European decision-making institutions on the other. But more conventional actors also have a difficult time establishing clear constituencies and, therefore, representativeness, as we have seen in the cases of European Party Federations and of regional representatives in the CoR. The future will show whether the difficulty to identify and to represent a clearly demarcated constituency in a supranational context will accentuate a development in which mechanisms of control and accountability become even more important.

Considering the diversity of existing forms and actors of representation, it is necessary to detach the concept of representation from one single form of institutionalization (through elections), and to consider the dynamic practice of representation (Taylor 2010: 170). Often, in this book, this dynamic perspective has been inspired by the terminology of representative claims-making, as introduced by Michael Saward (2006, 2010). With this notion, Saward succeeded in establishing a terminological innovation that has conceptual repercussions. However, we can see that such terminology is far more easily adopted than implemented in empirical research, not least due to methodological challenges. Attempting to embrace a more dynamic research approach requires different data and methods than research on formal practices of representation. As can be seen in the chapters of de Wilde, Michailidou and Trenz, and Jentges, who implement the claims-making notion, such research needs a combination of quantitative and qualitative methods of discourse analysis in order to make the dynamics of the representative relationship visible. Such a methodological approach is, for instance, capable of illustrating how the representativeness of CSOs is constructed through the discursive relationship of claims-making beyond the existing formalized representative practices. It might thus, for instance, be useful to obtain a deeper understanding of the results, such as those presented by Rodekamp (Chapter 6), who suggests that, despite shortcomings in formalistic and participatory representation, a positive assessment of substantive representation is observable.

Besides these methodological considerations, the claims-making terminology also conceptually challenges representation theory. What exactly are we observing when we analyse claims made in a political arena? Are we merely observing claims, or are we observing representative claims and what makes a claim representative? Are we, while talking about claims-making, still talking about political representation? And, considering the communicative resolution of representation as representative claims-making at the expense of authorization and accountability, what is the difference between a representative claim and the utterances of actors in what is described as the weak public sphere (Fraser 2007), to which the theory of deliberative democracy has pointed so strongly?

The influence of EU institutions on the organization of representation

It is important to examine the way European integration as such and/or individual EU institutions influence and, eventually, transform established forms and practices of political and democratic representation in order to gauge the extent to which these changes deter the norm of political equality, which democratic representation is meant to assure. Institutions select, and therefore restrict, access to them (the European Commission, the European Parliament); they can represent disproportionally (the Council, the European Parliament); or they can re-orient the activities and strategies of collective actors, for example, towards professionalization or a change of priorities.

Throughout the analysis of different actors and different forms of representation, the empirical studies convey an interesting duality of two seemingly opposed results. On the one hand, and dominating this volume, there is the view that representation in the context of EU integration functions as a negative, rather than as a positive, sum game. The more a representative actor is included in EU policy-making, the weaker the link to its respective constituency seems to be. On the other hand, other results suggest that (sub-) national actors do strive to strengthen their representative function in EU policy-making.

The first observation is supported, for instance, by Raunio's (Chapter 10) analysis of the changing role and self-perception of national parliamentarians in the context of European integration. He concludes that, in EU policy-making, national parliamentarians shift their focus away from electoral representation towards controlling the government, that is, towards governmental accountability. This finding bears brisance in that it sees the core function of national parliamentarians challenged, that of (electoral) representation (Gallagher et al. 2006; O'Flynn 2010). The sub-national assemblies of Italy also seem to be going in this direction, as pointed out by Elena Griglio (Chapter 11), although the Spanish ones are in line with the opposite observation.

Three contributions show how the Commission influences the activities of CSOs. Sandra Kröger (Chapter 13) and Heiko Pleines (Chapter 14) observe that European integration tends to uncouple representatives from their constituencies, as they turn towards 'Brussels'. Kröger makes the case that non-electoral representation in the EU is heavily dependent upon the funding and consultation practices of the EU, notably the European Commission, thereby confirming the analysis that CSOs 'may be trapped by the need to adapt to the "logic of influence" prevailing in Brussels' (Kohler-Koch et al. 2008: 6). Hereby she questions the transmission-belt expectations of CSO involvement in EU governance (see Rodekamp, Chapter 6) and highlights the pressure on CSOs for professionalization and expertise (similar Johansson, Chapter 5, and Jentges, Chapter 9). Examining the representation of trade unions from East European countries in EU policy-making, Pleines (Chapter 14) shows that national trade unions represent European interests domestically, instead of representing the interests of their members at EU level, where they are not actively engaged in the political processes. Instead, the trade unions act, on some occasions, as watchdogs for the European Commission in the national implementation process of social policy legislation. Thus, the trade unions act as the trustees of what they believe to be in the interest of their constituency, irrespective of whether these assumptions hold true or not. Stijn Smismans (Chapter 12), in his analysis, uncovers the political opportunity structure that the Commission provides for CSOs in the context of its consultation regime. Inevitably, the way in which the Commission consults and how it incorporates societal interests constitutes a 'mobilization of bias' which will 'privilege particular conceptions of group relations over others' (Beyers et al. 2008: 1118). Hence, a common result of these contributions is that the Commission privileges the deliberator and the expertise function of CSOs at the expense of their potential to represent a constituency and to hold EU actors accountable.

Griglio (Chapter 11) observes both sides of the duality. With a view to the Spanish case, she finds that those sub-national assemblies that have a strong aspiration to autonomy tend to be more proactively trying to shape EU policy-making, that is, to strengthen their role of territorial representation, rather than restricting themselves to controlling national authorities. Although Fasone's (Chapter 3) investigation of interparliamentary cooperation also suggests that national parliamentarians tend to neglect their representative function vis-à-vis their national electorate, unlike Raunio, she expects a change, and thus a strengthening of territorial representation in EU policy-making in the wake of the Treaty of Lisbon's new parliamentary procedures.

One can thus conclude that the more actors are part of EU policy-making, the more focused their actions are on accountability and control of the different executives. The more firmly they are locally or regionally grounded, the more they try to strengthen their representative functions. Overall, however, there seems to be a pull-dynamic towards the institutional and political centre of the EU, which entails a preference of a trustee model or representation on the part of the EU institutions. The extent to which this pull-factor determines the way in which representative practices are organized, or the extent to which different actors are able to uphold a voluntaristic character in organizing their relationship with 'Brussels', as suggested, for instance, by Pleines' concept of 'opportunistic Europeanization' and by the research into the voluntarism of national parties in their adoption of Euro-parties' manifestos (see Chapter 2 by Sigalas and Pollak), needs to be established by further research.

Normative considerations for political representation

At this point, we wish to discuss two issues that are related to substantive representation, that is, the question of how the representative relationship works, but from a more normative perspective than has been done so far. First, we will engage with the concept of claims-making, and ask to what extent the concept lives up to the norm of political equality which forms the normative core background of political representation. Second, we will address the issue of the representation of weak interests or parties, equally relating it to the norm of political equality.

Political equality is a 'foundational idea' of democracy (Christiano 2003; Saward 1998: 15). It stipulates that 'no compelling justification for democracy could oppose the view that people ought to be treated as political equals' (ibid.). Although there are different justifications for this principle, all scholars defend the position that each individual is of equal moral worth, a position that ultimately dates back to the tradition of natural law and social contract theory as developed by Hobbes, Locke, and Rousseau. They all postulated that individuals, in their natural condition, possess equal rights, as was also mirrored in the categorical imperative of Kant, who defended the equality postulate of universal human worth, which became one of the guiding themes of the French Revolution, along with freedom and fraternity. Ever since, and since the parallel fusion of democracy and representation (see the Introduction to this volume), *democratic* governments were understood to be those which recognize the principle of political equality and, thereby, at least in principle, treat all citizens with equal concern and respect. On the other side of the representative relationship, all those who are bound by collective decisions are entitled to an equal say in their making, a goal that was translated into the rule of one person, one vote. To say 'this much is merely to say that the principle of political equality is integral to the meaning and practice of democracy' (O'Flynn 2010: 283).

(1) The claims-making literature does not (explicitly) deal with issues relating to the principle of political equality, namely, which act can count as a representative act, and whether all citizens count as equals. It would seem to us that the claims-making literature needs to engage in a discussion about the political nature of (representative) claims and their institutional environment. A claim might be representative if it is a public statement made by a speaker towards an audience that, at least partially, accepts the claim. However, is this social representation, similar to the concept of social legitimacy which is based upon the social acceptance of politics or policies, or is it still political representation? If, as presented, for example, in the contribution by de Wilde (Chapter 7), journalists or other commentators on public life make public claims in the media about EU budget negotiations, it is implied that we observe an instance of *political* representation, arguably because the claim is linked to a political issue. But, if anyone can be a maker of a claim, as suggested by Jentges (Chapter 9), the result of unchaining the concept of political representation too far from any linkages to authorization and accountability may be conceptual overstretching. Many social relations in highly complex societies with divisions of labour are representative in nature. But does this suffice as a characterization of a claim to be politically representative? We argue that social legitimacy is not sufficient for democratic representation, which requires normative legitimacy as can be derived from the principle of political equality.

Furthermore, Saward criticizes Pitkin's model of accepting the represented as being unproblematically given, as being 'prior' to representation (Saward 2006: 301). However, he is in danger of reversing the relationship to the point where the represented exists by virtue of the representative (Severs 2010), subordinated to a representative relationship that is constructed/dominated by the representative. Such a conceptualization implies that only those individuals for whom there are claims-makers will be represented, while the others will go unnoticed, thereby harming the principle of political equality. In short, the application of the claims-making terminology is valuable for carving out the depths of a representative relationship, thus complementing the more conventional research approaches of representation. But this perspective is in danger of focusing too strongly on performative aspects of representation, of de-coupling the representative claim from democratic political representation, which must live up to the principle of political equality (Pitkin 1972, cop. 1967: 224), and of giving up the independence of the represented.

(2) As elaborated in the Introduction to this volume, the subject of the representation of weak interests or parties has recently received significant attention, in particular in regard to the representation of women and ethnic minorities or other categories of groups that have historically been disadvantaged or currently face social disadvantages. The idea is that, in order to realize the norm of political equality, that is, the equal contribution of all citizens to will-formation, and the exercise and control of political power, equal opportunities to do so are essential. In order to assure equal opportunities, democratic institutions have to be designed in such a way that the socially disadvantaged can also fully participate in democratic politics. However, at times the core concern of democracy – political equality – may actually imply treating people or groups of people in a dissimilar way in order to obtain equality (Taylor 1992).

The political system of the EU bears both opportunities and dangers for both electoral and non-electoral forms of representing weak interests. The system's complexity, and the numerous institutions and actors across different levels might favour the strong, well-organized interests over the weaker voices. However, the very same complexity potentially opens up several paths of inserting the voices of CSOs, speaking in the name of weak interests, into European politics. Adopting an EU level perspective, Johansson (Chapter 5) very thoroughly describes the presence of the voices of the socially excluded through the EAPN. Although the EAPN has to date been a very influential voice in shaping the

European discourse on social exclusion, its invention was triggered by the European Commission, thus from the top, as also shown more generally by the contributions by Kröger and Smismans.

These findings suggest that the EU affects the way in which weak interests are included in political representation across the EU. However, the contributions did not reveal evidence that there is a systematic trend towards strengthening inclusiveness by means of fostering descriptive forms of representation. Instead, citizenship reforms point towards universalization, whereas the inclusion of CSO representation tends to follow the logic of efficiency and expertise, of which improvements in more equal representation of difference and diversity are side effects rather than intended goals pursued by EU institutions.

Democracy and representation in the EU

It is, at the same time, both self-evident and surprising that we compiled a book on the issue of representation and democracy in the EU. It is self-evident, because democracy and representation belong closely together in all modern democracies. But it is also surprising because the representative avenue to strengthen democracy in the EU has seemingly failed, despite the significant gains that the EP has made in terms of competence. At least, these changes were unsuccessful in stopping the scholarly and political debates about democracy and democratic legitimacy in the EU (Kohler-Koch and Rittberger 2007; Jensen 2009). Consequently, in recent years, the academic focus has shifted away from the parliamentary route, towards the participation and deliberation of CSOs in EU policy-making processes. However, after some years of optimism, recent research has shown the limits of participation and deliberation in democratizing the EU via the civil society route (Friedrich 2011; Hüller 2010; Kohler-Koch and Quittkat 2011; Kröger 2008).

What, then, can we say about political representation in the EU? For one, there is the prevalence of national demoi. Traditionally, most advocates of (representative) democracy have pre-supposed that 'a people already exists' (Dahl 1989: 3) within the confines of a state. The deepening and widening scope of European integration, however, has brought the nation-state model of representation into question. Yet, neither the formal definition of the European people as all those who possess European citizenship, nor, as it is argued in several chapters here, the existing practices of representation, are capable of fostering a European constituency. To the contrary, representation in the contemporary EU is, in many instances, still organized along national lines. Hence, it seems that the diversification of representative practices does not possess sufficient strength to counter those voices that perceive a common identity and/or a common demos as a social prerequisite to democracy (Kielmansegg 1996; Offe 2003).

Furthermore, although forms of non-electoral representation bear a democratic opportunity in that the elitist character inherent in traditional representation is challenged, the contributions to this book clearly show the limits of non-traditional forms of representation. For instance, several contributions show that CSOs are trapped between the logic of influence of the EU institutions, with a strong focus on expertise and professionalism which tears representatives away from their constituents, and the logic of delegation, with internal structures of democratic representation. The pressure to adapt to the institutional needs of the European Commission, in particular, is hampering the implementation of internal democratic structures as these need time to function, while the EU institutions are interested in a quick response.

Altogether, many contributions have revealed tendencies towards a decoupling of representative actors from those whom they claim to represent. In such cases, CSOs, sub-national assemblies, and even national parliaments tend to lose contact with their bases while engaging in the EU-universe of Brussels. Having said this, it is, admittedly, much harder to organize non-electoral representation in a democratic manner, that is, in a manner that does not violate political equality, than it is through the formula of one –person, one vote. Yet, the multiple forms of political representation have the potential to express the existing diversity in the EU and to feed this diversity into the public sphere, where claims are publicly discussed and, to some degree, inserted into the decision-making arenas. A model of EU representation would thus encompass different mechanisms of representation, both electoral and non-electoral. Moreover, it would fit the multi-level structure of the EU, where different levels of political action necessitate different forms of representation.

Overall, it is to be welcomed that alternatives to the conventional model of representation, as the dominant form of organizing politics in the EU, are increasingly implemented and conceptually reflected upon. However, the empirical insights given by the assembled contributions give little reason for enthusiasm. Whereas governance functions spread from the national level to the different levels of the EU, representative democratic qualities do not, it is apparent, follow at the same pace. That we are now able to understand that political representation is more than formal authorization and accountability through elections does not mean that the conventional form of representation has become irrelevant altogether. To the contrary, in the EU this conventional understanding lies at the heart of the political system. Parliaments continue to be at the very centre of European democracies; research is therefore well advised to engage in studies which focus on representative fields (Crum and Fossum 2009) of which parliaments are an important, if not crucial, part. It also does not mean that we should dissolve representation into performative acts of claims-making, be they in conventional modes or newer ones, thereby running the danger of losing sight of our core interest, namely, democratic representation as the implementation of political equality.

This book started with the observation that the link between democracy and representation is challenged through a variety of diversification processes, and with the diagnosis of the dilution of traditional representative politics (Warren and Castiglione 2004). Its guiding interest was to gain further knowledge regarding the question of whether the current system of representation in the EU has contributed to a re-configuration of the link between democracy and representation, so that one could speak of a transformation of democratic representation in the EU. In the light of the book's contributions, we can conclude that the diagnosis of the dilution seems to hold empirically. The chapters suggest that electoral, functional, and sub-national forms of representation, and actors of these kinds, are adapting their ways of organizing representation. Consequently, we can say with some confidence that the transformation of representation in the EU is characterized by diversification processes, albeit with an uncertain ability to re-configure the link between representation and democracy. Political representation, to be democratic, requires a strong linkage to the institutional centre of decision-making and, as of now, it is undecided whether the ongoing transformation of political representation in the EU will provide for such strong linkages in the future.

While we cannot deduce large generalizations from the contributions to this volume, they nevertheless point to a number of avenues for future research. Empirically, the interactions of different actors require further research, above all the interactions of the multiple actors of political representation. Conceptually, if different forms and practices of representation simultaneously overlap, the consequences for political representation need consideration. Also, the interaction of the different governance levels needs attention; for example, how democratic theory can usefully take advantage of the insights of the Europeanization literature. Normatively, we need to ask ourselves how far we are moving towards a post-representative space in the EU in which democracy is realized *ex post*, through mechanisms of accountability, and whether political equality can still be ensured under such conditions.

Bibliography

Aben, H. (1992), 'Het prijskaartje van Maastricht', *Algemeen Dagblad*, 7 March: 6.

Ahern, B. (2005), 'Regrets but we must remain optimistic about the Union', *Irish Independent*, 20 June.

Alexa Internet, Inc. (2011) Homepage of Alexa, the Web information company, http://www.alexa.com/, date accessed 3 January 2011.

Alexander, J. (2009), 'The Democratic Struggle for Power: The 2008 Presidential Campaign in the USA', *Journal of Power* 2(1): 65–88.

Altheide, D. L. (2004), 'Media Logic and Political Communication', *Political Communication* 21(3): 293–96.

Altides, C. and Kohler-Koch, B. (2009) 'Multi-level accountability via civil society associations?' Paper presented at the conference 'Bringing Civil Society In: The European Union and the rise of representative democracy', Robert Schuman Centre for Advanced Studies – European University Institute (EUI), 13–14 March 2009, Florence.

Álvarez Conde, E. (2006), 'Los Parlamentos regionales y la Unión europea: el mecanismo de alerta temporanea' in E. Álvarez Conde, L. Pegoraro and A. Rinella (eds), *Regional Councils and Devolved Forms of Governments* (Bologna: Clueb), 21–55.

Anderson, J. (1991), 'Skeptical Reflections on a Europe of the Regions: Britain, Germany and the ERDF', *Journal of Public Policy* 10(4): 417–47.

Arnull, A. and Wincott, D. (2002), *Accountability and Legitimacy in the European Union* (Oxford: Oxford University Press).

Auel, K. (2007), 'Democratic Accountability and National Parliaments: Redefining the Impact of Parliamentary Scrutiny in EU Affairs', *European Law Journal* 13(4): 487–504.

Auel, K. and Benz, A. (eds) (2005), 'The Europeanisation of Parliamentary Democracy', *Journal of Legislative Studies* 11(3–4): 446–65.

Avdagic, S. (2005), 'State-Labour Relations in East Central Europe. Explaining Variations in Union Effectiveness', *Socio-Economic Review* 3(1): 25–53.

Bache, I. (1999), 'The Extended Gate-keeper: Central Government and the Implementation of EC Regional Policy in the UK', *Journal of European Public Policy* 61(March): 28–45.

Bagehot, W. (1867) [2009], *The English Constitution* (Oxford: Oxford University Press).

—— (1873), *The English Constitution,* 2nd edn (London: Chapman).

Barber, B. (1950), 'Participation and mass apathy in associations', in A. Gouldner (ed.), *Studies in Leadership: Leadership and Democratic Action (*New York: Harpe), 477–504.

—— (1984), *Strong Democracy: Participatory Politics for a New Age* (Berkeley: University of California Press).

Barrett, G. (ed.) (2008), *National Parliaments and the European Union: The Constitutional Challenge for the Oireachtas and Other Member State Legislatures* (Dublin: Clarus Press).

Bartolini, S. (2005), *Restructuring Europe: Centre Formation, System Building and Political Structuring between the Nation-State and the European Union* (Oxford: Oxford University Press).

Bauer, M. W. (2002) 'Limitations to Agency Control in EU Policy Making: The Commission and the Poverty Programmes', *Journal of Common Market Studies* 40(3): 381–400.

Beck, U. (1997), *The Reinvention of Politics: Rethinking Modernity in the Global Social Order* (Cambridge: Polity).

Beetham, D. and Lord, C. (1998), *Legitimacy and the European Union* (London: Longman).

Behnke, T. (1992), 'Nej til dyr union', *Berlingske Tidene*, 15(December): 10.

Bellamy, R. and Castiglione, D. (2010), 'Democracy by Delegation? Who Represents Whom and How in European Governance', *Government and Opposition* 46(1): 101–25.

Bengtson, C. (2007), 'Interparliamentary cooperation within Europe', in J. O'Brennan and T. Raunio (eds), *National Parliaments within the Enlarged European Union: From 'victims' of Integration to Competitive Actors?* (Abingdon: Routledge), 46–65.

Bennett, W. L. and Entman, R. M. (eds) (2001), *Mediated Politics: Communication in the Future of Democracy* (Cambridge: Cambridge University Press).

Bentham, J. (1843), 'Chapter 11', in M. James, C. Blamires and C. Pease-Watkin (eds) *Political Tactics* (Oxford: Clarendon Press).

Benz, A. (1998), 'From Cooperative Federalism to Multi-Level Governance: German and EU Regional Policy', *Regional & Federal Studies* 10(3): 505–22.

—— (2000), 'Two Types of Multi-Level Governance: Intergovernmental Relations in German and EU Regional Policy', *Regional and Federal Studies*, 10(3): 21–44.

Bercusson, B. and Van Dijk, J. J. (1995), 'The Implementation of the Protocol and Agreement on Social Policy of the Treaty on European Union', *International Journal of Comparative Labour Law and Industrial Relations* 3(3): 3–30.

Bergman, T. and Damgaard, E. (eds) (2000), 'Delegation and Accountability in European Integration: The Nordic Parliamentary Democracies and the European Union', *Journal of Legislative Studies* 6(1) (Special Issue).

Bergman, T., Muller, W.C., Strom, K. and Blomgren, M. (2003), 'Democratic Delegation and Accountability: Cross-national Patterns' in K. Strøm, W. C. Müller and T. Bergman (eds), *Delegation and Accountability in Parliamentary Democracies* (Oxford: Oxford University Press), 109–221.

Bergman, T. and Strøm, K. (eds) (2011), *The Madisonian Turn: Political Parties and Parliamentary Democracy in Nordic Europe* (Ann Arbor, MI: University of Michigan Press).

Best, E., Christiansen, T. and Settembri, P. (eds) (2008), *The Institutions of the Enlarged European Union: Continuity and Change* (Cheltenham, UK: Edward Elgar).

Bexell, M., Tallberg, J. and Uhlin, A. (2010), 'Democracy in Global Governance: The Promises and Pitfalls of Transnational Actors', *Global Governance* 16(1): 81–101.

Beyers, J., Eising, R. and Maloney, W. (2008), 'The Politics of Organised Interests in Europe: Lessons from EU Studies and Comparative Politics', *West European Politics* 31(6): 1103–1128.

Beyers, J. and Kerremans, B. (2007), 'Critical Resource Dependencies and the Europeanization of Domestic Interest Groups', *Journal of European Public Policy* 14(3): 460–481.

Bignami, F. (2004), 'Three Generations of Participation Rights Before the European Commission', *Law and Contemporary Problems* 68(1): 61–83.

Bilbao Ubillos, J. M. (2003), 'El control parlamentario de la politica europea de las Comunidades Autónomas', in P. Biglino Campos (ed.), *La Politica europea de las Comunidades Autónomas y su control parlamentario* (Valencia: Tirant Lo Blanch), 203–273.

—— (2009), 'Membership Recruitment and Internal Democracy in Interest Groups: Do Group-Membership Relations Vary Between Group Types?', *West European Politics* 32(3): 657–78.

Binderkrantz, A. (2008), 'Different Groups, Different Strategies: How Interest Groups Pursue Their Political Ambitions', *Scandinavian Political Studies* 31 (2): 173–200.

Bolduc, V. L. (1980), 'Representation and Legitimacy in Neighborhood Organizations: A Case Study', *Nonprofit and Voluntary Sector Quarterly* 9(1–4): 165–178.

Bourdieu, P. (2000), *Pascalian Meditations* (Stanford: Stanford University Press).

—— (2001), *Das politische Feld. Zur Kritik der politischen Vernunft* (Konstanz: UVK).

—— (2005), 'The mystery of ministry: from particular wills to the general will', in L. J. D. Wacquant (ed.), *Pierre Bourdieu and Democratic Politics: The Mystery of Ministry* (Cambridge, UK and Malden, MA: Polity), 55–63.

Bovens, M. (2007), 'Analysing and Assessing Public Accountability: A Conceptual Framework', *European Law Journal* 13(4): 447–468.

Bozzini, E. (2007) 'Why get involved in Brussels? A cross-sectoral and cross-national comparison of the involvement of civil society organisation in EU policy processes' in *CINEFOGO Mid Term Conference* (Roskilde (DK)).

Broscheid, A. and Coen, D. (2007), 'Lobbying Activity and Fora Creation In the EU: Empirically Exploring the Nature of the Policy Good', *Journal of European Public Policy* 14(3): 346–365.

Brown, T. (2003), 'National Parliaments in the Convention on the Future of Europe', *The Federal Trust Online Paper* 31(March).

Brunazzo, M. and Domorenok, E. (2008), 'New Members in Old Institutions: The Impact of Enlargement on the Committee of the Regions', *Regional & Federal Studies* 18(4): 429–488.

Burgess, M. (2006), *Comparative Federalism: Theory and Practice* (Routledge: London).

Busemeyer, Marius R., Kellermann, C., Petring, A. and Stuchlik, A. (2007), 'Overstretching solidarity? trade unions' national perspectives on the european economic and social model', http://library.fes.de/pdf-files/id/04751.pdf, 8 March 2011.

Buss, T. F., Redburn, F. S. and Guo, K. (2006), *Modernizing Democracy: Innovations in Citizen Participation* (Armonk, NY: M. E. Sharpe).

Cambalikova, M. (2008), 'Slovak Trade Unions in EU Governance', in J. Kusznir and H. Pleines (eds), *Trade Unions from Post-Socialist Member States in EU Governance* (Stuttgart: Ibidem Publishers), 141–154.

Carter, A. (1998),'Vaclav Havel: civil society, citizenship and democracy', in A. Carter and G. Stokes (eds), *Liberal Democracy and Its Critics* (Cambridge: Polity Press), 58–76.

Casale, G. (2000), 'Experiences of Tripartite Relations in Central and Eastern European Countries', *International Journal of Comparative Labour Law and Industrial Relations* 16(2): 129–42.

Castiglione, D. and Warren, M. E. (2008), 'Rethinking democratic representation: eight theoretical issues'. Paper prepared for the workshop on 'Rethinking Representation', 30 September–3 October 2008, Bellagio.

Chadwick, A. and Howard, P. N. (2009), *Routledge Handbook of Internet Politics* (London: Routledge).

Charnovitz, S. (2006), 'Accountability of non-governmental organizations in global governance' in L. Jordan and P. van Tuijl (eds), *NGO Accountability: Politics, Principles and Innovation* (London: Earthscan), 21–42.

Christiano, T. (2003), 'An argument for democratic equality', in T. Christiano (ed.), *Philosophy & Democracy* (Oxford: Oxford University Press), 39–67.

Christiansen, T. (1996), 'Second Thoughts on Europe's "Third Level": The European Union's Committee of the Regions', *Publius: The Journal of Federalism* 26(1): 93–116.

Clarence, A. L., Jordan, G. and Maloney, W. A. (2005), 'Activating participation. Generating support for campaign groups', in S. Rossteutscher (ed.), *Democracy and the Role of Associations* (London: Routledge), 121–137.

Cnaan, R. A. (1991), 'Neighborhood-Representing Organizations: How Democratic Are They?', *The Social Service Review* 65(4): 614–634.

Cohen, J. (2004), 'Whose Sovereignty? Empire versus International Law', *Ethics & International Affairs* 18(3): 1–24.

Cole. T. (2005), 'The Committee of the Regions and Subnational Representation to the European Union. Maastricht', *Journal of European and Comparative Law* 12(1): 49–72.

Copeland, G. W. and Patterson, S. C. (1994), 'Changing an Institutionalized System', in G. W. Copeland and S. C. Patterson (eds), *Parliaments in the Modern World: Changing Institutions* (Ann Arbor: The University of Michigan Press), 151–160.

Committee of the Regions (2009), White Paper on Multi-Level Governance – Building Europe in Partnership (CoR 89/2009, CONST-IV-020), http://www.cor.europa.eu/pages/CoRAtWork.Template.aspx, date accessed 30 January 2011.

—— (2010), *Consultation Report. White Paper on Multi-Level Governance – Building Europe in Partnership* (CoR 25/2010), http://www.cor.europa.eu/pages/CoRAtWork.Template.aspx, date accessed 30 January 2011.

COSAC (2005), *Fourth Bi-Annual Report: Developments in European Union Procedures and Practices Relevant to Parliamentary Scrutiny* (Brussels: COSAC Secretariat).

—— (2008), *Ninth Bi-Annual Report: Developments in European Union Procedures and Practices Relevant to Parliamentary Scrutiny* (Brussels: COSAC Secretariat).

—— (2009), *Eleventh Bi-Annual Report: Developments in European Union Procedures and Practices Relevant to Parliamentary Scrutiny* (Brussels: COSAC Secretariat).

—— (2010), 'Report on "The evolution of COSAC over the last 20 years"', by H. Haenel and H. De Croo, XLIII COSAC 1 June 2010, http://www.cosac.eu/en/meetings/Madrid2010/ordinary.doc/, date assessed 20 February 2011.

Crespy, A. and Fimin, O. (2011), 'Euroscepticism in the 2009 European election in France and French-speaking Belgium' in P. De Wilde, A. Michailidou and

H. J. Trenz, *Online Euroscepticism: Contesting EU Legitimacy in 2009 European Parliament Election Campaigns* (forthcoming, Colchester, UK: ECPR Press), 76–102.

Crowley, S. (2004), 'Explaining Labor Weakness in Post-Communist Europe', *East European Politics and Society* 18(3): 394–429.

Crum, B. and Fossum, J. E. (2009), 'The Multilevel Parliamentary Field: A Framework for Theorising Representative Democracy in the EU', *European Political Science Review* 1(2): 249–271.

Culpepper, P. D. and Fung, A. (2007), 'Do All Bridges Collapse? Possibilities for Democracy in the European Union', *Politische Vierteljahresschrift* 48(4): 730–739.

Dahl, R. (1989), *Democracy and Its Critics* (New Haven and London: Yale University Press).

Dáil Éireann (1997), 'Agenda 2000 Proposals: Statements', Volume 483, Oireachtas – Dáil Éireann, 27 November.

—— (2005a), 'Ceisteanna – Questions. European Council Meetings', Volume 610, Oireachtas – Dáil Éireann, 23 November 2005.

—— (2005b), 'European Union: Statements (Resumed)', Volume 610, Oireachtas – Dáil Éireann, 23 November.

Dalton, R. J. (1985), 'Political Parties and Political Representation: Party Supporters and Party Elites in Nine Nations', *Comparative Political Studies* 18(3): 267–99.

Daly, M. (2008), 'Whither EU Social Policy? An Account and Assessment of Developments in the Lisbon Social Inclusion Process', *Journal of Social Policy* 37(1): 1–19.

Dankert, P. (1997), 'Geef Europa waar het recht op heeft', *Algemeen Dagblad*, 18 December 2011.

Dann, F. (2003), 'European Parliament and Executive Federalism: Approaching a Parliament in a Semi-Parliamentary Democracy', *European Law Journal* 9(5): 549–574.

Decker, F. (2002), 'Governance Beyond the Nation State. Reflections on the Democratic Deficit of the European Union', *Journal of European Public Policy* 9(2): 256–272.

Della Sala, V. and Ruzza, C. (eds) (2007), *Governance and Civil Society: Policy Perspectives* (Manchester: Manchester University Press).

Dewey, J. (1927), *The Public and Its Problems* (Chicago: Gateway Books).

De Wilde, P. (2010), 'Contesting the EU Budget and Euroscepticism: A Spiral of Dissent?', *ARENA Working Paper Series* 2010(2), (ARENA Centre for European Studies, University of Oslo).

De Wilde, P., Michailidou, A. and Trenz, H. J. (2011), *Online Euroscepticism: Contesting EU Legitimacy in 2009 European Parliament Election Campaigns* (forthcoming: ECPR Press).

Di Napoli, M. (2009), 'Gli obiettivi delle relazioni interparlamentari', in C. Decaro and N. Lupo (eds), *Il 'dialogo' tra parlamenti: obiettivi e risultati* (Rome: Luiss University Press), 305–312.

Domorenok, E. (2010), 'The Committee of the Regions in Search of Identity', *Regional & Federal Studies* 19(1): 143–163.

Donsbach, W. and Patterson, T. E. (2004), 'Political News Journalists: Partisanship, Professionalism, and Political Roles in Five Countries', in F. Esser and B. Pfetsch (eds), *Comparing Political Communication: Theories, Cases, and Challenges* (Cambridge: Cambridge University Press), 251–70.

Dorussen, H. and Nanou, K. (2006), 'European Integration, Intergovernmental Bargaining, and Convergence of Party Programmes', *European Union Politics* 7(2): 235–256.

Dougan, M. (2008), 'Direct Democracy and the European Union...Is that a Threat or a Promise?' *Common Market Law Review* 45(1): 929–940.

Dovi, S. (2002), 'Preferable Descriptive Representatives: Or Will Just Any Woman, Black, or Latino Do?', *American Political Science Review* 96(4): 745–754.

Downing, J. (1992), '£8b EC fund: we'll lose aid if economy not in order', *Irish Independent*, 1 (August): 3.

EAPN (1991), *'The fight against poverty continues'*, n interim report from the European anti-poverty network to the European Commission. September 1991 (Brussels: EAPN).

—— (1993), 'Minutes from the EAPN General Assembly Meeting, Athens, November 1992. Appendix 3', *Final report from the European anti-poverty network to the European Commission on progress achieved to the end of March 1993* (Brussels: EAPN).

—— (2000), *Minutes EAPN General Assembly*, Barcelona, November 2000 (Brussels: EAPN).

—— (2001a), *Minutes from Executive Committee meeting*, November 2001 (Brussels: EAPN).

—— (2001b), *Minutes EAPN General Assembly*, 23–25 November (Brussels: EAPN).

—— (2002), *Minutes from Executive Committee meeting*, January 2002 (Brussels: EAPN).

—— (2003a), *Minutes from Executive Committee meeting*, March 2003 (Brussels: EAPN).

—— (2003b), *2nd European Meeting of People Experiencing Poverty*. A conference of the Greek presidency of the EU. 10–11 May (Brussels: EAPN).

—— (2005), *EAPN Membership. Directory of European Organizations in Membership of EAPN and of Member Organizations of EAPN National Networks* (Brussels: EAPN).

—— (2007a), *EAPN Network News*. July/September 2007 (Brussels: EAPN).

—— (2007b), *Minutes from National Coordinators Meeting*. 8 December (Brussels: EAPN).

—— (2009a), *8th European Meeting of People Experiencing Poverty*. A conference of the Czech presidency of the EU. 15–16 May 2009 (Brussels: EAPN).

—— (2009b), *Small Steps – Big Changes. Building Participation of People Experiencing Poverty* (Brussels: EAPN).

—— (2009c), *Minutes from Follow-Up Participation Meetings – Developing Proposals for Increasing Participation in the European Work of EAPN*, 26 June (Brussels: EAPN).

—— (2009d), Standing Orders (Brussels: EAPN).

—— (2009e), Statutes (Brussels: EAPN).

—— (2011), 'The Making of a European Civil Society: "Imagined", "Practised" and "Staged"', in U. Liebert and H. J. Trenz (eds) *The New Politics of European Civil Society* (London: Routledge), 40–54.

Eder, K. (2009) 'The making of a European Civil Society: "Imagined", "Practised" and "Staged"', *Policy and Society* 28, 23–33.

Edquist, K. (2006), 'EU Social-Policy Governance: Advocating Activism or Servicing States?', *Journal of European Public Policy* 13(4): 500–518.

Einbock, J. (2008), 'Polish Trade Unions in EU Governance', in J. Kusznir and H. Pleines (eds), *Trade Unions from Post-Socialist Member States in EU Governance* (Stuttgart: Ibidem Publishers), 113–128.

Eising, R. (2008), 'Interest groups in EU policy-making', *Living Reviews in European Governance* 3(4), http://www.livingreviewPp.org/lreg-2008-4, date accessed 2 February 2009.

Elias, N. (1978), *What Is Sociology?* (London: Hutchinson).

Eriksen, E. O. (2007), 'Conceptualising European Public Spheres: General, Segmented and Strong Publics', in J. E. Fossum and P. Schlesinger (eds), *The European Union and the Public Sphere: A Communicative Space in the Making?* (Abingdon: Routledge), 23–43.

Eriksen, E. O. and Fossum, J. E. (2000), 'The EU and Post-National Legitimacy', *ARENA Working Papers* – WP 00/26.

—— (2002), 'Democracy through Strong Publics in the European Union?', *Journal of Common Market Studies* 40(3): 401–424.

—— (2007), 'Europe in transformation: How to reconstitute democracy?', *RECON Online Working Paper Series 2007/1*, http://www.reconproject.eu, 8 March 2011.

Erne, R. (2006), 'European Trade-Union Strategies: Between Technocratic Efficiency and Democratic Legitimacy', in S. Smismans (ed.), *Civil Society and Legitimate European Governance* (Cheltenham: Edward Elgar), 219–240.

Etzioni, A. (ed.) (1998), *The Essential Communitarian Reader* (Lanham: Rowman & Littlefield).

EU Citizenship Report (2010), 'Dismantling the Obstacles to EU Citizens' Rights', http://ec.europa.eu/justice/policies/citizenship/docs/com_2010_603_en.pdf, date accessed 11 October 2010.

Eurobarometer (2007), 'Standard Eurobarometer No. 67 June 2007', http://ec.europa.eu/public_opinion/archives/eb/eb67/eb67_en.htm, 8 March 2011.

—— (2008), *Special Eurobarometer 307. The role and impact of local and regional authorities within the European Union. Opinions on the different levels of public authorities and awareness of the Committee of the Regions*, http://www.cor.europa.eu/pages/CoRAtWorkTemplate.aspx, date accessed 30 January.

European Commission (1993a), *Communication on 'An Open and Structured Dialogue between the Commission and Special Interest Groups'* (OJ 93/C 63/02).

—— (1993b), *Communication on 'Increased Transparency in the Work of the Commission'* (OJ 93/C 63/03).

—— (1993c), *Communication Concerning the Application of the Agreement on Social Policy*, COM (93) 600 final.

—— (2000), *'The Commission and NGOs: Building a Stronger Partnership'*, COM (2000) 11 final, Brussels, 18 January 2000.

—— (2001), *'European Governance: A White Paper'*, COM (2001) 428 final.

—— (2002a), *Communication from the Commission: Towards a Reinforced Culture of Consultation and Dialogue – General Principles and Minimum Standards for Consultation of Interested Parties by the Commission*, COM (2002) 704 final.

—— (2002b), *Communication on General Principles and Minimum Standards for Consultation*, Brussels: European Commission.

—— (2002c), *Communication 'Towards A Reinforced Culture of Consultation and Dialogue. General Principles and Minimum Standards for Consultation of Interested Parties by the Commission'*, COM (2002) 704 final, Chapter 12.

—— (2003), *Report on European Governance, 2003*, Official Publications of the EU, Luxembourg.

—— (2005), *Decision Of The European Parliament and of the Council Establishing for the Period 2007–2013 the Programme 'Citizens For Europe' To Promote Active European Citizenship*, COM (2005) 116 final, Brussels, 6 April 2005.

—— (2006), *Green Paper on the European Transparency Initiative*, COM (2006) 194 final.

—— (2007a), *EU Consumer Policy Strategy 2007–2013. Empowering Consumers, Enhancing Their Welfare, Effectively Protecting Them*, COM (2007) 99 final, 13 March.

—— (2007b), *Follow-Up to the Green Paper 'European Transparency Initiative'*, COM (2007) 127 final. Chapter 12.

—— (2008), *Communication 'European Transparency Initiative: A Framework for Relations with Interest Representatives* (Register and Code of Conduct)', COM (2008) 323 final.

European Convention (2003), *Draft Treaty Establishing a Constitution for Europe*, CONV 850/03, Brussels, 18 July 2003.

European Economic and Social Committee (1999), *Opinion 'The Role and Contribution of CSOs in the Building of Europe'*, 22 September 1999, OJ C329, 17 November 1999.

European Parliament (2006), *Resolution on European Political Parties (2005/2224 (INI))*, P6_TA (2006) 0114.

European Parliament and Council (2003), 'Regulation (EC) No 2004/2003 of 4 November 2003 on the Regulations Governing Political Parties at the European Level and the Rules Regarding their Funding', *Official Journal of the European Union* L297/: 1–4.

—— (2007), 'Regulation (EC) No 1524/2007 of 18 December 2007 Amending Regulation (EC) No 2004/2003 on the Regulations Governing Political Parties at the European Level and the Rules Regarding their Funding', *Official Journal of the European Union* L343/: 5–8.

European Union (2006), 'Consolidated Versions of the Treaty on European Union and of the Treaty Establishing the European Community', *Official Journal of the European Union* C321/: 1–331.

—— (2007), 'Treaty of Lisbon', *Official Journal of the European Union* C306/: 1–270.

Ewing, K. D. (2005), 'The Function of Trade Unions', *Industrial Law Journal* 34(1): 1–22.

Fabbrini, S. (2007), *Compound Democracies: Why the United States and Europe Are Becoming Similar* (Oxford: Oxford University Press).

Falkner, G. (2000), 'The Council or the Social Partners? EC Social Policy Between Diplomacy and Collective Bargaining', *Journal of European Public Policy* 7(5): 705–724.

—— (2006), 'Forms of Governance in European Union Social Policy: Continuity and/or Change?', *International Social Security Review* 59(2): 77–103.

—— (2007), 'The EU's social dimension', in M. Cini (ed.), *European Union Politics*, 2nd edn (Oxford: Oxford University Press), 271–285.

Fasone, C. (2009), 'Le assemblee legislative regionali e i processi decisionali comunitari: un'analisi di diritto comparato', *Le istituzioni del federalismo*, 409–436.

Finer, S. E. (1974), 'Groups and political participation', in R. Kimber and J. J. Richardson (eds), *Pressure Groups in Britain* (London: J. M. Dent/Aldine Press), 255–275.

Finke, B. (2007), 'Civil society participation in European governance', *Living Reviews in European Governance* 2(2), www.livingreviews.org/lreg-2007-4-2, date accessed 8 October 2010.

Fitzmaurice, J. (1976), 'National Parliaments and European Policy-Making: The Case of Denmark', *Parliamentary Affairs* 29(3), 282–292.

Foley, M. W. and Edwards, B. (1997), 'Escape From Politics? Social Theory and the Social Capital Debate', *American Behavioral Scientist* 40(5): 550–561.

Follesdal, A. and Hix, S. (2006), 'Why There is a Democratic Deficit in the EU: A Response to Majone and Moravcsik', *Journal of Common Market Studies* 44(3): 533–562.

Fossum, J. E. and Trenz, H. J. (2005), 'The EU's Fledgling Society: From Deafening Silence to Critical Voice in European Constitution-Making', *Journal of Civil Society* 2(1): 57–77.

Franssen, E. (2002), *Legal Aspects of the European Social Dialogue* (Intersentia: Antwerpen).

Fraser, N. (1992), 'Rethinking the Public Sphere: A Contribution to the Critique of Actually Existing Democracy', in C. Calhoun (ed.), *Habermas and the Public Sphere* (Cambridge, MA: MIT Press), 109–142.

—— (2007), 'Die Transnationalisierung der Öffentlichkeit. Legitimität und Effektivität der öffentlichen Meinung in einer postwestfälischen Welt', in P. Niesen and B. Herborth (eds), *Anarchie der kommunikativen Freiheit. Jürgen Habemas und die Theorie der internationalen Politik* (Frankfurt am Main: Suhrkamp), 224–253.

Friedrich, D. (2011), *Democratic Participation and Civil Society in the European Union* (Manchester: Manchester University Press).

Fukuyama, F. (1995), *Trust: Social Virtues and the Creation of Prosperity* (New York: Free Press).

Gajewska, K. (2008), 'Polish Trade Unions for the European Cause: The Case of the EU Directive on Services in the Internal Market', in J. Kusznir and H. Pleines (eds), *Trade Unions from Post-Socialist Member States in EU Governance* (Stuttgart: Ibidem), 89–104.

—— (2009), *Transnational Labour Solidarity: Mechanisms of Commitment to Cooperation within the European Trade Union Movement* (Abingdon, NY: Routledge).

Gallagher, M., Laver, M., Mair, P. (2006), *Representative Government in Modern Europe* (Boston: McGraw-Hill).

Galtung, J. and Ruge, M. H. (1965), 'The Structure of Foreign News: The Presentation of the Congo, Cuba and Cyprus Crises in Four Norwegian Newspapers', *Journal of Peace Research* 2(1): 64–91.

Garofalo, D. (2006), 'Regional Competences, Community and International Regulation in Italy', *Transition Studies Review* 13(1): 28–33.

Gates, A. M. (2006), *Promoting Unity, Preserving Diversity? Member-State Institutions and European Integration* (Lanham, MD: Lexington Books).

German Law Journal (2009), Special Issue on the 'The Lisbon Judgment of the German Federal Constitutional Court?', 10(8).

Goetz, K. H. and Meyer-Sahling, J. H. (2008), 'The Europeanisation of National Political Systems: Parliaments and Executives', *Living Reviews in European Governance* 3(2).

Goodin, R. E. (2003), 'Democratic accountability: the third sector and all', Harvard: The Hauser Center for Nonprofit Organizations, Working Paper No. 19.

Grant, W. (2001), 'Pressure Politics. From "Insider" Politics to Direct Action', *Parliamentary Affairs,* 54(2): 337–348.

—— (2003), 'Pressure Politics. The Challenges for Democracy', *Parliamentary Affairs* 56(2): 297–308.

Grant, R. W. and Keohane, R. O. (2005), 'Accountability and Abuses of Power in World Politics', *American Political Science Review* 99(1): 29–43.

Greenwood, J. (2007a), 'Review Article. Organized Civil Society and Democratic Legitimacy in the European Union', *British Journal of Political Science* 37(2): 333–357.

—— (2007b), *Interest Representation in the European Union*, 2nd edn (New York: Palgrave Macmillan).

—— (2010), 'Regulating NGO participation in the EU. A *de-facto* accreditation system built on "representativeness"?', in Kristina Hahn and Jens Steffek (eds), *Evaluating International NGOs: Legitimacy, Accountability, Representation* (Houndmills, Basingstoke, Hampshire: Palgrave Macmillan), 200–219.

Grosse, T. (2010), 'Social Dialogue During Enlargement: The Case of Poland and Estonia', *Acta Politica* 45(1/2): 112–135.

Guo, C. and Musso, J. A. (2006), 'Representation in Nonprofit and Voluntary Organizations: A Conceptual Framework', *Nonprofit and Voluntary Sector Quarterly* 35(4): 1–19.

—— (2007), 'Representation in Nonprofit and Voluntary Organizations: A Conceptual Framework', *Nonprofit and Voluntary Sector Quarterly* 36(2), 308–326.

Habermas, J. (1998), *Die Postnationale Konstellation. Politische Essays* (Frankfurt am Main: Suhrkamp).

Hall, S. (1997), *Representation: Cultural Representations and Signifying Practices* (Newbury Park: Sage).

Halpin, D. R. (2006), 'The Participatory and Democratic Potential and Practice of Interest Groups: Between Solidarity and Representation', *Public Administration* 84(4): 919–940.

Harvey, B. (1990), *European Working Group Against Poverty,* Final Interim report (Belfast: Northern Ireland Council for Voluntary Action).

—— (1991), *European Working Groups Against Poverty,* Final Report, March 1991 (Belfast: Northern Ireland Council for Voluntary Action).

—— (1993), 'Lobbying in Europe: The Experience of Voluntary Organizations', in S. Mazey and J. Richardsson (eds), *Lobbying in the European Community* (Oxford: Oxford University Press), 188–200.

Harvey, B. and Kiernan, J. (1991), *The Foundation of the European Anti-Poverty Network: From Working Group to Launch* (Belfast: Northern Ireland Council for Voluntary Action).

Hendriks, C. M. (2009), 'The Democratic Soup: Mixed Meanings of Political Representation in Governance Networks', *Governance: An International Journal of Policy, Administration, and Institutions* 22(4): 689–715.

Hirst, P. (1997), *From Statism to Pluralism* (London: UCL Press).

Hix, S. (1996), 'The Transnational party federations', in J. Gaffney (ed.), *Political Parties and the European Union* (London and New York: Routledge), 308–329.

—— (2008), *What's Wrong with the European Union and How to Fix It* (Cambridge, UK: Polity Press).

Hix, S. and Marsh, M. (2007), 'Punishment or Protest? Understanding European Parliament Elections', *Journal of Politics* 69(2): 495–510.

Hix, S., Noury, A. and Roland, G. (2007), *Democratic Politics in the European Parliament* (Cambridge: Cambridge University Press).

Hobson, C. (2008), 'Revolution, Representation and the Foundations of Modern Democracy', *European Journal of Political Theory* 7(4): 449–471.

Holzhacker, R. (2005), 'The Power of Opposition Parliamentary Party Groups in European Scrutiny', *The Journal of Legislative Studies* 11(3–4): 428–445.

Holzhacker, R. and Albæk, E. (eds) (2007), *Democratic Governance and European Integration: Linking Societal and State Processes of Democracy* (Cheltenham: Edward Elgar).

Holzhauer, J. (2006), 'Lobbyismus der Kirchen in der Bundesrepublik', in T. Leif and R. Speth (eds), *Die fünfte Gewalt. Lobbyismus in Deutschland* (Berlin: bpb), 259–271.

Hooghe, L. (1995), 'Sub-national Mobilization in the European Union', *West European Politics* 18(3): 175–198.

—— (ed.) (1996), *Cohesion Policy and European Integration: Building Multi-Level Governance* (Oxford: Clarendon Press).

Hooghe, L. and Michael, K. (1994), 'The Politics of European Union Regional Policy', *Journal of European Public Policy* 1(3): 367–393.

Hönnige, C. and Kaiser, A. (2003), 'Opening the Black Box: Decision-Making in the Committee of the Regions', *Regional & Federal Studies* 13(2): 1–29.

Hüller, T. (2007), 'Assessing EU Strategies for Publicity', *Journal of European Public Policy* 14(4): 563–581.

—— (2010), *Demokratie und Sozialregulierung in Europa. Die Online-Konsultationen der EU-Kommission. Serie Staatlichkeit im Wandel* (Frankfurt am Main: Campus).

Hyman, R. (2005), 'Trade Unions and the Politics of the European Social Model', *Economic and Industrial Democracy* 26(1): 9–40.

Irish Times (2005), 'Barroso sets out growth plan for EU', 27 January: 23.

Jansen, T. (2000), 'Europe and Religions: The Dialogue between the European Commission and Churches or Religious Communities', *Social Compass* 47(1): 103–112.

Jeffery, C. (1997), *The Regional Dimension of the European Union. Towards a Third Level in Europe?* (London: Frank Cass).

—— (2000), 'Sub-National Mobilization and European Integration: Does It Make Any Difference?', *Journal of Common Market Studies* 38(1): 1–23.

—— (2005), 'Regions and the European Union: Letting Them in, and Leaving Them Alone', in S. R. Weatherill and U. Bernitz (eds), *The Role of Regions and Sub-National Actors in Europe* (Oxford: Hart Publishing), 33–47.

Jensen, T. (2009), 'The Democratic Deficit of the European Union', *Living Reviews in Democracy* 1(4), http://democracy.livingreviews.org/index.php/lrd/article/view/lrd-2009–2/8, date accessed 8 March 2011.

Jentges, E. (2010), *Die soziale Magie politischer Repräsentation. Charisma und Anerkennung in der Zivilgesellschaft* (Bielefeld: Transcript).

Johansson, H. (2010), *The History of a European Anti-Poverty Lobby* (Lund: Lund University School of Social Work).

Johansson, K. M. and Tallberg, J. (2010), 'Explaining Chief Executive Empowerment: EU Summitry and Domestic Institutional Change', *West European Politics* 33(2): 208–236.

Johansson, K. M. and Zervakis, P. A. (2002), 'Historical-Institutional framework', in K. M. Johansson and P. A. Zervakis (eds), *European Political Parties between Cooperation and Integration* (Baden-Baden: Nomos), 11–28.

Jordan, L. and van Tuijl, P. (eds) (2006), *NGO Accountability: Politics, Principles and Innovation* (London: Earthscan).

Jordan, G. and Maloney, W. A. (2007), *Democracy and Interest Groups: Enhancing Participation?* (Basingstoke and New York: Palgrave Macmillan).

Judge, D. and Earnshaw, D. (2008), *The European Parliament*, 2nd edn (Basingstoke: Palgrave Macmillan).

Katz, R. (1999), 'Representation, the Locus of Democratic Legitimation and the Role of National Parliaments in the European Union', in R. Katz and B. Wessels (eds), *The European Parliament, the European Integration* (Oxford: Oxford University Press), 21–44.

Katz, R. and Mair, P. (1995), 'Changing Models of Party Organization and Party Democracy', *Party Politics* 1(1): 5–28.

Keating, M. (2008), 'A Quarter Century of the Europe of the Regions', *Regional and Federal Studies* 18(5): 629–635.

Kielmansegg, P. G. (1996), 'Integration und Demokratie', in M. Jachtenfuchs and B. Kohler-Koch (eds), *Europäische Integration* (Opladen: Leske + Budrich), 47–71.

Kiiver, P. (2006), *The National Parliaments in the European Union: A Critical View on EU Constitution-Building* (The Hague: Kluwer Law International).

—— (ed.) (2006), *National and Regional Parliaments in the European Constitutional Order* (Groningen: Europa Law Publishing).

—— (2007), 'European scrutiny in national parliaments: individual efforts in the collective interest?', in J. O'Brennan and T. Raunio (eds), *National Parliaments within the Enlarged European Union. From 'victims' of Integration to Competitive Actors?* (New York: Routledge), 66–77.

King, A. (1976), 'Modes of Executive-Legislative Relations: Great Britain, France, and West Germany', *Legislative Studies Quarterly* 1(1): 11–36.

Klintmann, M. and Kronsell, A. (2010), 'Challenges to Legitimacy in Food Safety Governance? The Case of the European Food Safety Authority (EFSA)', *Journal of European Integration* 32(3): 309–327.

Knudsen, M. and Carl, Y. (2008), 'COSAC – its role to date and its potential in the future', in G. Barrett (ed.), *National Parliaments and the European Union: The Constitutional Challenge for the Oireachtas and Other Member State Legislatures* (Dublin: Clarus Press), 455–483.

Kohler-Koch, B. (2007a), 'The organization of interests and democracy in the European Union', in B. Kohler-Koch and B. Rittberger (eds), *Debating the*

Democratic Legitimacy of the European Union (Lanham: Rowman & Littlefield), 255–271.

—— (2007b), *Political Representation and Civil Society in the EU*, paper presented at the CONNEX thematic conference on political representation, EUI, May 2007.

—— (ed.) (2008), 'Representation, Representativeness, and Accountability in EU-Civil Society Relations', in CONNEX Final Conference, *Efficient and Democratic Governance in a Multi-Level Europe. Workshop 5: Putting EU civil society involvement under scrutiny. Panel: A Normative View on Civil Society Involvement* (Mannheim: CONNEX).

—— (2009), 'The Three Worlds of European Civil Society – What Role for Civil Society for What Kind of Europe?', *Policy & Society* 28(1): 47–57.

—— (2010), 'Civil Society and EU Democracy: "Astroturf" Representation?', *Journal of European Public Policy* 17(1): 100–116.

—— (2011), 'The three worlds of "European civil society". Different images of Europe and different roles for civil society', in U. Liebert and H. J. Trenz (eds), *The New Politics of European Civil Society* (London: Routledge), 57–72.

Kohler-Koch, B. and Buth, V. (2009), 'Civil society in EU governance. lobby groups like any other?', http://www.sfb597.uni-bremen.de/pages/pubApBeschreibung.php?SPRACHE=en&ID=148, 8 March 2011.

—— (2011), 'Der Spagat der europäischen Zivilgesellschaft – zwischen Professionalität und Bürgernähe', in B. Kohler-Koch and C. Quittkat (eds), *Die Entzauberung partizipativer Demokratie: Zur Rolle der Zivilgesellschaft bei der Demokratisierung von EU-Governance* (Frankfurt am Main: Campus), 167–210.

Kohler-Koch, B. and Edler-Wollstein, S. (2008), 'It's about Participation, Stupid. Is It? Civil-Society Concepts in Comparative Perspective', in B. Jobert and B. Kohler-Koch (eds), *Changing Images of Civil Society: From Protest to Governance (Routledge Studies in Governance and Public Policy)* (London: Routledge), 195–214.

Kohler-Koch, B. and Finke, B. (2007), 'The Institutional Shaping of EU-Society Relations – A Contribution to Democracy via Participation?', *Journal of Civil Society* 3(3): 205–221.

Kohler-Koch, B. and Quittkat, C. (2011), *Die Entzauberung partizipativer Demokratie. Zur Rolle der Zivilgesellschaft bei der Demokratisierung von EU-Governance* (Frankfurt am Main: Campus).

Kohler-Koch, B., Quittkat, C. and Buth, V. (2008), 'Civil Society Organisations under the Impact of the European Commission's Consultation Regime'. Paper presented at the *CONNEX Final Conference*, Workshop 5: Putting EU civil society involvement under scrutiny. Mannheim University, 6–8 March 2008, Mannheim.

Kohler-Koch, B. and Rittberger, B. (eds) (2007), *Debating the Democratic Legitimacy of the European Union* (Lanham: Rowman & Littlefield).

Koopmans, R. (2002), 'Codebook for the analysis of political mobilisation and communication in European public spheres', Europub.com Project, http://europub.wz-berlin.de, 8 March 2011.

Koopmans, R. and Erbe, J. (2004), 'Towards a European Public Sphere? Vertical and Horizontal Dimensions of Europeanized Political Communication', *Innovation* 17(2): 97–118.

Koopmans, R. and Statham, P. (1999), 'Political Claims Analysis: Integrating Protest Event and Political Discourse Approaches', *Mobilization: An International Quarterly* 4(2): 203–221.

Kragh, C. (2004), 'Enighed om næste års EU-budget', *Berlingske Tidene*, 27 November: 8.

Krech, B. (2008), 'Presence and visibility of polish, Czech and Slovak trade unions at the EU level', in J. Kusznir and H. Pleines (eds), *Trade Unions from Post-Socialist Member States in EU Governance* (Stuttgart: Ibidem Publishers), 57–68.

Kreppel, A. (2002), *The EP and Supranational Party System* (Cambridge: Cambridge University Press).

Kröger, S. (2008), 'Nothing but consultation: The place of organised civil society in EU policy-making across policies'. *European Governance Papers* (EUROGOV) No. C-08-03, http://www.connex-network.org/eurogov/pdf/egp-connex-C-08-03.pdf, date accessed 20 July 2008.

—— (ed.) (2009), 'What we have learnt: Advances, pitfalls and remaining questions in OMC research'. Special issue of *European Integration Online Papers* 1(13).

Külahci, E. (2010), 'Europarties: Agenda-Setter or Agenda-Follower? Social Democracy and the Disincentives for Tax Harmonization', *Journal of Common Market Studies* 48(5): 1283–1306.

Kymlicka, W. (1995), *Multicultural Citizenship: A Liberal Theory of Minority Rights* (Oxford: Oxford University Press).

Ladrech, R. (2010), *Europeanization and National Politics* (Basingstoke: Palgrave Macmillan).

Laffan, B. (1997), *The Finances of the European Union* (London: Palgrave MacMillan).

—— (2000), 'The Agenda 2000 Negotiations: La Présidence Coûte Cher?', *German Politics* 9(3): 1–22.

Larhant, M. (2005), 'La cooperation interparlementaire dans l'UE', *Notre Europe Policy paper no 16.*

Lavalle, A. G., Houtzager, P. P. and Castello, G. (2005), *In Whose Name? Political Representation and Civil Organisations in Brazil* (Brighton: Institute of Development Studies).

Lefkofridi, Z. and Kritzinger, S. (2008), 'Battles Fought in the EP Arena: Developments in National Parties' Euromanifestos', *Österreichische Zeitschrift für Politikwissenschaft* 37(3): 279–296.

Leiber, S. (2009), 'Europäisierung sozialpolitischer Interessenvermittlung. Erosion oder Aufwertung korporatistischer Strukturen in den Mitgliedsstaaten?', in B. Rehder, T. von Winter and U. Willems (eds), *Interessenvermittlung in Politikfeldern. Vergleichende Befunde der Policy- und Verbändeforschung* (Wiesbaden: VS Verlag), 248–266.

Liebert, U. (2002), 'Regional Parliaments and Good Governance in the EU', *CEuS Working Paper,* August 2002.

Liesbet, H. and Keating, M. (1994), 'The Politics of European Union Regional Policy', *Journal of European Public Policy,* 1(3): 367–393.

Lijphart, A. (1971), 'Comparative Politics and the Comparative Method', *American Political Science Review* 65(3): 682–93.

Lindner, J. (2006), *Conflict and Change in EU Budgetary Politics* (Abingdon: Routledge).

Lis, A. (2008), 'Trade union strength in an EU-wide comparison', in J. Kusznir and H. Pleines (eds), *Trade Unions from Post-Socialist Member States in EU Governance* (Stuttgart: Ibidem Publishers), 43–56.

—— (2012), 'Europeanization as Interests Re-Framing: Polish Trade Unions in EU Governance', *Europe-Asia Studies*, forthcoming (under revision).

Liston, V. (2009), 'Microcosms of Democracy? A Study of the Internal Governance of International NGOs in Kenya', *Journal of Civil Society* 5(1): 61–82.

Loewenberg, G. and Kim, C. L. (1978), 'Comparing the Representativeness of Parliaments', *Legislative Studies Quarterly* 3(1): 27–49.

López Castillo, A. (1992), 'Creation y aplication del derecho comunitario europeo y comunidades autonomas', *Revista Española de Derecho Constitucional* 35: 111–151.

Lord, C. (2004), 'Political parties and the European union. What kind of imperfect competition?' in P. Delwit, E. Külahci and C. van de Walle (eds), *The Europarties Organisation and Influence* (Brussels: Editions de l'Université de Bruxelles), 45–67.

—— (2006), 'The Aggregating Function of Political Parties in EU Decision-Making', *Living Reviews in European Governance* 1(2), http://www.livingreviews.org/lreg-2006–2, 15 February 2011.

—— (2010), 'The Aggregating Function of Political Parties in EU Decision-Making', *Living Reviews in European Governance*, 5(3), http://www.livingreviews.org/lreg-2010–3, 15 February 2011.

Lord, C. and Pollak, J. (2010), 'The EU's Many Representative Modes: Colliding? Cohering?', *Journal of European Public Policy* 17(1): 117–136.

Lupo, N. (2008), 'Le Regioni in Parlamento: la mancata adozione di metodi della legislazione adeguati alle esigenze delle autonomie (e le sue conseguenze nefaste sull'attuazione del Titolo V Cost)', in V. Antonelli (ed.), *Città, province, regioni, Stato. I luoghi delle decisioni condivise* (Roma: Donzelli), 215–240.

Mahoney, C. (2004), 'The Power of Institutions: State and Interest-Group Activity in the European Union', *European Union Politics* 5(4): 441–466.

Mailand, M. and Due, J. (2004), 'Social Dialogue in Central and Eastern Europe. Present State and Future Development', *European Journal of Industrial Relations* 10(2): 179–197.

Mair, P. (2006), 'Ruling the Void? The Hollowing of Western Democracies', *New Left Review* 42, Nov–Dec. 2006, 25–51.

Mair, P. and Thomassen, J. (2010), 'Political Representation and Government in the European Union', *Journal of European Public Policy* 17(1): 20–35.

Majone, G. (1998), 'Europe's Democratic Deficit: The Question of Standards', *European Law Journal* 4(1): 5–28.

—— (1999), 'The Regulatory State and Its Legitimacy Problems', *West European Politics* 22(1): 1–24.

—— (2002), 'Delegation of Regulatory Powers in a Mixed Polity', *European Law Journal* 8(3): 319–339.

Maloney, W. (2007), 'The Professionalization of representation: biasing participation', in B. Kohler-Koch, D. de Bièvre and W. Maloney (eds), *Opening EU Governance to Civil Society: Gains and Challenges,* Connex Report Series, 5, 69–86.

—— (2009), 'Interest Groups and the Revitalisation of Democracy: Are We Expecting too Much?', *Representation* 45(3): 277–287.

Manin, B. (1997), *The Principles of Representative Government* (Cambridge: Cambridge University Press).

Mansbridge, J. (1999), 'Should blacks represent blacks and women represent women? a contingent "yes." ', *Journal of Politics* 61(3): 628–657.

—— (2003), 'Rethinking Representation', *American Political Science Review* 97(4): 515–528.

Mansfeldova, Z. (2008), 'Czech trade unions in EU governance', in J. Kusznir and H. Pleines (eds), *Trade Unions from Post-Socialist Member States in EU Governance* (Stuttgart: Ibidem Publishers), 129–140.

Manzella, A. (2002), 'Il Parlamento federatore', *Quaderni costituzionalim* 22(1): 35–49.

—— (2009), 'The role of parliaments in the democratic life of the union', in S. Micossi, S. Cassese, and G. L. Tosato (eds), *The European Union in the 21st Century: Perspectives from the Lisbon Treaty* (Brussels: Centre for European Policy Studies), 257–270.

Mardell, M. (2009), A Walk on the Wilders side (Mark Mardell's Euroblog: BBC News online), http://www.bbc.co.uk/blogs/thereporters/markmardell/2009/06/almere_near_amsterdam_three_bl.html, date accessed 15 November 2010.

Marquand, D. (1979), *Parliament for Europe* (London: Jonathan Cape).

Marsh, M. (1998), 'Testing the Second-Order Election Model after Four European Elections', *British Journal of Political Science* 28(4): 591–607.

—— (2005), 'The results of the 2004 European parliament elections and the second-order model', in O. Niedermayer and H. Schmitt (eds), *Europawahl 2004* (Wiesbaden: VS Verlag für Sozialwissenschaften/GWV Fachverlage), 142–158.

Martin, A. and Ross, G. (2001), 'Trade Union organizing at the European level', in D. Imig and S. Tarrow (eds), *Contentious Europeans. Protest and Politics in an Integrating Europe* (Lanham: Rowman & Littlefield), 53–76.

Matthes, C. and Terletzki, P. (2005), 'Tripartite Bargaining and Its Impact on Stabilisation Policy in Central and Eastern Europe', *International Journal of Comparative Labour Law and Industrial Relations* 21(3): 369–403.

Maurer, A. (2002), 'National parliaments in the European architecture: elements for establishing a best practice mechanism. the european convention'. Working document 8, http://european-convention.eu.int/docs/wd4/1380.pdf, date accessed 28 August 2010.

—— (2008), 'The Lisbon treaty: new options for and recent trends of interparliamentary cooperation', Paper presented at the Annual Conference of Correspondents, in Brussels, 9–11 October 2008.

Maurer, A. and Wessels, W. (eds) (2001), *National Parliaments on Their Ways to Europe: Losers or Latecomers?* (Baden-Baden: Nomos).

McLaverty, P. (2002), 'Civil Society and Democracy', *Contemporary Politics* 8(4): 303–318.

Mendonca, R. F. (2008), 'Representation and Deliberation in Civil Society', *Brazilian Political Science Review* 2(2): 117–137.

Mény, Y. (2002), 'De la démocratie en Europe: Old Concepts and New Challenges', *Journal of Common Market Studies* 41(1): 1–13.

Meyer, J. et al. (1997), 'World Society and the Nation-State', *American Journal of Sociology* 103: 144–180.

Michailidou, A., Trenz, H. J. and de Wilde, P. (2010), *(W)e the peoples of Europe: Assessing the contours of the EU online public sphere*, RECON WP5 – Civil society and the public sphere – Euroscepticism project, http://www.reconproject.eu/projectweb/portalproject/KrakowMay10.html, date accessed 18 November 2010.

Michel, H. (2008), 'Incantations and Uses of Civil Society by the European Commission', in B. Jobert and B. Kohler-Koch (eds), *Changing Images of Civil Society: From Protest to Governance Routledge Studies in Governance and Public Policy* (London: Routledge), 107–119.

Montilla Martos, J. A. (2004), 'La articulación normativa bases-desarrolo al incorporar el Derecho europeo en el Estado autonómico', *ReDCE* 2: 207–231.

Moravcsik, A. (1998), *The Choice for Europe: Social Purpose and State Power from Messina to Maastricht* (London: Routledge/UCL Press).

—— (2002), 'In Defense of the "Democratic Deficit": Reassessing the Legitimacy of the European Union', *Journal of Common Market Studies* 40(4): 603–634.

—— (2008), 'The Myth of Europe's "Democratic Deficit"', *Journal of European Economic Policy* November–December 2008: 331–340.

Morgan, G. (2005), *The Idea of a European Superstate: Public Justification and European Integration* (Princeton, NJ: Princeton University Press).

Moschonas, G. (2004), 'The party of European socialists: the difficult "construction" of a European player', in P. Delwit, E. Külahci and C. van de Walle (eds), *The Europarties Organisation and Influence* (Brussels: Editions de l'Université de Bruxelles), 113–134.

Nanz, P. and Steffek, J. (2005), 'Assessing the Democratic Quality of Deliberation – Criteria and Research Strategies', *Acta politica* 40(3): 368–383.

Neal, A. (ed.) (2004), *The Changing Face of European Labour Law and Social Policy* (The Hague: Kluwer).

Neunreither, K. (2005), 'The European Parliament and National Parliaments: Conflict or Cooperation?', *Journal of Legislative Studies* 11(3–4): 466–489.

Nielsen, O. B. (1998), 'Discount-udvidelse af EU', *Berlingske Tidene*, 20 March: 15.

Norris, P. (1997), 'Representation and the Democratic Deficit', *European Journal of Political Research* 32(2): 273–282.

Norton, P. (1990), *Legislatures* (Oxford: Oxford University Press).

—— (1993), *Does Parliament Matter?* (Hemel Hempstead: Harvester Wheatsheaf).

—— (1995), 'Conclusion: Addressing the Democratic Deficit', *Journal of Legislative Studies* 1(3): 177–193.

—— (1996), 'National Parliaments in Western Europe', in E. Smith (ed.), *National Parliaments as Cornerstones of European Integration* (The Hague: Kluwer), 19–35.

Nouvelobs.com (2009), *'L'Europe contre l'Europe'* (Le Nouvele Observateur Tchats), http://tchat.nouvelobs.com/recherche/tchat,20090525183358686.html, date accessed 18 November 2010.

Nu.nl (2009), 'Steun Nederlanders voor EU is breed maar broos' (NU.nl: Verkietzingen EU), http://www.nu.nl/verkiezingen-eu/1966210/steun-nederlanders-voor-eu-is-breed-maar-broos.html, date accessed 20 November 2010.

O'Brennan, J. and Raunio, T. (2007), 'Introduction: deparliamentarization and European integration', in J. O'Brennan and T. Raunio (eds), *National Parliaments within the Enlarged European Union: From 'Victims' of Integration to Competitive Actors?* (Abingdon: Routledge), 1–26.

—— (eds) (2007), *National Parliaments within the Enlarged European Union: From 'Victims' of Integration to Competitive Actors?* (Abingdon: Routledge).

Obradovic, D. and Vizcaino, J. M. A. (2006), 'Good Governance Requirements for the Participation of Interest Groups in EU Consultations', *Working Papers of the Research Centre for East European Studies* 76, 19–44.

Offe, C. (1998), Demokratie und Wohlfahrtsstaat: Eine europäische Regimeform unter dem Stress der europäischen Integration', in W. Streeck (ed.), *Internationale Wirtschaft, nationale Demokratie. Herausforderungen für die Demokratietheorie* (Frankfurt am Main: Campus), 99–136.

—— (2003), 'Is there, or can there be a "European society"?', in I. Katenhusen and W. Lamping (eds), *Demokratien in Europa. Der Einfluss der europäischen Integration auf Institutionenwandel und neue Konturen des demokratischen Verfassungsstaates* (Opladen: Springer), 71–89.

O'Flynn, I. (2010), 'Democratic Theory and Practice in Deeply Divided Societies', *Representation* 46(3): 281–293.

Ost. D. (2006), 'After postcommunism: legacies and the future of unions in eastern Europe', in C. Phelan (ed.), *The Future of Organised Labour: Global Perspectives* (Oxford: Lang), 305–331.

Packenham, R. (1970), 'Legislatures and Political Development', in A. Kornberg and L. D. Musolf (eds), *Legislatures in Developmental Perspective* (Durham, NC: Duke University Press), 521–582.

Palanza, A. (2009), 'I Parlamenti come attori autonomi nelle nuove forme della politica internazionale', in C. Decaro and N. Lupo (eds), *Il 'dialogo' tra parlamenti: obiettivi e risultati* (Rome: Luiss University Press), 251–256.

Papadopoulos, Y. (2007), 'Problems of Democratic Accountability in Network and Multilevel Governance', *European Law Journal* 13(4): 469–486.

—— (2010), 'Accountability and Multi-level Governance: More Accountability, Less Democracy?', *West European Politics* 33(5): 1030–1049.

Pateman, C. (1970), *Participation and Democratic Theory* (Cambridge: Cambridge University Press).

Peeters, M. A. (2003), 'The principle of participatory democracy in the new Europe. a critical analysis', American Enterprise Institute for Public Policy Research, http://www.aei.org/docLib/20040402_20030611_Peeters.pdf, date accessed 8 March 2011.

Pennings, P. (2006), 'An Empirical Analysis of the Europeanization of National Party Manifestos, 1960–2003', *European Union Politics* 7(2): 257–270.

Pérez Tremps, P. (1991), 'Il rafforzamento dell'Esecutivo come conseguenza della integrazione nella Comunità europea', in G. Rolla (ed.), *Le forme di governo nei moderni ordinamenti policentrici* (Milano: Giuffrè), 93–111.

Pernice, I. (2002), 'Multilevel Constitutionalism in the European Union', *European Law Review* 27(5): 511–529.

Peruzotti, E. (2006), 'Civil society, representation and accountability: restating current debates on the representativeness and accountability of civic associations', in L. Jordan and P. van Tuijl (eds), *NGO accountability: Politics, Principles and Innovation* (London: Earthscan), 43–60.

Peters, A. (2009), 'Dual democracy', in J. Klabbers, A. Peters and G. Ulfstein (eds), *The Constitutionalization of International Law* (Oxford: Oxford University Press), 263–340.

Peterson, E. (1970) 'Forms of Representation: Participation of the Poor in the Community Action Program', *The American Political Science Review* 64 (2), 491–507.

Peterson, J. and Shackleton, M. (2002), 'Conclusion', in J. Peterson and M. Shackleton (eds), *The Institutions of the European Union* (Oxford: Oxford University Press), 219–234.

Piattoni, S. (2008), 'The committee of the regions: multi-level governance after enlargement', in E. Best, T. Christiansen and P. Settembri (eds), *The Institutions of the Enlarged European Union* (Cheltenham, UK: Edward Elgar), 162–182.

—— (2010a), *The Theory of Multi-Level Governance: Conceptual, Empirical and Normative Challenges* (Oxford: Oxford University Press).

—— (2010b), 'The Problematic Coexistence of Territorial and Functional Representation in the EU', Paper presented at the second IPSA International Conference, University of Luxembourg, 18–20 March 2010.

Piewitt, M., Rodekamp, M. and Steffek, J. (2010), 'Civil Society in World Politics: How Accountable Are Transnational CSOs?', *Journal of Civil Society* 6(3): 237–258.

Pitkin, H. F. (1967), *The Concept of Representation* (Berkeley: University of California Press).

—— (2004), 'Representation and Democracy: Uneasy Alliance', *Scandinavian Political Studies* 27(3): 335–342.

Pleines, H. (2008a), 'Already arrived in Brussels? interest representation of trade unions from the New EU member states at the EU level. Documentation of interview results', *Working Papers of the Research Centre for East European Studies,* 91, http://www.forschungsstelle.uni-bremen.de/images/stories/pdf/ap/fsoAP91.pdf, 8 March 2011.

—— (2008b), 'Conclusion', in J. Kusznir and H. Pleines (eds), *Trade Unions from Post-Socialist Member States in EU Governance* (Stuttgart: Ibidem Publishers), 155–164.

Plotke, D. (1997), 'Representation Is Democracy', *Constellations* 4(1): 19–34.

Pollack, M. (1995), 'Regional actors in an inter-governmental play: the making and implementation of EC structural funds', in J. Richardson and S. Mazey (eds), *The State of The European Union: Building a European Polity?,* 3rd edn (Boulder, CO: Lynne Rienner), 361–390.

—— (2007), 'Contested Meanings of Representation', *Comparative European Politics* 5(1): 87–103.

Pollak, J., Bátora, J., Mokre, M., Sigalas, E. and Slominski, P. (2009), 'On political representation: myths and challenges', *RECON Online Working Paper Series* 2009/2, http://www.reconproject.eu, 8 March 2011.

Putnam, R, D. (1988), 'Diplomacy and Domestic Politics: The Logic of Two-Level Games', *International Organization* 42(3): 427–460.

—— (1993), *Making Democracy Work* (Princeton: Princeton University Press).

—— (1995), 'Bowling Alone: America's Declining Social Capital', *Journal of Democracy* 6(1): 65–78.

Radaelli, C. M. (2004), 'Europeanisation. Solution or Problem?', *European Integration Online Papers* 8(16).

Rant, V. and Mrak, M. (2010), 'The 2007–13 Financial Perspective: Domination of National Interests', *Journal of Common Market Studies* 48(2): 347–372.

Raunio, T. (1999), 'Always One Step Behind? National Legislatures and the European Union', *Government and Opposition* 34(2): 180–202.

—— (2007), 'National Legislatures in the EU Constitutional Treaty', in J. O'Brennan and T. Raunio (eds), *National Parliaments within the Enlarged European Union: From 'Victims' of Integration to Competitive Actors?* (Abingdon: Routledge), 79–92.

—— (2009a), 'The gatekeepers of European integration? The function of national parliaments in the EU political system', paper presented at the RECON Workshop on 'With or Without Lisbon: Continuous Institutional Change in the European Union', Amsterdam, 15–16 May 2009.

—— (2009b), 'National Parliaments and European Integration: What We Know and Agenda for Future Research', *The Journal of Legislative Studies* 15(4): 317–334.

—— (2010), 'Destined for Irrelevance? Subsidiarity Control by National Parliaments', *Real Instituto Elcano Working Paper* 36/2010.

Raunio, T. and Hix, S. (2000), 'Backbenchers Learn to Fight Back: European Integration and Parliamentary Government', *West European Politics* 23(4):, 142–168.

Raunio, T. and Wiberg, M. (2009), 'How to Measure the Europeanisation of a National Legislature?', *Scandinavian Political Studies* 33(1): 74–92.

Rehfeld, A. (2005), *The Concept of Constituency: Political Representation, Democratic Legitimacy, and Institutional Design* (Cambridge: Cambridge University Press).

—— (2006), 'Towards a General Theory of Political Representation', *The Journal of Politics* 68(1): 1–21.

—— (2009), 'Representation Rethought: On Trustees, Delegates, and Gyroscopes in the Study of Political Representation and Democracy', *American Political Science Review* 103(2): 214–230.

Reif, K. and Schmitt, H. (1980), 'Nine Second Order National Elections: A Conceptual Framework for the Analysis of European Election Results', *European Journal of Political Research* 8(1): 3–44.

Risse, T. (2010), *A Community of Europeans? Transnational Identities and Public Spheres* (Oxford: Oxford University Press).

Rittberger, B. (2005), *Building Europe's Parliament: Democratic Representation Beyond the Nation-State* (Oxford: Oxford University Press).

—— (2009), 'The Historical Origins of the EU's System of Representation', *Journal of European Public Policy* 16(1): 43–61.

Rivosecchi, G. (2009), 'Le assemblee legislative regionali nel processo decisionale europeo: una questione aperta', *Le istituzioni del federalismo*, 381–407.

Roig, A. (2003), *La deslegalización: orígenes y límites constitucionales, en Francia, Italia y España* (Sevilla: Editorial Dykinson).

Rojot, J. (2004), 'European collective bargaining: new prospects or much ado about little?', in A. Neal (ed.), *The Changing Face of European Labour Law and Social Policy* (The Hague: Kluwer), 13–38.

Ross, G. (1995), 'Assessing the delors era and social policy', in S. Leibfried and P. Pierson (eds), *European Social Policy: Between Fragmentation and Integration* (Washington, DC: Brookings Institution), 357–388.

Rossteutscher, S. (2000), 'Associative democracy – fashionable slogan or constructive innovation? in M. Saward (ed.), *Democratic Innovation: Deliberation, Representation and Association*, (London: Routledge), 172–183.

Rumford, C. (2003), 'European Civil Society or Transnational Social Space? Conceptions of Society in Discourses of EU Citizenship, Governance and the

Democratic Deficit: An Emerging Agenda', *European Journal of Social Theory* 6(1): 25–43.

Ruzza, C. (2005), 'EU public policies and the participation of organized civil society'. Working Papers del Dipartimento di studi sociali e politici, Università degli studi di Milano, 23 November 2005.

Šabič, Z. (2008), 'Building Democratic and Responsible Global Governance: The Role of International Parliamentary Institutions', *Parliamentary Affairs* 61(2): 255–271.

Sanchez-Salgado, R. (2007), 'Giving a European Dimension to Civil Society Organizations', *Journal of Civil Society* 3(3): 253–269.

Sartori, G. (1987), *The Theory of Democracy Revisited* (Chatam, NJ: Chatham House Publishers).

—— (2005), *Parties and Party Systems*, 2nd edn (Colchester: ECPR Press).

Saurugger, S. (2008), 'Interest Groups and Democracy in the European Union', *West European Politics* 31(6): 1274–1291.

Saward, M. (1998), *The Terms of Democracy* (Cambridge, Oxford: Polity Press).

—— (2006), 'The Representative Claim', *Contemporary Political Theory* 5(2): 297–318.

—— (2009), 'Authorisation and Authenticity: Representation and the Unelected', *The Journal of Political Philosophy* 17(1): 1–22.

—— (2010), *The Representative Claim* (Oxford and New York: Oxford University Press).

Scharpf, F. (1988), 'The Joint Decision Trap: Lessons from German Federalism and European Integration', *Public Administration* 66(3): 239–278.

—— (1997), 'Economic Integration, Democracy and the Welfare State', *Journal of European Public Policy* 4(1): 18–36.

—— (1999), *Regieren in Europa. Effektiv und demokratisch?* (Frankfurt am Main and New York: Campus).

—— (2006), 'The Joint-Decision Trap Revisited', *Journal of Common Market Studies* 44(4): 845–864.

Schäfer, A. and Leiber, S. (2009), 'The double voluntarism in EU social dialogue and employment policy', in S. Kröger (ed.), *What We Have Learnt: Advances, Pitfalls and Remaining Questions in OMC Research*, European Integration online Papers (EIoP), Special Issue 1, 13(9), http://eiop.or.at/eiop/texte/2009-009a.htm, 8 March 2011.

Scherpereel, J. A. (2005), 'Absorbing the Shock: Enlargement's Effects on the Committee of the Regions', Paper presented at the ninth biennial conference of the European Union Studies Association, Austin, TX, March–April.

Schlichte, K. and Jentges, E. (2009), 'What's the political? Bourdieu meets Weber', Paper presented at the ECPR Conference, Potsdam, 10–12 September 2009.

Schmidt, V. (1999), 'European "Federalism" and Its Encroachments on National Institutions', *Publius* 29(1): 19–44.

—— (2006), *Democracy in Europe: The EU and National Polities* (Oxford: Oxford University Press).

Schmitt, H. (2009), 'Introduction', *Journal of European Integration* 31(5): 525–535.

Schmitter, P. (2000), *How to Democratize the European Union…And Why Bother* (Lanhman, MD: Rowman & Littlefield).

—— (2002), 'Participation in governance arrangements: is there any reason to expect it will achieve "sustainable and innovative policies in a multi-level context"?', in J. Grote and B. Gbikpi (eds), *Participatory Governance: Political and Societal Implications* (Leske + Budrich: Opladen), 51–70.

Schöbel, N. (1997), *The Committee of the Regions: A Preliminary Review of the Committee's Work during the First Two Years of Operation* (Tübingen: European Centre for Research on Federalism).

Schumpeter, J. A. (1950), *Kapitalismus, Sozialismus und Demokratie* (Tübingen: A. Francke).

—— (1976) [1943], *Capitalism, Socialism and Democracy* (Chatham: George Allen & Unwin).

Sejersted, F. (1996), 'The Norwegian parliament and European integration, reflections from middle-speed Europe', in E. Smith (ed.), *National Parliaments as Cornerstones of European Integration* (The Hague: Kluwer), 124–156.

Semetko, H.A., De Vreese, C. H. and Peter, J. (2001), 'Europeanised politics – Europeanised media? integration and political communication', in K. H. Goetz and S. Hix (eds), *Europeanised Politics? European Integration and National Political Systems* (Abingdon: Frank Cass).

Severs, E. (2010), 'Representation as Claims-Making: Quid Responsiveness?', *Representation* 46(4): 411–423.

Sigalas, E., Mokre, M., Pollak, J., Slominski, P. and Bátora, J. (2010), 'Democracy models and parties at the EU level', *RECON Online Working Paper Series* 2010/13, http://www.reconproject.eu, 8 March 2011.

Sil, R. and Candland, C. (2001), 'Institutional legacies and the transformation of labour: late-industrializing and post-socialist economies in comparative-historical perspective', in C. Candland and R. Sil (eds), *The Politics of Labor in a Global Age: Continuity and Change in Late-Industrializing and Post-Socialist Economies* (Oxford: Oxford University Press), 285–308.

Skocpol, T. (2003), *Diminished Democracy: From Membership to Management in American Civil Life* (Oklahoma: University of Oklahoma Press).

Slaughter, A. M. (2004), *A New World Order* (Princeton: Princeton University Press).

Smets, I. (1998), 'Les Régions se mobilisent – Quel "lobby régional" à Bruxelles?', in Clays, P., Gobin, C., Smets, I., and Winand, P. (eds), *Lobbyisme, pluralisme et intégration européenne* (Bruxelles, Presses interuniversitaires européennes), 303–327.

Smismans, S. (2003), 'European Civil Society: Shaped by Discourses and Institutional Interests', *European Law Journal* 9(4): 482–504.

—— (2004a), 'The Constitutional Labelling of "the Democratic Life of the EU": Representative and "Participatory" Democracy', in A. Follesdal and L. Dobson (eds), *Political Theory and the European Constitution* (London: Routledge), 122–138.

—— (2004b), *Law, Legitimacy and European Governance: Functional Participation in Social Regulation* (Oxford: Oxford University Press).

—— (2006), *Civil Society and Legitimate European Governance* (Cheltenham: Edward Elgar).

—— (2009), 'The representativeness of organised civil society: generally desired ... until defined'. Paper presented at the conference 'Bringing Civil Society In: The European Union and the Rise of Representative Democracy', European University Institute, 13–15 March 2009, Florence.

Smith, J. (1999), *Europe's Elected Parliament* (Sheffield: Sheffield Academic Press).

Sofsky, W. and Paris, R. (1994), *Figurationen sozialer Macht: Autorität, Stellvertretung, Koalition* (Frankfurt am Main: Suhrkamp).

Song, S. (2009), 'Democracy and Noncitizen Voting Rights', *Citizenship Studies* 13(6): 607–620.

Statham, P. (2005), 'Forging Divergent and "Path Dependent" Ways to Europe? Political Communication over European Integration in the British and French Public Spheres', *European Political Communication Working Paper Series* 2005(11), EurPolCom, University of Leeds.

Steffek, J. and Ferretti, M. P. (2009), 'Accountability or "Good Decisions"? The Competing Goals of Civil Society Participation in International Governance', *Global Society* 23(1): 37–57.

Steffek, J. and Hahn, K. (eds) (2010), *Evaluating Transnational NGOs: Legitimacy, Accountability, Representation* (Basingstoke: Palgrave Macmillan).

Steffek, J. and Nanz, P. (2008), 'Emergent Patterns of Civil Society Participation in Global and European Governance', in J. Steffek, C. Kissling and P. Nanz (eds), *Civil Society Participation in European and Global Governance: A Cure for the Democratic Deficit?* (Basingstoke:Palgrave Macmillan), 1–29.

Steffek, J. et al. (2010a), 'Assessing the Legitimacy and Accountability of CSOs: Five Criteria', in K. Hahn and J. Steffek (eds), *Evaluating International NGOs: Legitimacy, Accountability, Representation* (Houndmills, Basingstoke, Hampshire: Palgrave Macmillan), 100–125.

—— (2010b), 'Whose Voice? Transnational CSOs and Their Relations with Members, Supporters and Beneficiaries', *TranState Working Paper No. 113* (Bremen: Universität Bremen).

Stewart, J. (1992), *Accountability to the Public* (London: European Policy Forum).

Stoffel, S. (2008), 'Rethinking Political Representation: The Case of Institutionalised Feminist Organisations in Chile', *Representation* 44(2): 141–154.

Strøm, K. (1998), 'Parliamentary Committees in European Democracies', *Journal of Legislative Studies* 4(1): 21–59. Reprinted in L. D. Longley and R. H. Davidson (eds), *The New Roles of Parliamentary Committees* (London: Frank Cass).

Strøm, K., Müller, W. C. and Bergman, T. (eds) (2003), *Delegation and Accountability in Parliamentary Democracies* (Oxford: Oxford University Press).

Sudbery, I. (2003), 'Bridging the Legitimacy Gap in the EU: Can Civil Society Help to Bring the Union Closer to Its Citizens?', *Collegium* 26(Spring): 75–95.

Swindell, D. (2000), 'Issue Representation in Neighborhood Organizations: Questing for Democracy at the Grassroots', *Journal of Urban Affairs* 22(2): 123–138.

Szalay, K. (2005), *Scrutiny of EU Affairs in the National Parliaments of the New Member States: Comparative Analysis* (Budapest: Hungarian National Assembly).

Tans, O., Zoethout, C. and Peters, J. (eds) (2007), *National Parliaments and European Democracy: A Bottom-Up Approach to European Constitutionalism* (Groningen: Europa Law Publishing).

Tarrow, S. (1989), *Democracy and Disorder: Protest and Politics in Italy 1965–1975* (Oxford: Oxford University Press).

Taylor, C. (1992), 'Multiculturalism and "The Politics of Recognition"' (Princeton: Princeton University Press).

Taylor, L. (2010), 'Re-founding Representation: Wider, Broader, Closer, Deeper', *Political Studies Review* 8(2): 169–179.

Thaa, W. (2008), 'Kritik und Neubewertung politischer Repräsentation: vom Hindernis zur Möglichkeitsbedingung politischer Freiheit,' *Politische Vierteljahreszeitschrift* 49(4): 618–640.

The Selection Process for Committee of the Regions Members. *Procedures in the Member States* (2009), ISBN 978–92-895–0468-3, Nr Catalogue: QG-80-09-625-EN-C, accessible on the webpage: http://www.cor.europa.eu/pages/DocumentTemplate.aspx?view=detail&id=046e4f93-3757-4e90-8297-9552c72f9271 <http://www.cor.europa.eu/pages/DocumentTemplate.aspx?view=detail&id=046e4f93-3757-4e90-8297-9552c72f9271, date accessed 30 January 2011.

Thym, D. (2009), 'Parliamentary control of EU decision-making in germany: supportive federal scrutiny and restrictive regional action', in O. Tans, C. Zoethout and J. Peters (eds), *National Parliaments and European Democracy; A Bottom-Up Approach to European Constitutionalism* (Groningen: Europa Law Publishing), 49–75.

Trenz, H. J. (2009a), 'European Civil Society: Between Participation, Representation and Discourse', *Policy and Society* 28(1) 35–46.

—— (2009b), 'Digital Media and the Return of the Representative Public Sphere', *Javnost – the Public* 16(1): 33–46.

—— (2010), 'In Search of the Popular Subject: Identity Formation, Constitution-Making and the Democratic Consolidation of the EU', *European Review* 18(1): 93–115.

Trenz, H. J. and De Wilde, P. (2009), *Denouncing European Integration: Euroscepticism as Reactive Identity Formation*, RECON Online Working Paper 2009/10, http://www.reconproject.eu/projectweb/portalproject/RECONWorkingPapers2009.html, date accessed 21 November 2010.

Trouw (1998), Boerenorganisaties eisen aanpassing beleid Brussel. 19 March: 6.

—— (2005), Balkenende ziet niets in voorstel Luxemburg. 11 June: 1.

Tsatsos, D. (1999), *Verfassung-Parteien-Europa* (Baden-Baden: Nomos).

Tweede Kamer (1997), 'Debat naar aanleiding van de Europese top', Handelingen 1997–1998, Tweede Kamer der Staten-Generaal, TK 38, 3055–3079.

—— (2005), 'Debat over de Europese Top van 16 en 17 juni 2005', Handelingen 2004–2005, Tweede Kamer der Staten-Generaal, TK 93, 5578–612.

Urbinati, N. (2000), 'Representation as Advocacy: A Study of Democratic Deliberation', *Political Theory* 28(6): 758–786.

—— (2004), 'Condorcet's Democratic Theory of Representative Government', *European Journal of Political Theory* 3(1): 53–75.

—— (2006), *Representative Democracy: Principles and Genealogy* (Chicago: University of Chicago Press).

Urbinati, N. and Warren, M. E. (2008), 'The Concept of Representation in Contemporary Democratic Theory', *Annual Review of Political Sciences* 11(1): 387–412.

Van der Knaap, P. (1994), 'The Committee of the Regions: The Outset of a "Europe of the Regions"?', *Regional Politics and Society* 4(2): 86–100.

Van Kersbergen, K. (1995), *Social Capitalism: A Study of Christian Democracy and the Welfare State in Europe* (London: Routledge).

Van Roermund, B. (2003), 'First-Person Plural Legislature: Political Reflexivity and Representation', *Philosophical Explorations* 6(3): 235–250, date accessed 5 March 2011.

Vanhuysse, P. (2007), 'Workers without Powers. Agency, Legacies and Labour Decline in East European Varieties of Capitalism', *Czech Sociological Review* 43(3): 459–522.

Vos, H. (2005), 'National/Regional Parliaments and EU-Decision Making under the New Constitutional Treaty', *EIPA Working Paper,* 2005/W/02.

Vos, H. et al. (2007), 'Belgian parliaments and EU decision-making: "In the government we trust"', in O. Tans, C. Zoethout and J. Peters (eds), *National Parliaments and European Democracy: A Bottom-Up Approach to European Constitutionalism* (Groningen: Europa Law Publishing), 99–121.

VZBV (2010), 'Jahresbericht 2009/2010. Verbraucherzentrale Bundesverband e.V. – Die Stimme der Verbraucher', http://www.vzbv.de/downloads/Jahresbericht_vzbv_2009_2010.pdf, date accessed 9 November 2010.

Warleigh, A. (1997), 'A Committee of No Importance? Assessing the Relevance of the Committee of the Regions', *Politics* 17(2): 101–107.

—— (1999), *The Committee of the Regions: Institutionalizing Multi-Level Governance?* (London: Kogan Page).

—— (2000), 'The Hustle: Citizenship Practice, NGOs and "Policy Coalitions" in the European Union – the Cases of Auto Oil, Drinking Water and Unit Pricing', *Journal of European Public Policy* 7(2): 229–243.

—— (2001), '"European" Civil Society: NGOs as Agents of Political Socialization' *Journal of Common Market Studies* 39(4): 619–639.

Warner, M. (2002), *Public and Counterpublics* (New York: Zone Books).

Warren, M. E. (2001), *Democracy and Association* (Princeton, NJ: Princeton University Press).

Warren, M. and Castiglione, D. (2004), 'The Transformation of Democratic Representation', *Democracy and Society* 2(1): 5–22.

Weatherill, S. R. (2005), 'The challenge of the regional dimension in the European Union', in S. R. Weatherill and U. Bernitz (eds), *The Role of Regions and Sub-National Actors in Europe* (Oxford: Hart Publishing), 1–33.

Weiler, J. H. H. (1994), 'Fin-de-siècle Europe: On Ideals and Ideology in Post-Maastricht Europe', in D. Curtin and T. Heukels (eds), *Institutional Dynamics of European Integration* (Dordrecht, Boston, London: Nijhoff Publishers), 23–41.

Weiler, J. H. H., Haltern, U. R. and Mayer, F.(1995), 'European Democracy and Its Critique', *West European Politics* 18(3): 4–39.

Weiss, J. (1984), 'Stellvertretung. Überlegung zu einer vernachlässigten soziologischen Kategorie', *Kölner Zeitschrift für Soziologie und Sozialpsychologie* 36 (1): 43–55.

—— (1998), *Handeln und Handeln lassen. Über Stellvertretung* (Wiesbaden: Westdeutscher Verlag).

Wessels, B. and Katz, R. (1999), 'Introduction: European Parliament, National Parliaments and European Integration', in R. Katz and B. Wessels (eds), *The European Parliament, the European Integration* (Oxford: Oxford University Press), 174–196.

White, J. (2010) 'Europe and the Common', *Political Studies* 58, 104–122.

Whiteley, P. (2011), 'Is the Party Over? The Decline of Party Activism and Membership Across the Democratic World', *Party Politics* 17(1): 21–44.

Wiercx, J. (2010), *All for One and One for All: The Democratic Legitimacy of European Social Movement Organisations* (Brussels: Vrije Universiteit Brussel).

Willems, U. (2007), 'Kirchen', in T. von Winter and U. Willems (eds), *Interessenverbände in Deutschland* (Wiesbaden: VS Verlag für Sozialwissenschaften), 316–340.

Williams, M. (1998), *Voice, Trust, and Memory: Marginalized Groups and the Failings of Liberal Representation* (Princeton, NJ: Princeton University).

Wikio.com (2011), Homepage of Wikio News, http://www.wikio.com, date accessed 6 January 2011.

Wüst, A. (2009), 'Parties in European Parliament Elections: Issues, Framing, and the Question of Supply and Demand', *German Politics* 18(3): 426–440.

Wüst, A. and Schmitt, H. (2007), 'Comparing the views of parties and voters in the 1999 elections to the European parliament', in W. van der Brug and C. van der Eijk (eds), *European Elections and Domestic Politics* (Notre Dame: University of Notre Dame Press), 73–93.

Yin, R. K. (2003), *Case Study Research: Design and Methods,* 3rd edn (Thousand Oaks: Sage Publications).

Young, I. M. (2000), *Inclusion and Democracy* (Oxford: Oxford University Press).

Zahn, R. (2008), 'The Viking and Laval Cases in the Context of European Enlargement', *Web Journal of Current Legal Issues* 3, http://webjcli.ncl.ac.uk/2008/issue3/zahn3.html, 8 March 2011.

Index